Software Design

INTERNATIONAL COMPUTER SCIENCE SERIES

Consulting Editor   **A D McGettrick** University of Strathclyde

SELECTED TITLES IN THE SERIES

Distributed Systems: Concepts and Designs   *G Coulouris and J Dollimore*
Software Prototyping, Formal Methods and VDM   *S Hekmatpour and D Ince*
High-Level Languages and Their Compilers   *D Watson*
Interactive Computer Graphics: Functional, Procedural and Device-Level Methods
      P Burger and D Gillies
Real Time Systems and Their Programming Languages   *A Burns and A Wellings*
Fortran 77 Programming (2nd Edn)   *T M R Ellis*
Prolog Programming for Artificial Intelligence (2nd Edn)   *I Bratko*
Introduction to Expert Systems (2nd Edn)   *P Jackson*
Logic for Computer Science   *S Reeves and M Clarke*
Computer Architecture *M De Blasi*
The Programming Process: An Introduction using VDM and Pascal   *J T Latham,*
      V J Bush and D Cottam
Analysis of Algorithms and Data Structures   *L Banachowski, A Kreczmar and*
      W Rytter
Elements of Functional Programming   *C Reade*
Handbook of Algorithms and Data Structures in Pascal and C (2nd Edn)   *G Gonnet*
      and R Baeza-Yates
Algorithms and Data Structures   *J H Kingston*
Principles of Expert Systems   *P Lucas and L van der Gaag*
Discrete Mathematics for Computer Scientists   *J K Truss*
Programming in Ada plus Language Reference Manual (3rd Edn)   *J G P Barnes*
Software Engineering (4th Edn)   *I Sommerville*
Distributed Database Systems   *D Bell and J Grimson*
Software Development with Z   *J B Wordsworth*
Program Verification   *N Francez*
Concurrent Programming   *A Burns and G L Davies*
Concurrent Systems: An Integrated Approach to Operating Systems, Database and
      Distributed Systems   *J Bacon*
Comparative Programming Languages (2nd Edn)   *L B Wilson and R G Clark*

Software Design

David Budgen

University of Keele

ADDISON-WESLEY
PUBLISHING
COMPANY

Wokingham, England · Reading, Massachusetts · Menlo Park, California ·New York
Don Mills, Ontario · Amsterdam · Bonn · Sydney · Singapore
Tokyo · Madrid · San Juan · Milan · Paris · Mexico City · Seoul · Taipei

Typeset by CRB (Drayton) Typesetting Services, Norwich, Norfolk.
Printed in Great Britain by T.J. Press, Padstow, Cornwall.

First printed 1993. Reprinted 1994.

ISBN: 0–201–54403–2

British Library Cataloguing in Publication Data
A catalogue record for this book is available from the British Library.

Library of Congress Cataloging in Publication Data applied for

Acknowledgement
The publisher wishes to thank the following for permission to reproduce material in this book: Potts C. and Bruns G. (1988), Figure 8.3 from *Proceedings of the 10th International Conference on Software Engineering* © 1988 IEEE; Curtis B., Krasner H. and Iscoe N. (1988), Figure 2.6 from *Comm ACM*; and Barry Boehm for the use of Figures 3.2 and 3.3.

Preface

Why you might benefit from reading this book

Why should software need to be designed at all? Well, you would not expect any other engineered artifacts such as bridges, cars or television sets to be built without someone first designing them and producing plans for their construction. And you certainly would not expect to modify them significantly without having some detailed documentation available either. Software is no different: throwing a few dozen programmers at a problem without having detailed plans is hardly likely to result in well-engineered software that actually works.

So, where does the design process fit in? It occurs somewhere between the optimistic phase where we decide what we would like our system to do (often termed 'Requirements Capture') and the increasingly pessimistic phase where we build it ('Implementation'), although it may appear in many different guises. Design is the highly creative stage in software development where someone (the *designer*) plans how the system or program should meet the customer's needs, be easy to implement, 'efficient' and easily extended to meet new needs.

If it's so creative a task, how will this book help? Mainly because any form of creativity is likely to be more effective when there are ways of learning from the experiences of others ('rules of form', design methods) and when there are well-developed notations that can be used for communicating the designer's ideas and plans to those whose task it is to implement them.

These are just the sort of issues that this book addresses: how to develop our ideas about a design, the criteria we might use to assess our ideas and the ways in which we might convey these ideas to programmers. This is a book about software design. It provides an analysis of a number of the currently-used approaches to the task of design, rather than being dedicated to describing just one representation or method.

v

OK, so who will benefit from reading it? Well, every author would like their work to be a best-seller that appears on every airport and railway station bookstall – but this one is perhaps a bit too specialist for that! It contains information and ideas that are relevant to anyone who is in the business of developing software (except, of course, those whom Tom De Marco has described as the 'Mugwump School, people who believe that design is for sissies'). However, it does assume a basic acquaintance with imperative programming languages (although it is certainly not language-specific), and with concepts such as abstract data types. It is suitable as a text for advanced undergraduate or postgraduate courses in software design or software engineering. Systems analysts/designers, programmers and project managers should benefit from the comparison of a broad spectrum of design methods.

Outline of the book

The main objective of **Part I** is to explore the nature of the design process and to identify the role that this plays in software development. In addition to examining the form of the process, we look at the wider influences that affect this, including ideas about quality as well as the ways in which we can describe the many different attributes of software.

Part II begins by providing a more detailed examination of a broad cross-section of design methods, starting with the well-established 'structural' approaches provided by JSP, Structured Systems Analysis and Structured Design. We then explore the more advanced design-modelling techniques used in JSD and the object-oriented forms. For each of these, we examine how the design ideas are represented, the transformations that the procedures of the method apply to these, and the heuristic practices provided by experience. These are supported by outline examples that illustrate these features without requiring an excess of detail. The final chapters then review a number of other systematic design forms in rather less detail (SADT, SSADM and MASCOT), and briefly examine how the 'formal methods' can be accommodated in the methodological framework that has been developed in the preceding chapters.

Why software design is important

Writing a computer program is a challenging and creative experience, motivated by the desire to solve problems. The task of developing even a small computer program is not an easy one. Programmers are continually required to keep their attention focused upon many different aspects of both problems and solutions. Even when the static structure of a program is complete (that is, the program 'compiles' successfully), the correctness of its dynamic behaviour still needs to be confirmed. Indeed, it is this need to keep both static form and eventual dynamic behaviour continually in mind when developing a solution that forms a significant part of the challenge that programming provides.

During the 1970s a number of advances in software technology were designed to improve the task of developing computer programs: higher-level programming languages, more efficient compilers, structured programming practices and symbolic debugging facilities. All of these have assisted programmers with developing, controlling and visualizing their ideas about a program, mainly through increased use of the concept of **abstraction**.

Abstraction has played a central role in the development of better programming techniques, allowing the designer of a program to reason about its structure and behaviour without needing to address the detailed issues of determining implementation forms at the same time. While the benefits arising from these improved techniques were at first identified mainly in terms of programming activities, there was also a growing realization of the need to develop better practices for programming-in-the-large, which is concerned with the design and development of 'systems' as a whole.

Programming-in-the-large

While the design of programs offers significant problems, the design of large systems provides a vastly increased degree of complexity. The increased levels of abstraction required for designing a large system make it more difficult for the designer to visualize and 'model' the behaviour of the eventual system. The greatly increased time interval that can occur between the origination of an idea and its actual realization leaves designers much more isolated from their actual creation, compounded by the likelihood that the task of implementation will be allocated to others. This means that designers also need to communicate their ideas to others in an unambiguous manner.

So the 1970s also saw the development of design representation forms, and the emergence of design methods intended to capture the experiences of other designers, and so to help designers describe their ideas and to control and structure their task. (Throughout this book the term design method has been used in preference to the much-abused design methodology when describing specific design techniques. According to the dictionary, *method* is 'a procedure for doing things', while *methodology* is the 'study of method'. What we will be doing in this book is methodological, as it involves the study of methods!) This process has continued, and many design methods have themselves been re-designed en route, and have gradually evolved far beyond their original forms. New ideas about design quality and new viewpoints describing the properties of software have emerged, and have in turn been incorporated into both new and existing design methods.

As software plays a central role in the operation of many systems, as varied as banking transactions, spreadsheet calculations, or aircraft control systems ('fly by wire'), it becomes increasingly important that such systems should be designed as well as possible. Faulty design can lead to disaster and can even be life-threatening.

It is increasingly accepted that the study of software based systems (whether we call it software engineering, computer science, information systems engineering, or even information technology) needs to involve some basic knowledge about the roles of design within the software development process. However, students of design are confronted with many of the same problems as the designer: the high level of abstraction required in the descriptive forms, and the resulting 'distance' from the eventual solution, can make it difficult to provide them with the necessary degree of 'feeling' for all the issues that are involved. As a further complication, the time required to develop a significant item of software from the abstract design to its final implementation usually makes it impractical for students to gain real feedback from carrying their designs through to fruition.

A field which provides a good (and partly comforting) analogy is that of the study of music. Musical composition is another highly creative task and, like software designers, composers need to use a complex static notation to describe the eventual dynamic performance of a piece of music. The student of music must become proficient in reading and interpreting musical scores, before ever attempting to master the rules of composition. In the case of software design the novice needs to learn to program effectively, and to be familiar with the manipulation of various forms of abstraction, before proceeding to design a system of any size or complexity.

The analogy should not be pushed too far (few symphonies have been produced by 'composition teams', organized by project managers), but we do need to realize that teaching design *methods* does not teach a student *about* design, or even necessarily how to *do* design. The would-be designer needs to study widely and to gain a thorough understanding of the many issues that influence the design process before taking on the role of a system designer, whether or not this involves the use of specific design methods.

How this book came about

I was fortunate enough to spend some time at Carnegie-Mellon's Software Engineering Institute (SEI) during 1986, during which an initial curriculum on software design was developed for the Graduate Curriculum Project. This was then extensively revised in 1988, taking on board subsequent thinking and experience. The aim of this work was to develop a 'road-map' for use by instructors which identified the principal issues in the teaching of design knowledge and suggested ways in which these might be introduced to the student, supported by a bibliographical survey.

In compiling the curriculum, one of the major problems that emerged was the lack of textbooks suitable for teaching *about* software systems design. There are relatively few books that address the subject of design in general (not just in terms of software), and nearly all textbooks about software design are centred on describing the use of one particular method. These can be considered as being books about how to *do* design, rather than what design *is*. While these books cater for a very important set of skill needs, teaching one approach does make it difficult for almost all authors to avoid some degree of proselytizing!

One of the aims of this book is therefore to redress the balance by providing a book that can act as a 'road-map' to the issues of software systems design, and survey the roles that design methods play in this. This book is therefore about design (with particular attention to software and its needs), rather than about method, although in the process of describing the one, we necessarily have to discuss the other. It is not meant to replace those books that teach specific design methods in detail, but rather to provide a broad intermediate level of understanding that might usefully precede any detailed study of one or more methods, or the selection of a design method to be used in a project.

Acknowledgements

Design in any sphere can be a pleasurable and creative act for those involved in it, whether it involves building simple sand-castles on the beach, engineering a complex structure such as the Thames Barrier, or writing a fugue. Writing books is a creative act, and can also give the writer pleasure (at times), especially so once the task is completed! Like so many creative tasks it also depends upon the help, advice and encouragement of many others, and I would like to thank the many people who have helped and sustained my efforts on this book from its original inception to the final product. These include: my friends and mentors at the SEI, especially Jim Tomayko, Mary Shaw, Carol Sledge and the other members of the Education Program; my friends and collaborators in industry, Mike Looney, Ken Jackson, Hugo Simpson, Ray Foulkes and Alastair O'Brien; my former colleagues at the University of Stirling, with special thanks to Chic Rattray and Maurice Naftalin for the many exchanges of ideas; and my present colleagues at the University of Keele, including Mike Brough and my other research collaborators, Mustafa Marashi, Andrew Reeves and Grant Friel, who have put in so much work on some of my ideas. All of them have had to labour long and hard to correct my misconceptions and to further my education on the subject of software design. The mistakes that remain are all my own.

I should also like to acknowledge the contribution of my various student classes, in the Universities of Stirling and of Keele, as well as in industry. It has been their unfortunate lot to provide some of the testing ground for the frameworks that have been used in this book, and their feedback has been invaluable for this.

Last (but certainly not least) grateful thanks to my family, who have put up with 'not another book' for so long; and to Simon Plumtree of Addison-Wesley for his encouragement, and amazing patience in waiting for the final manuscript!

David Budgen
November 1993

Contents

Preface   v

Part I   The Role of Software Design   1

1   The Nature of the Design Process   3

   1.1   What is design?   4
   1.2   Objectives for the design activity   13
   1.3   Design as a problem-solving process   17
   1.4   Design as a 'wicked' problem   19

2   The Software Design Process   25

   2.1   Building models   26
   2.2   Structuring the design process   30
   2.3   Constraints upon the design process and
         product   35
   2.4   Recording design decisions   37
   2.5   Designing with others   38

3   Design in the Software Development Process   43

   3.1   A context for design   44
   3.2   Economic factors   48
   3.3   Software production models and their
         influence   51
   3.4   Prototyping roles and forms   52

4   Design Qualities   57

   4.1   The quality concept   58
   4.2   Assessing design quality   60

4.3	Quality attributes of the design product	67
4.4	Assessing the design process	76

5 Expressing Ideas about a Design — 81

5.1	Representing abstract ideas	82
5.2	Design viewpoints for software	85
5.3	Forms of notation	89

6 Some Design Representations — 95

6.1	A problem of selection	96
6.2	The Data-Flow Diagram (DFD)	97
6.3	The Entity–Relationship Diagram (ERD)	104
6.4	The Structure Chart	108
6.5	The Structure Graph	111
6.6	The Jackson Structure Diagram	115
6.7	Pseudocode	120
6.8	The State Transition Diagram (STD)	123
6.9	The Statechart	127
6.10	The Petri Net	131

Part II Design Practices — 139

7 The Rationale for Method — 141

7.1	What is a software design method?	142
7.2	Why design methods are needed	146
7.3	Why methods don't work miracles	151
7.4	Problem domains and their influence	153

8 Design Strategies — 159

8.1	Strategy and method	160
8.2	Top-down strategies for design	166
8.3	Design by composition	168
8.4	Organizational methods of design	170
8.5	Design by template and design reuse	171

A Brief Interlude — 175

9 Jackson Structured Programming (JSP) — 177

9.1	Some background to JSP	178
9.2	JSP representation forms	179
9.3	The JSP process	181
9.4	Some JSP heuristics	189

10 **Structured Systems Analysis and Structured Design** 205

10.1 Origins, development and philosophy 206
10.2 Representation forms for SSA/SD 207
10.3 The SSA/SD process 211
10.4 The role of heuristics in SSA/SD 221
10.5 Extended forms of SSA/SD 223
10.6 SSA/SD: an outline example 223

11 **Jackson System Development (JSD)** 239

11.1 The JSD model 240
11.2 JSD representation forms 242
11.3 The JSD process 247
11.4 JSD heuristics 260

12 **Object-Oriented and Object-Based Design** 265

12.1 Introducing the notion of the 'object' 266
12.2 Design practices for the object-oriented paradigm 276
12.3 Object-Based Design (HOOD) 279
12.4 Object-Oriented Design 287
12.5 HOOD: an outline example 293

13 **Some Other Systematic Approaches to Design** 305

13.1 Systematic design methods in perspective 306
13.2 Traditional analysis revisited: SADT 307
13.3 Organizational design practices: SSADM 312
13.4 Designing real-time systems: MASCOT 324

14 **A Formal Approach to Design** 337

14.1 The case for rigour 338
14.2 Model-based strategies 343
14.3 Property-based strategies 353

15 **The Evolution of Software Design Practices** 363

15.1 Experiences from the past 364
15.2 Present practices 365
15.3 Future developments 368

Bibliography 371

Index 377

Part I

The Role of Software Design

Chapter 1	**The Nature of the Design Process**	3
Chapter 2	**The Software Design Process**	25
Chapter 3	**Design in the Software Development Process**	43
Chapter 4	**Design Qualities**	57
Chapter 5	**Expressing Ideas about a Design**	81
Chapter 6	**Some Design Representations**	95

1 The Nature of the Design Process

1.1 What is design?
1.2 Objectives for the design activity

1.3 Design as a problem-solving process
1.4 Design as a 'wicked' problem

This opening chapter is concerned with examining the role that design plays in a wide range of spheres. It looks at the ideas of design theorists and examines these in the light of some simple examples of design activity. In particular, it contrasts the use of design as a problem-solving technique with that of scientific method, and shows how these differ in a number of highly significant ways.

1.1   What is design?

Various artifacts that are the outcome of many different applications of the design process extensively influence our lives. We ride in cars, trains, aeroplanes; we live in houses or flats; we use everyday domestic appliances such as washing-machines, television sets, vacuum cleaners; we sit on chairs, lie on beds, walk around in shoes; we play games, listen to music. All of these are artifacts because they have been devised and created by human beings, and all of them in some way are the products of some form of design process – whether a good one (shoes are comfortable, a washing-machine works reliably) or a poor one (the flat roof of a house leaks, or the chair collapses when the user leans back on two legs).

Our perception of the importance of the roles that design may play in producing these different artifacts will vary, although it may not always be correct. No-one is likely to deny the importance of using well-proven design practices for the design of motorway bridges, aeroplanes and buildings, not least because of the safety issues concerned with the use of such objects. Yet equally, good design is important for a wide range of less safety-critical objects – such as a domestic refrigerator: we do not want to have to de-ice it continually, nor to replace bottles that fall out when we open the door. Similarly, we also want to have well-designed footwear so that we do not find ourselves suffering from foot complaints.

Obviously design is not the only factor that matters in the production of artifacts. The fabrication process matters too, and a customer is unlikely to distinguish faulty design from faulty fabrication if shoes leak in the rain, or if the door falls off a car when it is opened. However, while good design may be marred by poor fabrication, usually no amount of constructional skill can disguise poor design.

Design is just as important with software systems also. Most people will readily accept that the software used in an aeroplane needs to be well designed and rigorously tested, not least because they might find themselves as passengers on that aircraft one day. Yet good design is equally desirable for smaller systems too, since the user still requires efficiency (if it can only be defined) and reliability (which suffers from a similar problem of being difficult to define in a precise manner). A word processor may not be a safety-critical item, but its user is unlikely to appreciate the occasional lost paragraph occurring at apparently random points in a document. The same techniques may not be used in designing a word processor as in designing safety-critical avionics systems, but the need for a well-designed product is still there. The same parallel might apply to the design of major road-bridges and the design of seating in the dentist's waiting room: the structural complexities are very different, but both of them are expected to function well enough to meet our needs.

Despite extensive exposure to the products of the design process in general (with an associated awareness that good design practices cannot always ensure success in terms of design quality), people's awareness of how design is carried out is often rather unstructured and piecemeal. In the domain of computing science and software engineering, designing software is a major problem-solving technique, to be ranked alongside the concepts of theory and of abstraction (Denning *et al.*, 1989). Yet all too rarely do we have a clear idea of the nature and purpose of the design process, and our ideas about design are all too often muddled in with notions derived from the more specific practices of design methods. So this first chapter aims to explore some ideas about the design process and its nature, in order to provide a basic framework for an understanding of design issues that can then be used to explore the ideas and concepts introduced in the subsequent chapters.

Although this book is focused largely on the application of design ideas and methods to the production of software, the task of design involves the use of many ideas and concepts that can be applied more widely. To help reinforce this point, the examples used in these introductory chapters will be drawn from a wide range of fields, and not just from the field of software development.

So what is design exactly, what sort of activities does it involve, and what can we observe about the products of that process? Perhaps a good starting point is to consider the words of one of the foremost design methodologists, J. Christopher Jones, taken from his classic work, *Design Methods: Seeds of Human Futures* (Jones, 1970).

'The fundamental problem is that designers are obliged to use current information to predict a future state that will not come about unless their predictions are correct. The final outcome of designing has to be assumed before the means of achieving it can be explored: the designers have to work backwards in time from an assumed effect upon the world to the beginning of a chain of events that will bring the effect about.'

This concise description of the design process is more than sufficient to show that its form is very different from that of the 'analytical' technique that lies at the root of the scientific approach to problem-solving which will perhaps be more familiar to many readers. The scientific approach to problem-solving involves making measurements, building a theory that explains these, making predictions from this theory, and then seeking to verify these predictions through further measurements. The approach used in design is focused on achieving a goal rather than on investigation, and so begins by assuming the end result and then seeks ways of bringing this about. In both cases one builds 'models' of the problem, but they are used for very different purposes as is shown in Figures 1.1 and 1.2, which summarize and contrast the forms of the scientific and design processes.

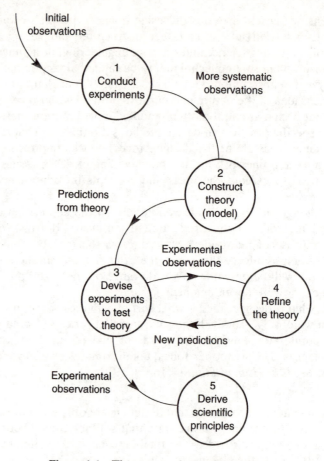

Figure 1.1 The nature of scientific analysis.

Since software can be considered a prime example of an artifact, we can see why an understanding of the techniques of design are so important in its production. Indeed, this is true of the craft and engineering disciplines in general, in that they are usually concerned with the production of artifacts, whether these be bridges, buildings, statues, cars or space probes. The nature of software may make this design process more complex, but does not alter its essential nature.

So if we examine the quotation from Jones a little more closely, and rephrase it a little, we can identify the set of actions that need to be performed by a designer in deriving and specifying a solution to a problem. (There may, of course, be more than one possible solution; indeed, this is generally so, and this is again where the process of design differs somewhat from the case of scientific investigation, since for the latter it is unusual for

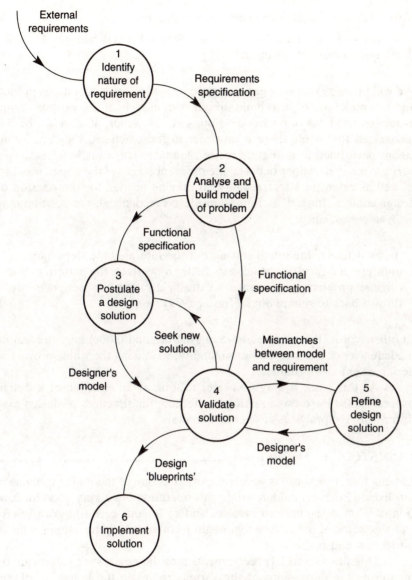

Figure 1.2 A model of the design process.

there to be more than one equivalent solution to a problem.) This set of actions can be summarized as:

- postulate a solution
- build a model of the solution

- evaluate the model against the original requirement
- elaborate the model to produce a detailed specification of the solution (a form of 'blueprint')

We will be using this very general 'process model' again at various points, and will make use of it to build up our own models of the various design processes used for software development. However, it should also be recognized that while there is an order to these actions, they are by no means performed in a single, precise sequence. It is usually necessary to perform many iterations between the different stages of the design process, as well as extensive backtracking that may be needed for the revision of design choices. Indeed, as Jones himself has recognized, the position may be even worse, since:

> 'If, as is likely, the act of tracing out the intermediate steps exposes unforeseen difficulties or suggests better objectives, the pattern of the original problem may change so drastically that the designers are thrown back to square one.' (Jones, 1970)

In other words, the act of elaborating the original model might reveal its inadequacies or even its total unsuitability, so making the whole process of design essentially unstable.

At this point it may be useful to look at an example of a design process, and to use this to demonstrate how the practices of design may differ from the practices of scientific analysis.

CASE STUDY 1   Moving house

Moving to a new house is widely regarded as one of the major traumas in our lives. However, hidden within this operation lies a very good illustration of what designing can involve, and so for our case study we briefly examine some of the actions that might be involved when planning a move into a new house.

One practice widely recommended to the new owner is to begin by measuring the dimensions of the various rooms in the house, to obtain some squared paper and to use this for drawing up a scale plan showing all the rooms, doors, windows and so on. The next step is to measure the dimensions of various items of furniture and to cut out cardboard shapes to represent these on the chosen scale. Together these form a representation of the new house and its future contents that can be considered as forming the **initial model**. Figure 1.3 shows an example of such an outline plan for a small single-storey house.

The design process itself then involves trying to identify the 'best' positions for the pieces of card on the plan of the new house. There is really

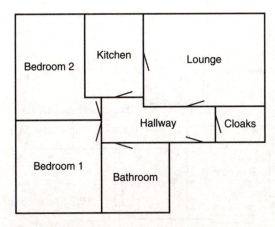

Figure 1.3 Outline plan of a single-storey house.

no analytical form that can be used to do this, since it is usually necessary to trade off different factors in making the choices. However, there are various **strategies** that can be adopted: for example, determine which rooms will take greatest priority, and then seek to find ways of producing a well-matched set of furniture for those rooms. This strategy may lead to greater mismatches in the remaining rooms than would occur if the owner tried for an overall best match.

Some of the **constraints** that apply to the various possible solutions will be more significant than others. Most people would not wish to place kitchen equipment in the living-room, for example, but might be prepared to position surplus fireside chairs in a bedroom. Other factors that might constrain the choice could be colour matches, style and so on. Equally, it is undesirable to obstruct power outlets – a point that leads on to our next issue.

The representation provided by the model as described above is somewhat incomplete, since it is only two-dimensional. On occasion it will be necessary to make vertical projections too, in order to avoid blocking windows with tall furniture, or to ensure that a power outlet will still be accessible through the legs of an item of furniture. Again, it may be necessary to make some trade-offs between what is desirable and what is practicable. Figure 1.4 shows how the model used in Figure 1.3 can be extended to describe these factors.

The final plan that is produced from this process can then be regarded as providing **a blueprint** for use by the removal team on the removal day. Indeed, not only will it determine just where in the house the various items are to be placed when the removal van arrives, but it may also affect the way that the removal process is to be organized, since the

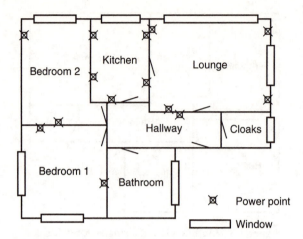

Figure 1.4 Expanded plan of a single-storey house.

removers might choose to pack their van in a particular way in order to make the unloading process easier.

From this relatively simple case study, we should be able to see some of the ways in which the process of design differs from that of scientific method. Rather than being able to identify a 'right' coordinate system that allows us to separate the variables and solve for each separately, we have to build a relatively complex model, and then make adjustments to this in order to produce a solution. There may be many possible 'solutions', and we may well have no very strong criteria that can be used to help us in choosing from a number of the better ones.

However, in some senses the problem that is presented in this case study provides a much simpler environment than is often available to the software designer. The form of the initial model used to describe the problem is directly related to that of the final blueprint used to describe the solution, in that both are scale drawings of the building. So there is no need to 'transform' between the representation used to describe the problem and that used to describe the solution, as is generally the case for software design. Similarly, the 'designer' is able to manipulate well-defined 'objects', in that each item of furniture already exists and its properties (that is, its dimensions) are fixed, and can easily be measured. The equivalent properties for software objects will generally not be so easily quantifiable or even identifiable.

Before going any further, it may be useful to take a brief look at another example of a design problem. Again, it is taken from a more traditional field than that of software development, but this problem possesses a set of constraints that some readers will probably be more familiar with.

CASE STUDY 2   The garden shed

The Lotsalogs timber company is chiefly concerned with operating sawmills and with producing various standard sizes of timber. As a side-line, they are developing a new production unit that will use the timber to construct a small range of garden sheds. These sheds will all need to be constructed by using a set of prefabricated panels, so that they can be assembled at the customer's home with relative ease.

The manager of the shed production unit therefore needs to produce a set of designs for a number of different sheds. Much of the process for doing this is relatively direct, but this time there are some constraints upon the form of the end result that are rather different from those of the previous problem. These do not constrain the form of the design process directly, but they influence it indirectly in terms of their effect upon the design product.

Apart from the cost of the timber, the main cost to consider in developing a new shed is the cost of fabricating the parts. Since sawing timber is very time-consuming, the amount of sawing needs to be kept to a minimum. Consideration of this factor has therefore led to the following set of design constraints.

- A shed should be assembled from a set of prefabricated panels for the sides and roof.

- Assuming that the boarding on the sides runs horizontally, each panel should be of a height that allows it to be constructed from a whole number of boards.

- Where possible, the panels used in one shed should be of a size that allows them to be used in another: for example, the side panel for a small shed could also be used as the back panel for a larger model.

- Windows and doors should be of standard dimensions, and again the height of each should correspond to a whole number of boards, in order to reduce the time needed for cutting out special shapes.

These effectively form constraints upon the design process too, and the designer will also need to consider a number of practical issues about size and shape of the range of products.

As we observed for the previous case study on moving house, there is no evident prescription that can be used to produce a set of designs for garden sheds that will automatically meet all of the criteria, as well as being visually pleasing and practical to use. Given the nature of the problem, the process will certainly be more direct than for the previous case study, but it will still involve some feedback and iteration of ideas.

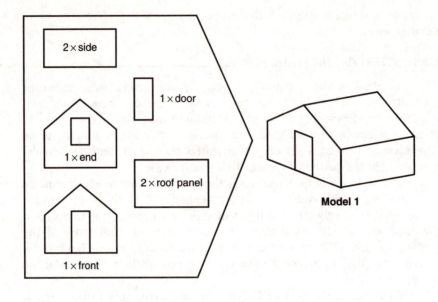

Model 1

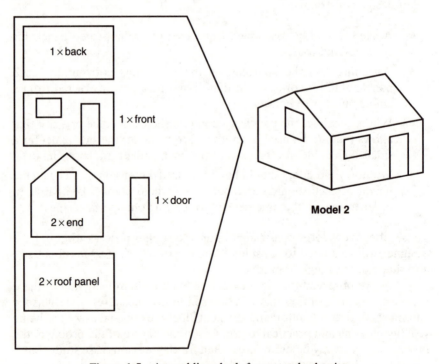

Model 2

Figure 1.5 Assembling sheds from standard units.

Given the original requirements that were identified by the company, and the constraints created by the nature of the material and the need for reuse of components, the outcome of the process will be a set of drawings showing the dimensions of each panel, the way that it should be assembled from the basic units of timber, and the ways that the panels can be assembled to create different sheds, as shown in Figure 1.5.

Obviously this problem could be explored further to provide more insight into the design process, but for the moment we can begin to see the importance of the basic idea of **modularity** and the way that it can be used in such a system. Modularity is an important tool in construction, and it is as important for constructing software as for constructing garden sheds, tower blocks and the like. However, it is not always quite so easy to see the most effective form it should take when we are designing software.

For both of the case studies introduced here, we can see how the concepts of design as described by Jones can be related to the processes involved in producing a solution, although the nature of the two problems is very different. In both cases the designer proceeds to build a model of what he or she wants to achieve – an organized house or a balanced range of products; modifies the model until satisfied that it can meet the particular constraints; and then elaborates it in order to specify clearly what needs to be done to turn the model into reality.

In one case the end product is an organizational plan for the removal men, in the other it is a set of plans and drawings that will be used by the joiners who produce the sheds. For both cases there are constraints operating upon the process, although these have very different forms, and in both cases the designer has some concept of **quality** to help with making choices. In the one case this may be the balance of style and colour for the furniture in a room, in the other it will be a matter of producing a shed that has the 'right' proportions. Quality is an elusive concept, although an important one, and it is one that we will be returning to later.

The next section seeks to establish a clearer picture of the designer's goals, and to clarify how these can be described for software systems.

1.2 Objectives for the design activity

As we saw in the previous section, the principal task for the designer is to specify the best solution to a problem and produce a description of *how* this is to be organized. This description then forms a 'blueprint' that can be used by the eventual implementors of the system.

Returning briefly to the two case studies that were introduced above, we can see that the objectives for these are somewhat different in form. They can be described as aiming to produce respectively:

- a plan that informs the removal men where each major item of furniture is to be positioned;

- a set of plans that inform the joiner about the dimensions of the panels and how the panels are to be jointed and so on.

The first of these is largely approximate (the extent to which this is true is, of course, variable: repositioning a chair is a less daunting task than re-positioning a piano). The second is more precise because a greater degree of precision is required, and so the degree of tolerance that is acceptable in the product may well need to be specified as a part of the plan. So the form of the output produced from the design process depends not only upon the nature of the problem, but also upon the nature of its eventual implementation.

In addition, the plans produced by the designer may need to indicate some information about the sequencing of operations in the eventual construction process. In the first example, some items of furniture may need to be positioned before or after others, perhaps because it will be difficult to move items past them; and in the second example, the directions for assembly may indicate any significant ordering that may be necessary. (We would generally expect to erect all of the walls before beginning to place the roof in position.)

Now that these two examples have introduced some basic ideas about the design process and its environment as it applies to static, physical artifacts, we can begin to explore how these ideas apply to designing software, which is dynamic and abstract. Before doing so, however, it will first be useful to review how the activity of design fits into the overall process of software development.

A number of models are used to describe the different approaches to software production. These models are neither rigid nor prescriptive, and should be treated chiefly as frameworks that can be used to aid discussion – which is how we will treat them here (Gladden, 1982; McCracken and Jackson, 1982). The most widely quoted model is that of the **software life-cycle**, which appears in a variety of forms in the software engineering literature. This model describes the software production process as being divided into a sequence of **phases**, which in turn can be divided into sub-phases. A fairly simple generic form of this is described below, and is shown in Figure 1.6 in a format that explains the term 'waterfall model' that has sometimes been applied to it (Royce, 1970). The major phases of the life-cycle can be identified as:

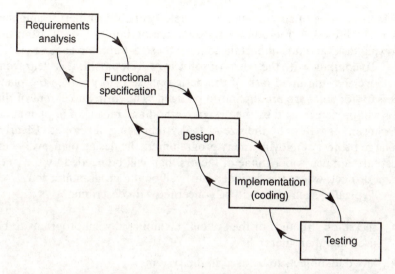

Figure 1.6 A simple form of the waterfall model describing the process of software development.

(1)   Requirements analysis, which is concerned with identifying what is *needed* from a system.

(2)   Specification, in which the objective is to state precisely and in an unambiguous manner what the system is to *do* in order to meet the overall requirements.

(3)   Design, which is concerned with describing *how* the system is to perform its tasks so as to meet the specification.

(4)   Implementation, which elaborates upon the design and translates this into a form that can be *used* on a computer system.

(5)   Testing, which is concerned with performing a *validation* of the implementation, in order to demonstrate how well it complies with the original requirements, the specification and the design.

As already mentioned, it is important that this is not considered as a rigid framework. Indeed, Chapter 3 will return to this theme and look at the role of design in greater detail, examining some of the other frameworks that are used. Similarly, one should not view the development life-cycle as simply forming a progression of operations from phase 1 to phase 5 in a neat, orderly sequence. As Figure 1.6 emphasizes, performing the task in each phase is apt to reveal the need to modify the outputs from the previous phases. Also, the actions of each phase usually involve a degree of iteration.

　　For the moment we will concentrate on using this framework to identify what the designer needs to do, and to see how the task of design differs from those of specification and implementation. In performing any task in the life-cycle, there is always some temptation to 'poach' from the following task, and it is important to keep these as separate as possible.

To continue with the needs of software development: it is clear from the above that the main task of the design phase is to produce the plans necessary for software production to proceed. The form and extent of the plans will be determined by the design method and means of implementation chosen, as well as by the size of the system being developed. Clearly, in a large project employing many programmers the design plans will need to capture a much wider range of factors than will be needed by the one-person project, where the designer may well be the programmer too.

Typically, such plans will be concerned with describing:

- the static structure of the system, including any subprograms to be used and their hierarchy;
- any data objects to be used in the system;
- the algorithms to be used;
- the packaging of the system, in terms of how components are grouped in compilation units (assuming that implementation will use a conventional imperative programming language);
- interactions between components, including the form these should take, and the nature of any causal links.

These are all concerned with specifying the form of the design product itself. But as was observed above, the overall design task may also involve producing process-oriented plans too, concerned with such matters as the preferred order of development for subprograms/modules and so on, and the strategy for their eventual integration into the complete system. (These are rather like the assembly directions that are needed for construction of the garden shed.) However, for the moment we will chiefly concern ourselves with the needs of the design product.

As in many more 'classical' forms of engineering, software designers produce plans that specify how the final product is to be assembled in terms of the items listed above. This usually requires the use of a variety of forms of representation, since each of these provides a different 'view' of a system. In a way, the use of these multiple views corresponds to the use of plan, elevation and end views in technical drawing, as well as to the cross-sectional forms used to indicate assembly details. (The concept of tolerance is perhaps lacking though, since software components generally have to 'fit' rather precisely.)

For software systems, however, a further degree of complexity has to be considered. For when one designs software one designs a *process*; and so one will need to model and describe its *behaviour* as well as its structure, and also the *functions* that it will perform. So the designer's

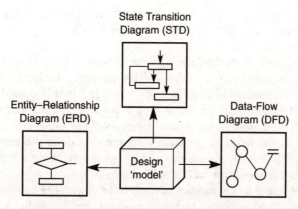

Figure 1.7 Examples of design viewpoints.

model will ideally include descriptions that also encompass these aspects of the eventual system.

To meet these needs, the designer will usually make use of a number of different forms of design representation to help with constructing the model, each representation providing a different **viewpoint** on the form of a design, as shown in Figure 1.7. The more complex the system, the more viewpoints are likely to be needed to understand its behaviour, and to provide a specification that is sufficiently complete for it to be used as an aid in the construction of the system.

We will return later to consider more fully the ways in which the dynamic nature of a software system influences (and complicates) the process of design; for the moment we will continue to focus our attention upon the nature of the design process in general.

1.3   Design as a problem-solving process

Having described the nature of the design process, and having examined its role and objectives in terms of software development, it is worth stepping back for a moment and reminding ourselves of the ultimate purpose of design.

The purpose of design is simply to produce a solution to a problem. The problem will typically be summarized by means of some form of requirements specification, and it is the designer's task to provide a description of how that requirement is to be met. Design is therefore essentially a problem-solving task, and the examples given show that it is not an analytical process. The process of design involves the designer in evaluating different options, and in making choices using decision criteria that may be complex and may involve trade-offs between factors such as size, speed and ease of adaptation, as well as other problem-specific factors.

Throughout all of this, the designer needs to keep in mind that the ultimate requirement is one of fitness for purpose. However elegant or efficient the final solution, the basic two needs are that it should work and that it should do the required job as well as possible. This is not to say that other factors and qualities are not important, but simply that they are subordinate to the need to produce a system that does the required job. However well structured, elegant or efficient a system may be, it will be assessed ultimately on how well it achieves its purpose.

The designer has a number of tools to help with the task of problem-solving. Design *methods* can provide strategies that will help to determine which choice may be most appropriate in a given situation. *Representations* can also help with the process of building models of the intended system and with evaluating its behaviour. In combination with these, *abstraction* plays a very important part, since to build manageable models of large and complex systems we need ways of abstracting their critical features for use in forming our models. Abstraction enables the designer to concentrate effort on building a logical model of a system, which is translated into a physical model at a relatively late stage in the design process.

The concept of abstraction is enormously important for all branches of engineering. Essentially, abstraction is concerned with the removal of detail from a description of a problem, while still retaining the essential properties of its structure. In our first case study, the outline plan on squared paper provided an abstraction of the idea of a house. It retained only those forms of information that were needed for solving the particular problem – namely two-dimensional areas – together with information about positioning of doors, windows, power outlets and so on. Clearly a house is a highly complex object, and the two-dimensional plan is the particular abstraction that is needed on this specific occasion. For the task of rewiring the house, a quite different abstraction would be needed, based on the use of some form of circuit diagram. Again, this would be a very incomplete description of the whole structure, but it would retain the basic information that was essential for the particular purpose.

This concept of abstraction is a very important one, and it is one that novice software designers are apt to find difficult to employ effectively (Adelson and Soloway, 1985). Programmers are accustomed to working with a wonderfully pliable medium, and so it is all too easy to be over-influenced by relatively detailed features of programming language structures when thinking about design. The designer needs to learn to think about a system in an abstract way – in terms of events, entities, objects, or whatever other key items are appropriate – and to leave questions of detail, such as the specific forms of loop construct to be used in a particular algorithm, until a relatively late stage in the design process.

Abstraction therefore plays a key role in this book, corresponding to its central role in design. In considering the forms of design representation that can be used for different purposes, we will be looking at ways of modelling a system using different abstract viewpoints. In looking at design methods, we will be seeing how the practices that they involve are intended to encourage the designer to think about a system in an abstract way. The effective use of abstraction is a key skill that any designer needs to learn and practise.

1.4   Design as a 'wicked' problem

Before concluding this general review of the nature of the design process, we should briefly consider some of the effects that the issues discussed in the previous sections have upon it. The major conclusion to draw is that the design process lacks any analytical form, with one important consequence being that there may well be a number of acceptable solutions to any given problem. Because of this, the process of design will rarely be 'convergent', in the sense of being able to direct the designer towards a single preferred solution. Indeed, the notion of the 'wicked' problem, which is sometimes used to describe a process such as that of design, suggests that it is potentially unstable.

A 'wicked' problem demonstrates some interesting properties. It can be characterized as a problem whose form is such that a solution for one of its aspects reveals an even more complex problem beneath. The term was coined by Rittel and Webber (1984), and arose from their analysis of the nature of social planning problems and of the design issues that were involved in these.

Social planning has many examples of such 'wicked' problems. One of the better-known is evident in many large cities in the UK, where rehousing in tower blocks of people who previously lived in substandard housing may have improved living conditions, but at the cost of destroying communities and other social frameworks. In some cases, the living conditions may also be little better or even worse, owing to architectural design decisions to construct the tower blocks with relatively untried materials. So removing the original problem has revealed or created new ones that are even less tractable. There is sometimes a similar effect during maintenance of software systems; adding one relatively innocuous feature may subsequently require massive redesign of internal data structures and reorganization of subprograms.

Rittel and Webber identified ten distinguishing properties of wicked problems, most of which can be seen as applying equally well to software design. The following four properties, taken from their list, are particularly relevant:

- There is no definitive formulation of a wicked problem. The difficulties of specifying the needs of software-based systems are well known, and the tasks of specification and design are often difficult to separate clearly. Rittel and Webber make the point that the understanding of such a problem is bound up with the ideas that we may have about solving it – which is why the simple life-cycle model in which the task of specification is followed neatly by that of design is rarely a realistic description of actual practices.

- Wicked problems have no stopping rule. Essentially this property implies that there is a lack of any criteria that can be used to establish when *the* solution to a problem has been found, such that any further work will not be able to improve upon it. For software, this is demonstrated by our lack of any quality measures that can be used to establish that any one system design is the 'best' one possible.

- Solutions to wicked problems are not true or false, but good or bad. For many scientific and classical engineering problems, we may be able to identify whether a solution is correct or false. Software designs usually come in 'shades of grey', in that there are usually no right or wrong solutions or structures. (This point will be evident to anyone who has ever had cause to mark a set of student programming assignments.)

- Every wicked problem can be considered to be a symptom of another problem. Resolving a discrepancy or inconsistency in a design may pose another problem in its turn. Again, in writing a computer program, a choice of data structure that helps with resolving one problem may well present an entirely new difficulty later.

A slightly different but related view of design problems is that of Herbert Simon (1984). He has introduced the idea of well-structured and ill-structured problems (WSPs and ISPs). There is no space here to elaborate further on these ideas but, as one might expect, the task of software design emerges as having the properties of an ISP.

These ideas are somewhat at variance with the ideas that are generally encountered in the 'classical' or 'scientific' approach to problem-solving, where we might expect that some form of convergence will occur, leading us to a single solution to a problem. The use of 'scientific' methods typically aims to reduce a problem in such a way that each step provides a set of simpler problems. As an example, separating the description of the motion of a system into descriptions of motion in each of three coordinates may result in the formulation of three separate equations that can then be solved independently, or nearly so. And if this fails to work, we can always try another criterion for separation, such as using a different coordinate system (we might try adopting polar coordinates rather than cartesian coordinates).

Unfortunately the process of producing a design is not like that at all. In working back from the initial model, one makes various choices, and the consequences of any of these choices may well be such as to make further choices much more complicated to resolve. In the extreme, the overall design itself may be shown to be inadequate. An example of just such a 'wicked' problem feature is often encountered in designing real-time systems. It may be possible to organize the system so that it can produce a response to one type of event within some required interval, but the way that this is achieved may place such constraints upon the operation of the system that it will then be unable to meet some other demand in an adequate time. Worse still (since the new problem might well be overcome by increasing the computer power available), the need to handle one event adequately might lead to the occasional exclusion of knowledge about some other event that can occur independently.

Problems like these can be hard to resolve, since concentrating upon solving one aspect in isolation (such as handling the single event) may eventually result in an inability to produce a solution for the second at all. In such cases our problem becomes one of producing a solution to the combined needs, since separating them out is not a valid option.

SUMMARY

This chapter has sought to examine the nature of the design process in fairly general terms. It has introduced a number of concepts, many of which will reappear later, and will be described in greater detail where appropriate. Some particularly important ideas presented in this chapter are:

- the design process is concerned with describing *how* a requirement is to be met by the design product;

- design *representation* forms provide means of modelling ideas about a design, and also of presenting the design plans to the programmer;

- *abstraction* is used in problem-solving, and is used to help separate the *logical* and *physical* aspects of the design process;

- the software design problem is a 'wicked' one and this imposes constraints upon the way in which the process of design can be organized and managed.

FURTHER READING

Jones J. Christopher (1970). *Design Methods: Seeds of Human Futures*. London: Wiley International

The opening chapters of this book provide an excellent degree of insight into the nature of the design process. The later chapters are less directly relevant to the issues of software design.

Cross N., ed. (1984). *Developments in Design Methodology*. London: Wiley

This collected set of articles and papers contains some significant contributions from authors such as Horst Rittel and Herb Simon. There is a strong and valuable input from a number of authors who bring the ideas of cognitive science to the study of design and designing.

Design Studies. London: Butterworth

This quarterly journal of the Design Research Society provides an insight into design issues affecting a wide range of fields of application for design techniques.

EXERCISES

1.1   You are asked to plan a journey by air from Manchester in England to Pittsburgh in the USA. Airline A is cheap, but involves flying to Chicago, waiting there for three hours and then flying on to Pittsburgh. Airline B is the most expensive, but offers a direct flight. Airline C has a package that is cheaper than that of airline A, but which involves flying from Manchester to Gatwick Airport near London, and then on to Pittsburgh via yet another airport in the USA.

      (a)   What factors besides price might affect your choice of airline?
      (b)   How does the decision about which airline and route to choose meet the 'wicked' problem criteria?

1.2   Imagine that you live in a world in which the only available means for telling the time of day are sundials and large pendulum clocks. Given the following requirements specification, suggest how you might begin exploring the ways of meeting it by creating a suitable design solution:

      The need is for a portable timepiece, to be carried in a pocket, or even (if possible) worn on one's wrist. It will have a circular dial, divided into twelve equal-sized portions, numbered 1 to 12. Two pointers will be fixed to a spindle in the centre of the dial: one (the longer one) will rotate once per hour, while the second (shorter) pointer will rotate once every 12 hours. The device should be capable of running unattended for at least 24 hours and should not need to be kept in a fixed position in order to work correctly.

This problem is a good demonstration of why the simplistic approach sometimes advocated in favour of stepwise refinement of a formal requirements specification as a means of producing a design is unrealistic and impractical for most real systems.

1.3   Sketch out a design for one or more of the following:

(a)   a rocking chair (to be made from timber)
(b)   a wooden storage rack for audio cassettes
(c)   a metal music stand that can be adjusted for height and taken apart for carrying and storage.

Then think about how you reached your design, and what changes you made to it as your thinking developed. What further changes do you think might occur if you had to produce detailed plans to help someone make this item?

1.4   Designing software is made more complex because we are designing for a sequence of actions. Sketch out a design for a set of instructions for making tea with a teapot and teabags. Try to consider the major problems that might arise (no water in the kettle, burst teabag, no kettle and so on). How would you organize the instructions for these exceptional situations so that they do not obscure the original design?

1.5   Planning a new garden is an example of design. Think about the abstractions that might arise in planning a new garden that is to have a lawn, patio, path and vegetable plot. Draw a diagram showing the different abstractions used as the plan develops.

2 The Software Design Process

2.1 Building models

2.2 Structuring the design process

2.3 Constraints upon the design process and product

2.4 Recording design decisions

2.5 Designing with others

This chapter takes the ideas about design that were introduced in Chapter 1 and considers how they particularly relate to the problem of designing software. It examines some of the conclusions that have been drawn from observation of software designers at work, and uses these to identify the forms of support that are required from a design method. Some of the other factors influencing software design are also surveyed, and their influence upon the evolution of software design techniques is considered.

2.1   Building models

The first chapter examined the characteristics of the general process of design and identified those features that made the act of designing a creative one. In this chapter the concern will be to examine the ways in which the design of software fits into this general pattern, and to identify any aspects in which it might differ significantly from design in other fields.

The difficulties involved in creating software-based systems have long been recognized. While apparently related technology such as hardware design and production has raced along gaining orders of magnitude in performance, and similarly reducing price and size, software development techniques seem to have inched along in a series of relatively small steps. Various reasons are cited for this, and in his widely acclaimed *No Silver Bullet: Essence and Accidents of Software Engineering*, Fred Brooks has pointed out some of the principal causes of this relatively slow progress (Brooks, 1987). In particular, Brooks cites the following properties of software as major factors affecting its development:

- *Complexity*. This is seen as being an essential property of software, in which no two parts are alike and a system may possess very many states during execution. This complexity is also arbitrary, being dependent upon the designer rather than the problem.

- *Conformity*. Software, being 'pliable', is expected to conform to the standards imposed by other components, such as hardware, or by external bodies, or by existing software.

- *Changeability*. Software suffers constant need for change, partly because of the apparent ease of making this (and the relatively poor techniques for costing it).

- *Invisibility*. Because software is 'invisible', any forms of representation that are used to describe it will lack any form of *visual* link that can provide an easily grasped relationship between the representation and the system – unlike, for example, a building plan which can be easily linked to the visible features of the building. This not only constrains our ability to conceptualize the characteristics of software, it also hinders communication among those involved with its development.

For these reasons (and especially the last one), while the act of designing software usually follows the general form identified for design activity in Chapter 1, it incorporates many additional problems for the designer. We therefore begin this chapter by considering the key design factor of model-building, used by a designer to posit a solution.

The construction of a model of the solution being proposed for a problem allows the designer to explore the potential limitations of a

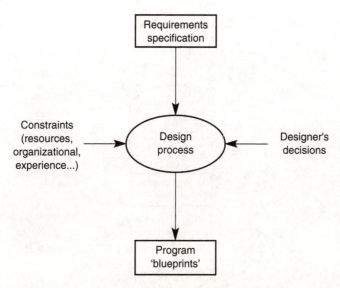

Figure 2.1 A general model of the software design process.

solution as well as to assess its behaviour and structure in an abstract way. However, the examples used in the first two case studies (Chapter 1) required the designer to construct only relatively simple models in order to explore the 'solution space'. Simple, that is, as compared with the models that are needed to assist with the process of software design. In this section we will try to identify some of the main features and characteristics of the models that are used in software design.

Figure 2.1 shows a (very general) 'model' of the software design process itself. The input to this process is provided by the Requirements Specification documents, while the outputs produced from it should consist of a set of detailed specifications that describe the form of the eventual program components. (Of course, we know from our discussion of the characteristics of wicked problems that this is a highly idealized account!)

In general, the process of software design can be elaborated into the form shown in Figure 2.2, in which the designer develops a highly abstract model of a solution (the 'architectural' or 'logical' design), and then transforms this into a very detailed design (the 'detailed' or 'physical' design) which can be used as a 'blueprint' for the programmer. The general structure shown in Figure 2.2 will be used quite extensively, in this and later chapters, in order to describe some of the different approaches to software design. However, for the moment we will concentrate chiefly upon the general role of model-building during design, rather than upon the exact forms that the models and transformations will take for specific design strategies.

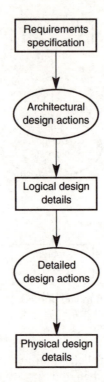

Figure 2.2   The major phases of the software design process.

The initial 'architectural model' that is used to describe the intended form that a system will take is generally highly abstract in its nature. The way that this is developed during the process of designing was examined in an interesting study of the ways that software designers work, made by Adelson and Soloway (1985). In their experiments, they studied the ways that both experienced and inexperienced designers set about the task of forming their models when they were faced with a range of different problems. The experiments were based upon situations where a designer was posed:

- a familiar problem;
- a problem that was unfamiliar in detail, but taken from a familiar domain; and
- a problem that was unfamiliar in all senses.

The study was limited in scope, in that they looked at only a small number of subjects, and concentrated their study to a single specialized problem domain. Also, for practical reasons, the problems themselves were relatively small in scale. However, their findings do seem to reflect more general experience with the software design process. Some key observations that were produced from this research included:

- The use of abstract 'mental models' by the designer to simulate the dynamic behaviour of the eventual system that will be derived from the design.

- Expanding the detail of a model in a systematic manner by keeping all elements of the design at the same level of detail as they are developed. This then aids with the task of simulation.

- The need to make any constraints affecting the design as explicit as possible when handling an unfamiliar problem.

- Reuse of previous design plans. This arises when part of a problem can be solved by using a previously developed design object or structure. Where this occurs, designers may use a 'label' to identify the plan, rather than describing it in detail at that point.

- Making notes about future (detailed) intentions, as an aid to systematic expansion of a design.

The last point is less directly concerned with the manner in which a model is developed and used, but it reflects the way in which an experienced designer avoids the pitfall of following one thread of a design in too much detail. (Fixing the details of one aspect of a design at too early a stage may severely, and inappropriately, later constrain the designer's choices for the other aspects.)

Unfortunately this experiment is so far the only significant one to have examined the activities involved in software design from the viewpoint of the actions of the designer and in a systematic manner. However, others have conducted some similar studies of design activity in more 'normal' working situations (Curtis *et al.*, 1988; Visser and Hoc, 1990). While this work concentrated on studying the process of software *design*, rather than on *programming*, many programmers will recognize that some of the observed techniques are also used for the more detailed design tasks that they undertake when 'programming in the small'. For instance, many programmers probably perform simulations by executing mental models for sections of their programs when coding conditional loop structures: modelling the entry/exit conditions that occur when the loop is first executed, and checking to ensure that the loop will terminate in the intended manner. In that sense, the idea of simulation is a fairly familiar one, and it is clearly rather important at all levels of abstraction.

Returning to the large-scale issues of design (such as arise for the type of problem that we term 'programming in the large'), we will see when we come to examine different software design methods that many of these provide quite extensive forms of support for a designer in building initial abstract models in order to explore ideas. The forms used for the models may be graphical, as in the case of 'systematic' methods, or mathematical, in the case of the more 'formal' methods. In each case, the use of an abstract model generally allows the designer to predict the likely behaviour of a system for different scenarios. In addition, the models can be used to aid a systematic expansion of the initial ideas of the designer towards the production of a detailed design description.

The models formed during the early stages of design are mainly concerned with assisting either the analysis or the specification of the problem (or with both, since they are often entwined). If we return briefly to the more general view of the design process that was given on page 5, based upon the quotation from the work of J. Christopher Jones, we can see that this use of an initial abstract model corresponds with the idea that a designer needs to 'predict a future state' and so needs to assume the outcome of the design process in order to begin that process.

A major role for a design method is therefore to provide the necessary set of transformations that will lead from this initial model to a detailed description of the eventual solution that corresponds to that particular model. The next section will explore the nature of a method a little more closely.

2.2 Structuring the design process

Chapter 1 examined the nature of the general design process and showed that it is quite unlike the 'scientific' approach to problem-solving. The act of designing is not based upon an analytic strategy, aimed at identifying the one true solution to a problem, as determined by physical laws. Instead, it is a highly creative process, and certainly very unlikely to lead to the identification of a single solution to any given problem.

Experimental study of software designers and their practices suggests that, as might be expected, some people are better designers than others (Curtis *et al.*, 1988). However, since the number of truly great designers is very small, we need to seek ways of providing appropriate design skills to a wider group in as effective a manner as possible.

In Curtis (1988), the exceptional designers were observed to possess three significant characteristics. As illustrated in Figure 2.3, these are:

- *Familiarity with the application domain*, enabling them to map between problem structures and solution structures with ease. (A domain in this sense may be one such as data processing, real-time, telecommunication systems, and so on.)

- *Skill in communicating technical vision to other project members*. This was observed to be so significant a factor that much of the design work was often accomplished while interacting with others.

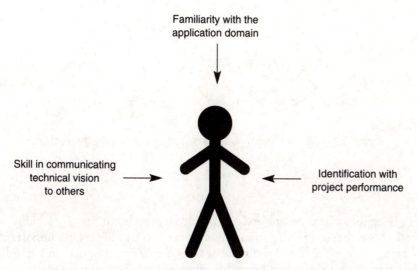

Figure 2.3   The characteristics of an exceptional designer.

- *Identification with project performance*, to the extent that they could be found taking on significant management responsibilities for ensuring technical progress.

Interestingly, though, the exceptional designers studied often did not possess particularly good programming skills.

Others too have identified the importance of the domain knowledge of the designer for producing successful designs (Adelson and Soloway, 1985), and clearly this aspect can only come from the accumulation of experience in a particular problem domain. It may well be, though, that the process of acquiring such knowledge can be accelerated and improved.

When we look at how successful designers work, there are other factors to consider, apart from those that were outlined in the previous section. Visser and Hoc (1990) have used the term 'opportunistic' to describe observations of software design activity. Even where designers aim to follow a strategy such as 'top-down' (systematically refining the description of the solution into ever smaller actions), they may deviate from this plan, either:

- to *postpone* a decision, if the information required is not yet available at this design level; or

- to process information that is readily to hand, and which can be used for defining modules in *anticipation* of further developments in the design.

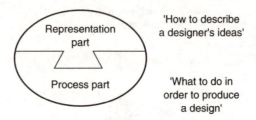

Figure 2.4 The two major components of a software design method.

Such opportunistic design activity is not unstructured; more probably it reflects the designer's experience and domain knowledge. One important consequence is that the developers of software design support tools should not give them an interface form that impedes this behaviour on the part of the designer.

Even if rigorous procedures for performing the transformations between the stages of a designer's model cannot be devised, there may still be benefits in seeking to codify design strategies in some way. Experienced designers can make use of opportunistic techniques precisely because they *are* experienced, and have extensive domain knowledge to guide their actions. However, such techniques are clearly inadequate where these characteristics are lacking, and one way in which to acquire the necessary knowledge is by the use of design methods. So the purpose of a design method can be regarded as being to provide the structure necessary to develop and elaborate a design in a systematic manner.

We will be looking further at the detailed form of the software development process in Chapter 7. This section will concentrate on what a design method should provide in the way of support for the designer, and on the factors that will limit its effectiveness.

For our purposes, a software design method can be considered as providing a supportive framework that consists of two major components (shown schematically in Figure 2.4).

- The *representation part* provides a set of descriptive forms that the designer can use for building models of the problem and their ideas for its solution, and for describing the structural features of the solution to the eventual implementors.

- The *process part* is concerned with describing how the necessary transformations between the representation forms are to be organized, as well as with any elaboration of their detail that might be required.

A further component is provided in most design methods:

- A set of *heuristics* that can be used to provide guidelines on the ways in which the activities defined in the process part can be organized for specific classes of problem. These are generally based upon experience of past use of the method within a particular domain or for a particular form of structure.

While these do not necessarily provide the domain knowledge that a designer needs, they may well aid in developing this knowledge.

The representation part of a design method will usually include forms that can be used for modelling the problem, as well as forms that reflect the significant structures of the implementation media. As an example of the latter form: in describing a garden shed, one would use drawings that described its plan, elevation and end view, and which showed how key joints were to be assembled. In describing software, one will typically use detailed design forms that describe the structures of the program subunits, the relationships that these have with one another, and the relationships that they have with the other entities in the system.

So representation forms generally reflect the properties of the objects in the design. Those forms that describe the detailed design may be concerned with fairly concrete properties such as the calling hierarchy, complex data structures, number of parameters and so on. On the other hand, the forms that are used for problem modelling will be concerned with more abstract properties of the problem objects and any relationships that may exist between these, based upon relatively abstract concepts such as operations and information flow.

The process part of design is rather more difficult to quantify and classify. Its structure may be derived from fairly general theory, from specific 'principles', or from heuristics ('it worked well when we did it this way before'). Most likely, it will reflect a mix of all three of these. In general there is a lack of strong theoretical underpinnings for existing design methods, and even the underlying principles may themselves be relatively empirical in nature. However, we can still identify some of the expectations that we have from the process part of a design method, which will include providing some degree of guidance for the following tasks:

- identification of the design actions to be performed;
- use of the representation forms;
- procedures for making transformations between representations;
- quality measures to aid in making choices;
- identification of particular constraints to be considered;
- verification/validation operations.

Most design methods provide strategic guidance for the designer, rather than detailed solutions to issues. To a large extent this is driven by the problem-oriented nature of many of the choices that a designer has to make: the role of the method is to help the designer to identify the choices available, and to evaluate these in terms of their likely consequences.

Akin (1990) has suggested that there are three 'classic' conditions that are observed in creative acts such as design. These are:

- The *recognition step*, sometimes termed the 'Aha!' response. This is a skill in which the designer recognizes a solution that has been there all along. (This form of creative act is perhaps more typical of scientific progress than of design progress.)

- The *problem restructuring* step, in which a change of viewpoint that is used to describe or model a problem leads to a major break-through in solving it. As an example, in solving a given problem, the designer may decide to store the data in an array. This choice may subsequently require a highly complex set of algorithms, and the designer may later realize that using a linked list in place of the array will result in much simpler algorithms.

- The *development of procedural knowledge* about how such problems are best solved, allowing the designer to perform many creative acts within a domain. (Again, Akin notes that there are many fields of human endeavour where this can be seen to apply.)

A major component of the process part of a design method is the structuring of the design transformations. The sequence that is expressed in the 'process diagram' used in Figure 2.2 is, of course, still a fairly abstract one, and omits any detail about the iterations that will normally occur as a designer explores and evaluates the design options. Any 'formal' inclusion of the heuristics is also omitted, since the nature of these is too strongly method-specific.

If we explore further the transformation steps themselves, we find that for each step we can identify a general structure of the form shown in Figure 2.5. Each transformation involves:

- an *input model* that may be described by using a suitable 'representation' (which may be graphical, textual or mathematical);

- an *output model* that, again, can have any of these forms;

- *design inputs* through which the designer adds information to the model.

In addition, we can identify two principal forms of design transformation, which respectively involve:

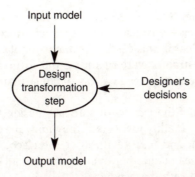

Figure 2.5   Transformation model of design activity.

- the *refinement* of structures, in which the input and output forms of the model are the same, but extra detail is added;
- the *transformation of viewpoint*, which may involve a change of representation form or of interpretation of the representation form.

In general, the transformations that involve refinement are apt to preserve the representation form while adding more detail; while those that involve a change of viewpoint add both decisions and a change of the structure of the design model. In the former case, the designer is chiefly concerned with reducing the eventual 'solution space' by making additional choices and decisions; whereas in the latter he or she may be adding information about new relationships between design objects.

The view of design as being a series of transformations is one that has been explored and used in a number of ways (Lehman *et al.*, 1984; Friel and Budgen, 1991). As a general model it provides a useful summary of design method structuring, and it will be used for this purpose in the chapters that describe specific design methods.

2.3   Constraints upon the design process and product

In practice, there are very few opportunities to design a system with a totally free hand, since each design task takes place within a particular context, and this will provide particular constraints upon the form of the design itself and possibly on the way that it is produced. We have already seen this in the case studies of developing designs for moving house and for a garden shed. In the example of moving house, the constraints were concerned both with functional issues (blocking power outlets or windows) and with aesthetic ones (clashes of style or colour, or putting a bed in the dining room...). These considerations largely act to constrain the form of the solution (or product in this case). For the example of designing garden sheds, the main constraints were again on the form of the product, and were driven by the need to provide a way of constructing sheds from easily prefabricated units.

This is generally the case with software design too. Constraints on the product are fairly readily identified: they may affect the file structures to be used, the 'look and feel' of the user interface, the choice of using several small processes or one big one – these are all constraints that are essentially concerned with the product.

Perhaps one of the most important constraints on the design task and the form of the design itself is that of the eventual form of implementation. For many years the approach used by most software development projects has been to purchase the hardware and select the major software facilities (operating system, programming language) before even beginning on the design task itself. While enlightenment may be (very slowly) dawning, the choice of the programming language is still more likely to be determined by external factors such as programmer skills and knowledge than by the features of the problem itself.

The imperative forms of programming language (COBOL, ALGOL, FORTRAN, Ada, C, Modula-2 etc.) have remained the dominant tool in software production. Indeed, the use of imperative language constructs is implicit in almost all design methods currently available, and so will be assumed throughout this book. However, the use of imperative forms is not essential to the design process, and the principles of design studied here are certainly not restricted to the imperative paradigm alone.

Constraints on the process of design are more difficult to identify. They may be concerned with designer skills and knowledge (experience with a particular method), or with a need to conform to a particular 'style' of design, in order to aid future maintenance. In some cases, a constraint upon the product leads to a constraint upon the process – where, say, the output form needs to be consistent with that generally produced from a particular design strategy.

Whatever form they take, constraints can be considered as forming a set of bounds upon the 'solution space'. Even if the process of design will not necessarily converge upon one solution for a given problem, the effects of the constraints may be to limit the amount of possible divergence that will be acceptable in particular circumstances.

In general, any significant constraints will be identified in the initial specification documents (or at least, they *should* appear here). After that, they mainly manifest themselves in the choices that the designer makes during the design process, since by limiting the choices that are available to the designer at any point, they effectively limit the overall solution space. Constraints are problem-specific in general, and as such they are rarely built into any method in any specific way. However, the process part of a design method needs to be able to accommodate their presence, at least by encouraging the designer to consider their influence when making design choices.

2.4   Recording design decisions

The need to record the decisions of the designer (or, for larger projects, of the design team) is important, from the viewpoint of the design task itself, and even more so from the viewpoint of the maintenance team who may later need to extend and modify the design. Unfortunately, while designers may diligently record the actual decisions, it is much rarer to record the reasons for the decisions. (Experience suggests that this is not a problem that is confined to software engineering alone: it seems to occur in many other branches of engineering practice too.)

Beginning with the original task of design, the recording of reasons is likely to be encouraged if the design process includes any form of **design audit**. Such an audit may consist of peer review of the designer's ideas, or may be something more formal that is conducted by the project manager. Whatever the form, if audits are held, they will be more systematically and usefully performed if the reasons for decisions are recorded.

There is an even stronger need on the part of the system mainten- ance task (which is thought to involve around 50–80 per cent of program- mer and designer effort). In order to modify or extend a design, the maintenance designers need to be able to recapture the original models that were used by the designers of a system. Only when they have a reasonably complete model can they reliably decide how to implement their changes in the most effective manner (Littman *et al.*, 1987). Possess- ing some record of the reasons for the existing structure can help both with recreating this model and with evaluating the effects of any changes. In turn, the reasons for the change need to be added to the records kept by the maintainers, in order to maintain a consistent and complete history of the system design.

So a major motivation for recording the reason for any design decisions is one of quality control, both at the design stage and also much later, during maintenance. Only if we have a complete picture can we hope to fully understand a design, and this is an essential factor in producing a good, reliable design.

Unfortunately, while software design methods generally provide good forms of support for recording decisions about product issues, usually through diagrams or other notation, they are generally weaker on process matters, such as recording the reasons for the decision. While the record- ing of decisions and their reasons can fairly easily be made a part of design practice, it is relatively hard to enforce it unless there is a strong quality control system in operation.

The way in which design decisions are recorded is obviously somewhat method-specific. Some work has been performed to look at ways of modelling this process of design deliberation – the 'Potts and Bruns model' (Potts and Brun, 1988; Lee, 1991) – and it has been demonstrated for the JSD method. As yet, though, there is little or no general tool support that can be used for this task.

An important issue in terms of recording decisions about a design has been raised by Parnas and Clements (1986). They have observed that, even if the design process actually used to produce a design is not a rational one, the documentation that is finally produced should still make it appear as though it were. In other words, the documentation should be written as though the 'ideal' design process was the one that was followed. Indeed, they argue that since design will never be a rational process (as we have been observing throughout this and the preceding chapter), any documentation produced will always need to 'fake' this appearance of rationality.

The principal benefits of such an approach are that new members of a design team should be able to absorb knowledge about the project much more easily, and also that the eventual task of maintaining the system will also be made easier. Parnas and Clements observe that for even a scientific document such as a mathematical proof, the form published is rarely the form of the initial derivation, since, as understanding grows, simplifications can usually be found. Readers need the simpler proof, since they are interested in the truth of the theorem, not the process of its discovery. In the same way, it is the structure of a design that matters to the new team member or the maintainer, and not the way it was developed.

The choice of the forms of documentation that should be used for documenting particular structures is a separate issue that will not be discussed here, since it merits a chapter to itself. However, we should note that this is one of those areas where the invisibility of software, and the complexity of its nature, become particularly evident.

2.5   Designing with others

While the development of a sound design is important for software development tasks of any scale, it is essential for any form of programming in the large, where a project is likely to involve a design team rather than a single designer. Given the nature of the design process, it is hardly surprising that designing as a team adds further complications, many of them in the form of added constraints upon the process, and hence upon the form of the product. (For medium-sized systems it sometimes appears as though there were an invariant 'law' of design that specified that the number of design modules should be equal to the number of members of the design team!)

Many of the very successful and 'exciting' software systems have been the work of one or a few 'great designers'. Brooks (1987) contrasts the 'excitement' of UNIX, Pascal, Modula, SmallTalk and similar systems with the 'blandness' of COBOL, PL/1, MVS/370 and MS-DOS as examples that support this point.

In the absence of any great designers, designing a system through the use of a team brings two major additional issues that need to be handled within the chosen design strategy. These are:

- how to split the design task among the team, and to determine the interfaces between the parts;

- how to integrate the individual contributions to the design, which may well involve a process of negotiation between the members of the team.

The first of these problems is at least partly aided by the increasing trend towards modular designs, an issue that will be examined at a later point. For the moment, it is sufficient to note that this strategy does help with the problem of subdividing the design operations among a team, although it is still necessary to ensure a fair balance of effort, where appropriate.

Bringing the elements of a design together, along with the accompanying negotiations, is again a mix of technical and managerial issues. While a process of negotiation may be right and necessary, it should not be allowed to reduce the integrity of the overall design.

Some of the original research studying how programming (and hence designing) is performed by teams was described in Gerald Weinberg's classic book *The Psychology of Computer Programming* (Weinberg, 1971). In this he observed the effects of different forms of group organization, ranging from groups that worked as an 'egoless' set of peers (in which different members of the group might take the lead for specific tasks), to those that had a highly hierarchical form.

The more hierarchical approach was at one time advocated by the exponents of the 'chief programmer' school (Baker, 1972; Brooks, 1975). Set in the design context, the chief programmer functions as a chief designer, acting in a highly centralized role, with the other members of the team performing functions that are solely intended to support his or her activity. The parallel usually drawn has been with the surgical team – which rather begs the question of the very different purpose of the latter. Members of the team might have specialized roles themselves, such as librarian, administrator or documentation expert, and there is a back-up who acts as the technical deputy to the chief programmer.

In practice, few design teams seem to act along such lines, perhaps because there are few great designers who can take on the very exacting central role it demands.

More recently, greater effort has been made to understand and model the psychological factors that influence team behaviour in designing (Curtis *et al.*, 1988; Curtis and Walz, 1990). The factors discussed in the references include:

- the size of a team (there seem to be pointers that a size of 10–12 members is probably an upper limit for productive working);
- the large impact that may be exerted by a small subset of the members of the team who possess superior application domain knowledge;
- the influence of organizational issues within a company (and particularly the need to maintain a bridge between the developers and the customer).

This last point raises an important issue in that:

> 'Designers needed operational scenarios of system use to understand the application's behaviour and its environment. Unfortunately, these scenarios were too seldom passed from the customer to the developer. Customers often generated many such scenarios in determining their requirements, but did not record them and abstracted them out of the requirements document.' (Curtis *et al.*, 1988)

This point is an interesting one, for it is not relevant only to the use of design teams, but addresses a much wider organizational issue in itself. (Figure 2.6 shows the full set of factors identified in Curtis *et al.*, 1988.)

For the present, however, the key issues of design team operation seem to lie more in the domain of group psychology than in that of design technology. Certainly few, if any, of the more widely used design methods offer any significant guidance on how they should be adapted for use by a team as opposed to an individual, and it would seem that they are probably correct to avoid doing so. To quote from Curtis and Walz (1990):

> 'Programming in the large is, in part, a learning, negotiation, and communication process.'

Unfortunately, to date far more effort has gone into technical research than into investigating team and organizational factors.

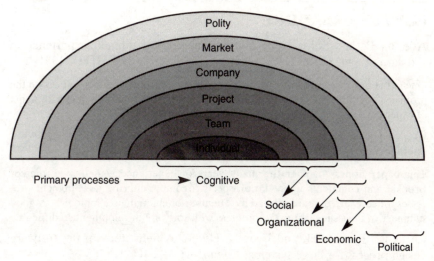

Figure 2.6 Factors influencing the software design process.

SUMMARY

This chapter has enlarged upon the issues that were raised in Chapter 1 by considering how they apply to the particular domain of software design. Major points from this chapter are:

- the complexity of the model-building processes for software systems, with their need to consider static forms as well as the dynamic behaviour of the eventual system;

- the influence of the invisible nature of software upon any attempts to describe it;

- the need for domain knowledge on the part of the designer;

- how the observed practices of software designers relate to the model of the general design process that was presented, and in particular, the use of opportunistic design practices by designers;

- the general form of a design method, and its three major components: the representation part, the process part, and the heuristics;

- how to go about recording the results of the design process, presenting an ideal view of design development by 'faking' an ideal development process;

- some of the factors that affect the operation of design teams, and how this differs from individual design practices.

FURTHER READING

Adelson B. and Soloway E. (1985). The role of domain experience in software design. *IEEE Trans. Software Engineering*, **SE-11**(11), 1351–9

One of the first papers to bring the research skills of cognitive science to bear on the problems of software design, in a series of experiments using designers with a mix of experience.

Brooks F.P. Jr (1987). No silver bullet: Essence and accidents of software engineering. *IEEE Computer*, 10–19

This paper brings together the many years of experience gained by Professor Brooks, and comments upon the prospects for improving the development processes for software that are offered by a number of emerging technologies. A good summary of the issues that make progress with software development so difficult.

Curtis B., Krasner H. and Iscoe N. (1988). A field study of the software design process for large systems. *Comm. ACM*, **31**(11), 1268–87

This paper describes an analysis performed on data gathered by interviewing personnel from 17 large projects. A particular feature is the consideration of the influence of various factors within the organization.

EXERCISES

2.1 Consider a recent item of software that you may have written. Thinking about how you developed it, are you aware of any way in which you might have reused experience from previous programs in deciding upon particular structures or algorithms?

2.2 The reuse of domain knowledge is clearly a feature that will take different forms in particular domains. Consider what particular forms of experience might be useful in the domains of

(a) processing financial transactions
(b) real-time process control for chemical plants
(c) writing compilers for imperative programming languages.

2.3 Design documentation, if available at all, often merely details the final structure of a system. Write down a list of the information about the development of a system that would be useful to you if you had to undertake a major revision of it in order to add new features.

2.4 Committees are a form of design team in some circumstances. Think back to when you were last a member of a committee that successfully produced a 'design' as a collective exercise, and identify the factors that made this possible.

3 Design in the Software Development Process

3.1 A context for design
3.2 Economic factors

3.3 Software production models and their influence
3.4 Prototyping roles and forms

Software design is but one of the many tasks that are required in Programming in the Large. In this chapter, we examine how design is influenced, both in its form and in its role, by the manner in which the overall development process is organized.

3.1   A context for design

The preceding two chapters have been concerned with examining the nature and form of the design process in general, and also with identifying the ways in which the design of software is 'different'. This chapter considers how the software design process is influenced by the context of its role within the overall task of software development.

The concept of a software life-cycle, which was introduced in Chapter 1 (page 14), provides a useful framework for describing the activities that are involved in software development – provided that we accept that it encompasses many forms and variations (Royce, 1970; Boehm, 1988; Davis *et al.*, 1988). Indeed however hard we try, it is almost always impossible to separate out completely the activities that are associated with the individual phases of development, since the overall development process involves so much iteration between tasks. This is not to say that it is not useful to have these activities recognized and classified, but rather that any form of classification is simply a tool to help us plan and manage software development. As Boehm (1988) points out:

'A software process model addresses the software project questions

(a)   What should we do next?
(b)   How long should we continue to do it?'

So methods give help by providing techniques for navigating through the detailed tasks involved in the different life-cycle phases, while process (life-cycle) models can provide guidance on the form of the overall development strategy.

Ideas about the software development process have undergone a process of evolution similar to the ways in which ideas about design have evolved. (A good overview of this evolution of thinking about life-cycle models, together with guidance on further reading, is given in Boehm (1988).) The idea of development 'steps' or 'stages' emerged in the 1950s, and Royce's formulation of the **waterfall model** (Royce, 1970), as shown in Figure 3.1, was a particularly influential refinement of earlier thinking that explicitly recognized the presence of 'feedback loops' between the various stages of development. (In many ways, this corresponds to recognizing that the task of development is a 'wicked problem', of course.)

As with design methods, there is always a danger that such a model may become institutionalized, and then used to constrain creativity rather than support it (McCracken and Jackson, 1982; Gladden, 1982). For this reason it is better to view the life-cycle model as a *descriptive* framework rather than a prescriptive one.

Two other life-cycle models that Boehm has identified as being significant are:

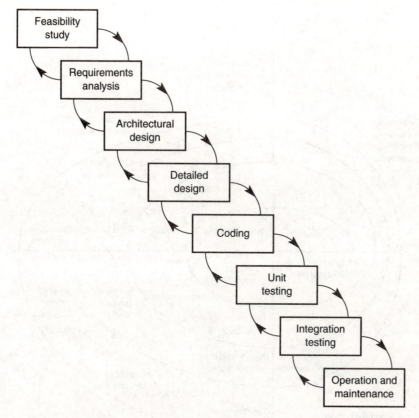

Figure 3.1 The waterfall model of the software life-cycle.

- The evolutionary development model, based upon developing high-level 'prototypes' that are gradually refined to produce the eventual system. This strategy is discussed further in Section 3.4, which examines the various roles that prototyping can have in system development.

- The transform model, based upon the automatic conversion of a formal specification of a software product into a program that satisfies the specification. Little practical progress has been made in this area, and the arguments of the preceding two chapters suggest some good reasons why this is so. However, more limited versions of this model do seem to offer more scope for real progress (Friel and Budgen, 1991).

More recently, Boehm's own **spiral model** has combined experience of the waterfall model with greater knowledge of how software projects have

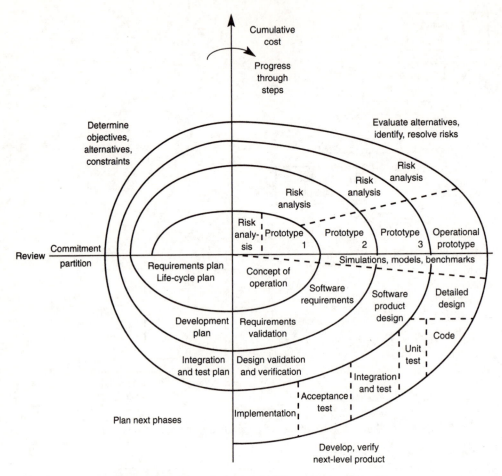

Figure 3.2   The spiral model of the software life-cycle.

actually been developed (Boehm, 1988); an outline of this is shown in Figure 3.2. Each stage in the spiral involves the following activities:

- the *objectives* of the stage are identified;
- the *options* and *constraints* are listed and explored;
- the *risks* involved in choosing between these options are evaluated;
- a *plan* for how to proceed to the next stage is determined, which may require the development of a prototype, or may more closely approximate to a traditional waterfall step, according to the conclusions of the risk analysis.

For our immediate needs, the exact form of the development process is less important than identifying the influences that the various development steps have upon the design stage, so we ignore for the moment the detailed forms of particular life-cycles. The major development tasks that are involved in software development were identified in Chapter 1 as including the following activities:

- requirements analysis, in which the objective is to identify what is needed from the system to be produced;
- specification, in which the objective is to state precisely and unambiguously what the system is to do in order to meet the overall requirements;
- design, in which the purpose is to describe how the system is to perform its tasks in order that its behaviour meets the specification;
- implementation, which involves translation of the design into suitable programming constructs and associated data and communication structures;
- testing, in which the implementation is validated in order to demonstrate how well it complies with the original requirements, the specification and the design.

This chapter will be concerned mainly with the two tasks that precede design, and with their relationship to the design task itself. To clarify exactly what their roles are, therefore, we shall examine the simple example of a computer system that is to support the issue, reservation and recall of books, cassettes and videos for the local branch of a library. Very briefly, these are as follows.

Requirements analysis will be concerned with identifying the needs of the library staff and users, in terms of the functioning of the library. An example of such a need might be the ability to check upon the number of books that have particularly long reservation lists, so that the library staff can consider ordering extra copies. Such an analysis will usually also consider the interactions and relationships between the various needs of the users of the end system.

Specification will translate those needs into a list of functions that the system must provide, and the behaviour that it should exhibit for given conditions. As an example, the book reservation function should specify the effects of a request when the maximum number of books that a borrower has on loan or requested is exceeded – or even when the borrower already has the requested book.

The specification for this system may also need to describe the way in which the users' interaction with the final system is to be organized (the 'look and feel' aspects). The design of human–computer interfaces is still a relatively specialized and difficult art, and one that is very domain- and application-dependent. In this example it will be a very important element, since the efficiency with which the librarians are able to perform their tasks will be strongly affected by the ease with which they can interact with the information on the screen. (In some ways, this relates to the designer's own use of 'mental models', since the interface should provide the librarians with a format that matches their own mental models of the processes that are involved.)

So the output from requirements analysis is *user*-oriented, while that from specification is *solution*-oriented.

Of course, these tasks are not performed in a rigid sequence, however desirable such a 'clean' solution structure might be. Some backtracking and revision to the outputs from earlier phases will be needed each time some inconsistency or omission is revealed in the work of later phases. Also, as we will see later, the use of prototyping may involve performing some design and implementation at an early stage of development, in order to refine ideas about the specification or requirements.

3.2 Economic factors

When the nature of the design process was examined in Chapter 1, a key point that emerged was that it is not *analytic* in any sense, and that it involves navigating through a 'solution space' that may be very – indeed, extremely – large. This is partly because of the abstract nature of software, which makes it difficult to specify complete needs, and also because the medium makes it possible to identify many solutions to a given problem.

A consequence of this is that, with so large and ill-defined a solution space, the design process can easily lead to a design that contains 'errors'. These might be of many kinds, but some particularly significant ones are:

- the design is not self-consistent, so that it cannot be successfully or efficiently implemented as it stands;
- the design and the specification are not consistent;
- the design and the requirements are not consistent.

Inconsistency in the form of the design itself may be revealed at various stages in its development. It may appear:

- when the design is being refined, perhaps arising from structural inconsistencies that emerge when comparing information that is obtained from different viewpoints – a widely used technique for seeking out such errors is that of the design review (Yourdon, 1979; Parnas and Weiss, 1987);
- while the design is being implemented (transformed into programming structures);

- while the implementation of the system is being tested, since this may reveal logical inconsistencies in the behaviour of the system.

The degree to which the design will need to be changed depends solely on the particular form and type of error.

Inconsistency between the design and the specification is more likely to be detected during testing (although if prototypes are constructed during development, it may well be detected earlier). The term 'verification' is usually used for this task of checking a design against the specification for the system.

Inconsistency between the design and the actual needs of the user (the requirements) is a much more difficult issue, although again it may be assisted by the use of prototypes. The procedure of checking for such inconsistencies is normally termed 'validation'.

Boehm has provided a very useful way to distinguish clearly between the actions of verification and validation (often referred to as 'V & V' – possibly to duck the question of making the distinction!):

Verification: are we building the product right?
Validation: are we building the right product?

Any inconsistencies in a design, whatever their form, need to be detected and identified at as early a stage as possible, so that a decision can be made about what to do. The later in development they are detected, the larger a task it will be to put them right. The results of a study by Boehm, shown in Figure 3.3, suggest that the cost of error detection and correction goes up by an order of magnitude at each stage in development (Boehm, 1981). That is, an error in the design costs ten times as much to fix if it is detected during the testing phase as it would if it were detected during the implementation phase.

Unfortunately, since the main error-detecting tasks are performed later on in the life-cycle, errors in specification and design can prove costly to fix when compared with errors in coding. Ideally, therefore, we need to find ways of evaluating designs and finding errors *before* proceeding to implement them. Prototyping offers one such approach, although there are some possible side-effects to this approach that can reduce its cost-effectiveness.

Another economic issue that needs to be considered is the cost of making *changes* to a system. Most software-based systems evolve with time, undergoing enhancements and changes as the needs of the users alter, the environment alters, and faults in performance are identified.

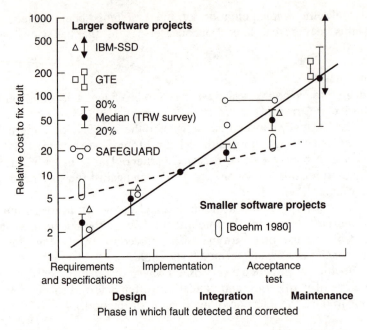

Figure 3.3 The cost of fixing 'bugs' at each stage of development.

Leintz and Swanson (1980) have studied the types of software maintenance activity that occur in practice, and have identified three main forms:

- *Perfective* maintenance is concerned with extending and improving a system once it is operational, typically by providing new forms of functionality requested by users.

- *Adaptive* maintenance is performed in order to meet needs for change that are imposed from outside (examples of these might be changes in legislation affecting a financial package, change of operating systems, or any similar type of change that arises from external factors).

- *Corrective* maintenance is performed to fix any 'bugs' that may be detected in the operational system.

In practice, the first of these is generally dominant, and it has been estimated that around 65% of all maintenance work falls into this category.

This reinforces the earlier point that the structure of a system should allow it to be modified fairly easily, so that it can be adapted to cope with likely changes (or, at least, with perfective and adaptive changes; it would be difficult to make much useful allowance for likely corrective changes!).

This is a principle that has been common in many other branches of engineering for a long time. (Examples of the design of components undergoing frequent revision can often be found in the design of cars and electronic goods.) As already observed, such practices may create constraints that limit the 'solution space' available to the designer, so increasing the initial cost while decreasing the long-term cost. Unfortunately, the way in which most organizations budget for software production is too short-term for such practices to be adopted as effectively as might be desired.

3.3 Software production models and their influence

Very broadly, the strategies used for organizing software development fall into two general classes. These can be summarized as follows.

Life-cycle forms: In essence, these assume that the production of software can be organized in the form of a sequential process, such as that described by the waterfall model. In such models it is assumed that each of the various tasks will be performed as an essentially self-contained activity, and that while there might be a degree of iteration between them, the tasks themselves, and the techniques required for them, can be readily identified. Most software design methods implicitly assume a framework of this form, although Boehm has sought to broaden this approach to recognize the use of feasibility studies and prototyping in his 'spiral model' of the life-cycle which was described in Section 3.1.

Incremental forms: These are based on the idea of developing the system through creating a sequence of 'enhancements' to a set of interim solutions. This strategy forms the basis for the various forms of prototyping that are used in software development.

Each of these forms has its strong points and its weaknesses. The life-cycle forms have the benefit of providing a strong management framework, permitting the setting of 'milestones' that can be used to record progress against some general plan of production. The well-defined stages of development can also be used to provide a framework for the development of documentation, and the management of changes to this too. However, this framework can quite easily become a straitjacket, as has been recognized in the past (Gladden, 1982; McCracken and Jackson, 1982), and it is far better at providing a description of what *has* been done than with assisting in the planning of what *is* to be done.

Incremental forms, on the other hand, lend themselves more readily to technical experiment, and to the involvement of the end user in such user-oriented tasks as developing specifications and evaluating design options. What exactly is meant by the term 'prototype' in terms of software is difficult to define in a precise manner (see the next section for a fuller discussion) and, for that and other reasons, it is less easily handled in terms of organizational and management frameworks, with their requirement for well-defined development paths. So we generally find that formulations of traditional software design methods make only occasional concessions to the use of such techniques – whatever the actual practice might be.

It can therefore be concluded that the main effect of production models is to influence the *organization* (and hence the form) of the software design process. Since life-cycle forms provide a stronger framework for management of the design process, it is not surprising to find that most design methods assume the use of a life-cycle structure. This in turn is reflected in the form of the method steps themselves. Indeed, most of the current software design methods are implicitly linked to the waterfall model, however limited this might be in terms of describing reality.

Since the life-cycle forms have already been described in outline, and their forms will be repeated in the later discussions of design methods, the remaining part of this chapter will concentrate on a discussion of the use of prototyping in design. Although prototyping is not generally included in the practices of design methods, it can provide a useful supplementary technique, and can aid in resolving some of the choices that appear during the process of design.

3.4 Prototyping roles and forms

One of the problems that arise in any discussion of prototyping in software production is to define exactly what we mean by the term 'prototype'. In traditional forms of engineering, a prototype is generally regarded as being a 'first of its kind', or some form of model that is produced to scale. We are all familiar with the idea of a prototype car, and with scale models of a building. (On a somewhat larger scale, the civil engineers constructing the Thames Barrage down-river from London built a scale working model of it in the nearby marshes.)

In the case of software, since duplication of the end product is simply a matter of making copies, these analogies do not really apply. In software production it is quite possible that the prototype will actually *be* the product in due course, and there is really no concept equivalent to that of a scale model. However, while the *forms* may be different, the basic *reasons* for building prototypes remain much the same as in other forms of engineering: prototypes are built in order to explore an idea more completely than would be possible by other means.

A useful categorization of the different roles that prototyping can play in software development has been produced by Floyd (1984). Her analysis recognizes three principal roles for software prototypes.

Evolutionary: This is the form closest to the 'incremental development' model. The software for a system is adapted gradually, by changing
the requirements step by step as these become clearer with use, and
changing the system to fit these. In this form, prototyping is used to
develop a product, and the prototype gradually evolves to form the end
product.

One benefit of this prototyping strategy is that it may be possible to
issue a release of the product while it is still technically incomplete,
although usable. Later releases can then provide the users with a gradual
increase in product functionality. While this approach to development may
not be appropriate for all purposes, it does have some attractions in
areas that involve a degree of 'pioneering', and where it is important to
get an early release of a system into the user's hands (or onto the
market).

Experimental: This role is distinguished by the use of the prototype
to evaluate a possible *solution* to a problem, by developing a prototype in
advance of large-scale implementation. The reasons for doing this may be
manifold, including the assessment of performance and resource needs,
evaluation of a form of user interface, assessment of an algorithm and so
on. This form of prototype is essentially a 'throw-away' item.

Exploratory: In this role a prototype is used to help with clarification
of user *requirements* and with other features of the system as a whole. One
purpose may be to help with the development of the analysis of the users'
needs by providing a series of possible models for their use. Essentially this
form of prototype is again a 'throw-away' item, and it can be considered as
enhancing the information that is provided from the requirements analysis
and functional specification activities.

Used in this role, the prototype assumes something of the nature of
a feasibility study. Much of it may be incomplete, since the purpose may be
focused on resolving only limited aspects of system functionality. Some
form of monitoring facility is a useful feature in such a prototype, giving it a
data-gathering role that will help when making the final evaluation.

In practice any actual use of prototyping may span these definitions,
since there may be a number of reasons for developing a prototype. At the
higher level of design, prototyping can be used to validate a design against
a specification through the use of 'executable specification' forms (Henderson, 1986). Such a use can be considered as a hybrid of the evolutionary
and exploratory forms, since the specification produced can itself be transformed into an implementation in turn.

The use of prototypes has been given greater attention in recent
years: Smith (1990) provides a useful review of some of its uses and roles.
For the purposes of this book, we can consider the experimental and
exploratory forms as being useful supplements to the strategies incorporated into the various methods, with the usual caveat that when building
prototypes we should avoid using these techniques in an *ad hoc* manner, so

that prototyping comes to act as a substitute for the use of sounder design practices.

SUMMARY

The role of design in the software development process needs to be considered, as it forms an important influence on the form and use of design approaches. In this chapter we have examined:

- design in the context of the life-cycle models, most notably the waterfall and spiral models;

- the associated roles of requirements analysis and specification, and their interaction with the design process;

- the identification of how well a design meets the users' needs, and the roles of

    verification: are we building the product right?
    validation: are we building the right product?

- the cost of fixing errors in design;

- the relationship between production models and design methods;

- the roles that software prototyping can play in supporting the design process.

FURTHER READING

Floyd C. (1984). A systematic look at prototyping. In *Approaches to Prototyping* (Budde R., Kuhlenkamp K., Mathiassen L. and Zullighoven H., eds.). Berlin: Springer-Verlag

The term 'prototype' is used with many different meanings in the context of software development. This conference paper seeks to clarify thinking about both the roles performed by prototypes and the terminology involved.

Boehm B.W. (1988). A spiral model of software development and enhancement. *IEEE Computer*, May, 61–72

This is a very clear exposition of the forms and roles of software life-cycle models from the pen of the guru himself. It provides a historical introduction and then the rationale for the form adopted for the spiral model.

EXERCISES

3.1   How do your techniques for testing an item of software conform to the objectives of

(a)   verification and
(b)   validation,

and how might they be improved for these purposes?

3.2   Consider the roles that prototypes could play (if any) in the development of the following software systems:

(a)   an interactive desk-top publishing system;
(b)   a compiler for the Pascal programming language;
(c)   a bank autoteller network for dispensing cash.

In each case, which group of people would be involved with reviewing any prototypes produced?

3.3   List reasons why each of the following systems may require 'maintenance' in the future, and identify the relevant form of maintenance for each case:

(a)   a spell-checking package used with a word processor that supports multiple languages;
(b)   a program used to list directory contents for the users of an operating system;
(c)   a system used to provide display information about the position of aircraft in an air traffic control system used at a number of busy airports.

Design Qualities

4.1 The quality concept
4.2 Assessing design quality

4.3 Quality attributes of the design product
4.4 Assessing the design process

Since one of the objectives of the software design process is to produce as 'good' a design as possible, this chapter is concerned with examining some of the ideas about what exactly constitutes a 'good' software design. It begins by examining some ideas about the properties associated with good quality in software, and then proceeds to consider how it is possible to make measurements at the design stage that might identify these properties and how the design process can be involved in meeting quality objectives.

4.1 The quality concept

The concept of quality is a familar one, although we tend to associate it with properties that arise from the tasks of construction rather than with those of design. Asked for examples of 'good' quality, many people are likely to identify such examples as well-made joints on an item of furniture, the quality of the paintwork on an expensive car, or the texture of a woven fabric. All of these are examples of quality of construction rather than of design, yet quality in construction depends upon good design: to achieve a high-quality product high standards are needed in both, and in order to achieve high standards of quality in design *products*, one needs to seek high standards of quality in the design *process*.

Unfortunately, quality is a concept that can rarely be related to any absolutes, and even for manufactured items ideas about quality usually cannot be usefully measured on any absolute scale. The best that we can usually do is to rank items on an ordinal scale, as when we say that we believe the construction of this coffee table is better than that of another, in terms of materials used and the workmanship it exhibits. However, we lack any means of defining *how much* better the one is than the other.

When it comes to assessing design, rather than construction, the problem is, if anything, worse. Quality in design is often associated with visual properties, as when we appraise the quality of typefaces, furniture, and clothes. We associate elegance with good design, yet it offers no help in quantifying our thinking and, even worse, is likely to have ephemeral aspects: it may be strongly influenced by our ideas about fashion – so creating a context for quality. (As an example, a 1930s radio set might look quite in place in a room that is furnished in 1930s style, but would be most unsuited to a room that was furnished in the style of the 1980s.)

Since software is such an abstract product, it is perhaps less apt to be influenced by fashion (a debatable point, perhaps, especially in relation to user interface design), but it is hardly surprising that the concept of quality is equally difficult to define for software. Few quality attributes can be quantified in any way, and those measures that we do possess are of uneven value. Furthermore, the idea of quality as applied to software is at least partly problem-related in nature, so it is certainly not guaranteed by the use of some particular form for the design process.

For software, as for other artifacts, it is also difficult to separate ideas about design quality from one's thinking about implementation quality. To return for a moment to the example of the garden shed that was introduced in Chapter 1: no matter how good the design is, in terms of proportions, efficient use of materials and ease of construction and modi-fication, our ideas about its quality will still be very largely influenced by the actual construction. If it is badly assembled, then, regardless of how good its design may be, we will not consider it to be of good quality.

Equally, if the design is poor, no amount of good craftsmanship applied to its construction will be able to disguise its fundamental failings. (The door may be well made and may close well, but if it is positioned so that we knock our elbow each time it is opened, then we will still find it inconvenient to use.)

We also encounter once again the dual nature of software in thinking about how we can identify its quality. Software has both static and dynamic attributes, and so any measures that we can develop should seek to assess both of these, and should recognize the potential for conflict between them. (A program may meet the specified real-time needs very well, but its internal structure may be so poorly organized that it is virtually impossible to modify it in any way. Equally, the structure of a program may be very good, while its run-time performance is awful!)

While our ideas of quality measures are perhaps essentially determined by the nature of the design object itself, it is still possible to find some very general measures of quality that are fairly universal, and which can be applied to software. In terms of the objectives for these, for any system the ultimate measure of quality should normally be that of *fitness for purpose*, since the end product must be capable of performing the task assigned to it. As an example, however elegant the design of a chair may be, it must still meet the basic requirement that we should be able to sit on it, and preferably in comfort. Therefore the quality factors to be used for assessing this will be selected and weighted by considering the role (purpose) of the system that is being designed.

This acts as a reminder that we should not seek to achieve elegance of form at the expense of function. So for software systems, we can reasonably expect to find that the final implemented system works, and works correctly in all the required situations. That is, it should perform the required tasks in the specified manner, and within the constraints of the specified resources. (Once again, we can only measure the ultimate success of a design through its implementation.)

This concept is related to the ideas of verification and validation that were introduced in the last chapter, since comparisons are being made with expectations as expressed in the requirements specification. As a measure for practical use, however, it can be assessed only by indirect means. So it may be better to consider fitness for purpose as an ultimate goal, and to look for ways of assessing it by finding a set of associated properties and then some system attributes that provide measures of these.

The next section begins by looking at a framework that enables us to identify some of the system properties that reflect our general ideas about quality. Section 4.3 examines some of the system attributes that relate to these properties, and briefly considers how these might be assessed. Finally, the influence of the design process itself in helping to produce the desired design attributes is considered.

4.2   Assessing design quality

'When you can measure what you are speaking about, and express it in numbers, you know something about it, but when you cannot measure it, when you cannot express it in numbers, your knowledge is of a meagre and unsatisfactory kind.' (Lord Kelvin.)

4.2.1   A framework for assessment

Fenton (1991) has observed that 'measurement is concerned with capturing information about *attributes* of *entities*', so at this point it is useful to identify more carefully how our ideas about quality can be tied to ideas about measurement.

Figure 4.1 shows an initial set of mappings that can be constructed to link these ideas. The key terms used in the figure can be interpreted as follows:

- **Quality concepts** are the abstract ideas that we have about what constitutes 'good' and 'bad' properties of a system, and which will need to be assessed by the designer when making decisions about design choices.
- **Measurable quantities** provide the mappings between the abstract concept of quality and the countable items (and therefore effectively corresponds to the general concept of a *metric*).

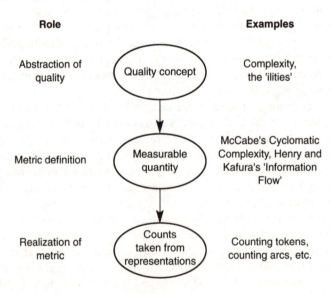

Figure 4.1   Mapping quality concepts to measurements.

- **Counts** are concerned with the realization of the mappings, that is, the attributes of a representation that will need to be counted in order to obtain some form of value for the metrics.

As an example of a widely used metric that fits into this framework, the quality of program code is often considered to be related to its structural complexity. One measurable quantity that can be used to assess this complexity is the number of possible control paths that exist within a program unit, as measured by McCabe's Cyclomatic Complexity measure (McCabe, 1976). This is measured by counting lexical tokens such as IF and WHILE in the source code, with the set of tokens used being specific to a particular implementation language.

The mapping from a measurable quantity to a set of good and unambiguous counting rules to be used with a particular implementation language is essentially one of transformation. However, the mapping from a quality concept to a set of measurable quantities is much more a case of making an *interpretation*. (This point tends to be glossed over in much of the literature on code metrics!) To help with this interpretation, we need a fuller model to help identify the mappings required. An expanded form of the framework provided in Figure 4.1 is shown in Figure 4.2: here the idea of a quality concept has been expanded into three further levels in which:

- *use* identifies the purpose of making measurements (and hence strongly differentiates between measuring static properties of a design and measuring dynamic behavioural qualities);
- *quality factors* determine the quality concepts that are associated with the purpose (these items are often referred to as the 'ilities');
- *quality criteria* relate the requirements-oriented properties of the intended system (the 'ilities') to the solution-oriented properties of the design itself, and these are then mapped onto a chosen set of metrics.

While this does not reduce the degree of interpretation involved, it does provide a clearer path between the need for quality assessments and the forms used.

An example of the mappings M1 and M2 from Figure 4.2 are shown in Figure 4.3, and are based on an example of the needs identified as being significant for a real-time system, and, for comparison, those that are considered as significant for a compiler.

In the previous section it was observed that any assessment incorporating the ultimate goal of fitness for purpose needed to recognize the nature of the problem and its domain. This balance is reflected in the weightings that we give to the uses, and hence the choice of weightings for the 'ilities' is strongly related to both the problem itself and its domain. For example, efficiency may be of greater importance for an embedded

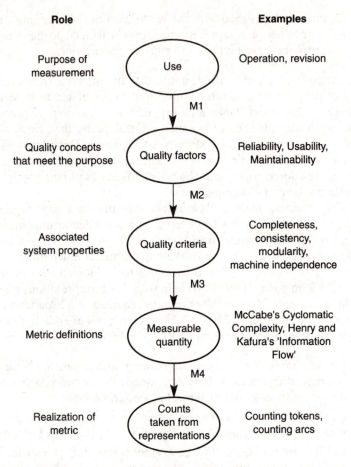

Role		Examples
Purpose of measurement	**Use**	Operation, revision
Quality concepts that meet the purpose	Quality factors	Reliability, Usability, Maintainability
Associated system properties	Quality criteria	Completeness, consistency, modularity, machine independence
Metric definitions	Measurable quantity	McCabe's Cyclomatic Complexity, Henry and Kafura's 'Information Flow'
Realization of metric	Counts taken from representations	Counting tokens, counting arcs

Figure 4.2 A fuller mapping from concepts of quality to countable attributes of a design/implementation.

control system than usability, while for an aircraft autopilot reliability might reasonably be regarded as by far the most important factor.

When we come to make use of these ideas, we find that the needs of the designer and the needs of any system of measurement unfortunately tend to create forces that pull in opposing directions. As was observed in Chapter 2, experienced designers will frequently seek to maintain a reasonably consistent level of abstraction in their reasoning at any given stage in the design process, and will avoid descending into detail at too early a stage in the development of this reasoning. However, it is difficult to measure abstractions, and so metrics analysis schemes seek to have available to them as much detail as possible about a design.

Even for program code, which at least possesses well-defined syntax and semantics, the process of defining properties and making measurements

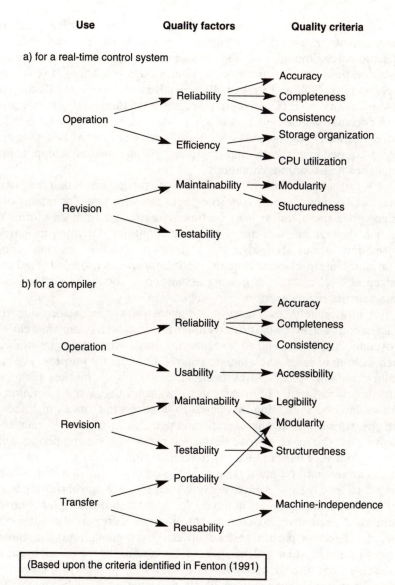

Use	Quality factors	Quality criteria

a) for a real-time control system

Operation → Reliability → Accuracy, Completeness, Consistency

Operation → Efficiency → Storage organization, CPU utilization

Revision → Maintainability → Modularity, Stucturedness

Revision → Testability

b) for a compiler

Operation → Reliability → Accuracy, Completeness, Consistency

Operation → Usability → Accessibility

Revision → Maintainability → Legibility, Modularity

Revision → Testability → Structuredness

Transfer → Portability → Machine-independence

Transfer → Reusability

(Based upon the criteria identified in Fenton (1991))

Figure 4.3   Mapping quality factors to quality criteria.

of these can be a difficult exercise requiring the careful specification of any counting rules to be used (Conte *et al.*, 1986; Fenton, 1991). For design description forms, the problem is compounded by the relatively poor syntax of most abstract design notations. (There are very few design notations that are unambiguous, and almost all graphical forms require careful use of the free-text component to make their purpose clear.)

So the automatic processing of design notations in order to extract measurements of particular attributes has not made a very significant impact to date, although a number of experiments have been conducted to extract various counts from systematic design notations (Troy and Zweben, 1981; Hall and Preiser, 1984; Budgen and Marashi, 1988). The growing use of CASE (Computer-Aided Software Engineering) tools as an aid to documenting designs and, in some cases, assisting with code generation, may improve the means for gathering such data, but weak syntax and semantics, needing careful interpretation of any textual components, remain problems for most notations.

A further problem with metrics analysis procedures is that they have so far been almost entirely concerned with assessing static attributes of a design, since these can at least be directly extracted from any forms of notation through some form of property counting. Attempts to extract information about the dynamic attributes require making some behavioural interpretations from the static information provided (Friel and Budgen, 1991), as well as making assumptions about the performance characteristics of any eventual implementation.

Unfortunately, as Figure 4.3 demonstrates, the factors that the designer considers to be particularly important may well relate most closely to dynamic attributes, and so assessing the static attributes is insufficient when seeking to assess the ultimate criteria of fitness for purpose. We can demonstrate why this is so, by using an analogy with musical notation. Music has some similar properties to software, in that a static notation is used to describe something that needs to be 'executed', and which therefore possesses a similar mix of static and dynamic attributes. (Again, it is relatively easy to make a broad distinction between good and poor quality in music, but very hard to quantify that distinction.)

The section of a musical score in Figure 4.4 shows that it should be possible to specify some form of analysis rules for checking basic properties such as the number of beats in a bar. We might also devise rules to check chords and sequences, to identify the intervals between the notes and hence to check for particular dissonances. Given enough musical knowledge, this might then tell us quite a lot about the piece of music it represents – but of course, the ultimate test is to hear it played. Only then can we be sure whether or not we like it, and whether it will be suitable for some particular purpose. (The 'mental' model applies here, too, as anyone with sufficient knowledge is likely to 'play' the score in his or her head in order to assess its qualities!)

4.2.2 The 'ilities'

The 'ilities' form a group of quality factors that need to be considered when making any attempt to assess design quality. Since there are many ilities,

Figure 4.4 Example of musical score notation.

our discussion in this section is limited to the group that can be considered as being the most widely applicable, namely:

- reliability
- efficiency
- maintainability
- usability

(The other ilities, such as testability, portability, reusability and so on are rather more specialized in purpose.)

Reliability

This factor is essentially concerned with the dynamic properties of the eventual system, and so involves the designer in making predictions about behavioural issues. In particular, for the purposes of design we are concerned with ways of determining whether the eventual system will be:

- *complete*, in the sense of being able to handle all combinations of events and system states;

- *consistent*, in that its behaviour will be as expected, and will be repeatable, regardless of the overall system loading at any time;

- *robust* when faced with component failure or some similar conflict (for example, if the printer used for logging data in a chemical process-control plant fails for some reason, this should not be able to 'hang' the whole system, but should be handled according to the philosophy summed up in the term 'graceful degradation').

As systems get larger and more complex, so the problems of ensuring reliability will also escalate.

For safety-critical systems, where this factor is paramount, various techniques have been developed to help overcome limitations in design and implementation techniques. For example, in a system used in a 'fly-by-wire' aircraft, in which the control surfaces are managed by computer links rather than direct hydraulic controls, the implementation will be by means of multiple computers, each programmed by a separate development team and tested independently. Any operational request to the control system is then processed in parallel by all the computers, and only if they concur will the requested operation be performed.

Efficiency

The efficiency of a system can be measured through its use of resources such as processor time, memory, network access, system facilities, disk space and so on. It is a relative concept, in that one system can be identified as more efficient than another in terms of some parameter such as processor use, but there is no absolute scale on which to specify an optimum efficiency.

In the early days of computers, when programs were small and computer time was relatively expensive, efficiency was considered a prime criterion, and was measured chiefly in terms of memory use and processor use. So systems that were implemented in machine code or assembler were generally considered to be highly efficient, but of course would rank very low on maintainability.

As a design factor, efficiency is a difficult property to handle, since it involves making projections from the design in order to estimate the effects of choices upon eventual resource needs. However, as these are of considerable importance in terms of the implementation of the eventual system, it is often necessary to make at least crude predictions of needs.

Maintainability

As systems get larger and more costly, the need for a long life-time in service increases in parallel. To help to achieve this, designs must allow for future modification.

Many of the factors that affect maintainability are related to implementation factors or, at least, to very detailed design issues. Examples of these are the choice of identifiers, comment structuring practices, and documentation standards. However, design is also an important factor since, by careful separation of concerns, the designers can help the future maintainers to gain a clear understanding of their original 'mental models' (Littman *et al.*, 1987). Some of the factors that affect this in terms of design structure will be discussed in the next section.

Usability

There are many issues that can affect usability, but for many systems the design of the user interface (usually termed the Human–Computer Interaction, or HCI) will form an important component, and will influence other design decisions about such features as module boundaries and data structures.

A good review of the issues that need to be considered in designing for 'ease of use' is provided in Branscomb and Thomas (1984), where the authors observe that the use of the term HCI is perhaps misleading, since 'people communicate via, not with, computer systems.' There is a strong cognitive element involved in this task, and a need for the designer to provide the user with a consistent 'mental model' of system behaviour. The techniques affecting the design choices are fairly specialized, and largely outside the scope of this book. Thimbleby (1990) provides a good introduction to this field of design.

Having examined some of the quality factors that designers would *like* to be able to assess in making their decisions, we now go on to consider what measures of quality we actually have available to us at the design stage. We can then consider how well these are able to provide help with assessing the extent to which a design meets the factors that have been described above.

4.3   Quality attributes of the design product

Now that a number of ideas about design quality concepts have been examined, it is clear that the two principal problems that they present for measurement are:

- to identify a set of design attributes that are related to these properties;
- to find ways of extracting information about these attributes from the available forms of design document.

In the first part of this section some of the attributes and criteria that are widely used for design assessment are described, and this is followed by a brief discussion of one of the ways in which these might be extracted.

4.3.1 Some design attributes

Simplicity

Characteristic of almost all good designs, in whatever sphere of activity they are produced, is a basic simplicity. A good design meets its objectives and has no additional embellishments that detract from its main purpose. (Perhaps this is why so many dual-purpose artifacts fail to achieve either of their objectives clearly and well. One example that comes to mind is a rucksack that expanded to become a tent, but was unsuccessful because it was much easier to have a good rucksack and a good tent as separate items. Most of us can probably think of similar examples.)

The often-quoted saying 'a solution should be as simple as possible, but no simpler', which is usually attributed to Albert Einstein, is more profound than it might seem at first. This is the opposite of the argument against unnecessary embellishment: it argues against attempting to over-simplify, since the result will be a product that will not be able to do its job. One important means of simplification is abstraction, but it is necessary to use an abstraction that preserves the key attributes if it is to be of any help in solving the problem.

While simplicity cannot easily be assessed, one can at least seek measures for its converse of *complexity*. A number of these, which measure different forms of complexity, have been developed for use with program code, including:

- complexity of control flow (McCabe, 1976), concerned with the number of possible paths of control during execution of a program unit;
- complexity of structure in terms of information flow around the system (Henry and Kafura, 1984; Kitchenham *et al.*, 1990);
- complexity of comprehension, as measured by the number of different identifiers and operators (Halstead, 1975).

Unfortunately none of these readily scale up for use in design, although they could possibly be applied to detailed design documentation forms.

There are no ready measures that can currently be used to help assess the architectural complexity of a design.

In terms of the design quality concepts, simplicity is clearly related to maintainability and testability as well as reliability and possibly efficiency.

Modularity

The use of an appropriate form of modular structuring makes it possible for a given problem to be considered in terms of a set of smaller components. Once again, modularity is not a concept that relates only to software: this principle has long been established in other forms of engineering. In electronics in particular, the idea of replacing one unit with another simply by unplugging one and plugging in the other has made the maintenance and upgrading of electrical and electronic equipment into a relatively straightforward task.

This is generally only possible where a well-defined set of interface standards is in existence. For electronic components this is generally achieved with some form of 'backplane' providing a data highway, together with the necessary signal lines. While this form of module connectivity is also possible with software (as is evident from the existence of libraries of subprograms), the standardization of the interfaces involved is much more limited.

To make good use of a modular structure, one needs to adopt a design practice based on a separation of concerns. Simply defining interfaces is not enough: a designer needs to group functions within modules in such a way that their interdependence is minimized. Such a grouping results in a less complex interface to the module: in the case of hardware, it may simply be that fewer interconnections are required; for software, we need to find other criteria in order to measure this factor.

Viewed generally, and also from a software perspective, the benefits of finding a suitable scheme of modularity to apply in solving a given problem will include:

- modules are easy to replace;
- each module captures one feature of a problem, so aiding comprehension (and hence maintenance), as well as providing a framework for designing as a team;
- a well-structured module can easily be reused for another problem.

So in terms of the design properties that we are seeking, the successful use of modularity should be related to such quality concepts as maintainability, testability, and (possibly) to usability and reliability too.

Two useful quality measures that have long been used for the purpose of assessing the extent of modular structuring in software are

Table 4.1 Forms of module coupling.

Form	Features	Desirability
Data coupling	Modules A and B communicate by parameters or data items that have no control element	High
Stamp coupling	Modules A and B make use of some common data type (although they might perform very different functions and have no other connections)	Moderate
Control coupling (i) Activating	A transfers control to B in a structured manner such as by means of a procedure call	Necessary
(ii) Coordinating	A passes a parameter to B that is used in B to determine the actions of B (a 'flag')	Undesirable
Common-environment coupling	A and B contain references to some shared data area (such as a FORTRAN COMMON block). Any change to the format of the block requires that all of the modules using it must also be modified	Undesirable

Note: The forms of coupling that can exist between modules A and B have been ranked in decreasing order of desirability.

'coupling' and 'cohesion'. These terms were defined in the early 1970s (Stevens *et al.*, 1974; Yourdon, 1979) and were used to identify the complexity of a system in terms of the form and interdependence of the component modules. In the original work, the basic unit of modularity was assumed to be the procedure, but the concepts are still valid for such modular forms as the Ada 'package' and the Modula-2 'module'.

Coupling is a measure of intermodule connectivity, and is concerned with identifying the forms of connection that exist between modules and the 'strength' of these connections. Table 4.1 summarizes the principal forms of coupling that are generally regarded as being significant in terms of design features.

In general, the forms of coupling listed are somewhat biased towards modules based on the procedure, or subprogram, rather than on such forms as the Ada package. The measures of coupling are generally related to the different ways of invoking procedures, and to the use of different parameter-passing mechanisms. However, the concept can also be applied to the 'uses' hierarchy (Parnas, 1979), concerned with the packaging of information, and so can be used as a guide in making design decisions at a number of different levels of abstraction.

A problem with the basic concepts involved in coupling and cohesion is the difficulty of quantifying these measures systematically. However, this is less of an issue for the design process than for assessing program structures, since there is only really scope to identify their *presence* during design, and determining their *extent* is rarely practicable. With coupling, there is at least the possibility of performing such operations as counting links, using sizes of data structures exchanged and so on, but even then the value of any such measures is somewhat limited.

As an example of the point about the extent of coupling being less critical in design assessment than the presence of particular forms, we can consider the case of coordinating control coupling, sometimes termed 'switch coupling'.

This form typically arises when one of the parameters of a procedure is used to determine the way that the procedure is to perform its task. This in turn may arise where a procedure is invoked from a number of different sections of a program, and where, at a fairly late stage, it may be realized that the task it performs may differ slightly according to section. The 'switch' parameter is then added to enable the invoking routine to indicate which variant of the task needs to be performed. In other words, it acts as a 'fix' for a design error! (A classic example of a situation in which this may occur is in writing any form of multi-pass program, such as an assembler, compiler or link-editor. These all have a number of fairly low-level tasks that need to be repeated, but which on inspection are seen to differ slightly on each pass.)

This form of coupling is therefore likely to arise from a failure to perform the detailed design tasks adequately. In making any form of design assessment the need is therefore to identify its presence. Any notion of its 'extent' is harder to determine, and of doubtful value if achieved.

Cohesion, in its turn, provides a measure of the extent to which the components of a module can be considered to be 'functionally related'. The ideal module is one in which all the components can be considered as being solely present for one purpose. Where the Ada package is the basis of modular structuring, an example of functional relatedness might be a stack module that provides only a set of procedures for accessing the stack, together with the data structure for the stack itself. Such a package can be considered as exhibiting functional cohesion, since all its components are present solely for the purpose of providing a stack facility.

Table 4.2 lists the main forms of cohesion (sometimes termed 'associations') that are generally recognized, As can be seen, cohesion is quite easily related to packaging forms of modular structure, as well as to procedural units. Perhaps the main exception to this is procedural association, which is very much concerned with sequencing of operations, and hence fits less easily with the packaging concept. (This form was not

Table 4.2   The principal forms of cohesion.

Form	Features	Desirability
Functional	All the elements contribute to the execution of a single problem-related task	High
Sequential	The outputs from one element of the module form the inputs to another element	Quite high
Communicational	All elements are concerned with operations that use the same input or output data	Fairly
Procedural	The elements of the module are related by the order in which their operations must occur	Not very
Temporal	The elements involve operations that are related by the time at which they occur, usually being linked to some event such as 'system initialization'	Not very
Logical	The elements perform operations that are logically similar, but which involve very different actions internally	Definitely not
Coincidental	The elements are not linked by any conceptual link (such modules may be created to avoid having to repeat coding tasks)	Definitely not

included in the original list (Stevens *et al.*, 1974) and was added later (Yourdon and Constantine, 1979).)

Cohesion is probably even more difficult to quantify than coupling, and again there is likely to be little benefit in seeking to do so during the design process. However, it does provide a measure that can be used to help the designer with assessing the relative merits of possible options.

The concepts of coupling and cohesion, and ways of applying these, are discussed in some detail in a number of texts (Yourdon and Constantine, 1979; Page-Jones, 1988).

Information-hiding

This concept is related to that of modularity, but it also incorporates additional notions about managing information in a system. The basic concept encourages the designer to keep information about the detailed forms of such objects as data structures and device interfaces local to a module, or unit, and to ensure that such information should not be made 'visible' outside that unit (Parnas, 1972).

Where this principle is applied, knowledge about the detailed form of any data structures within a module are kept concealed from any other

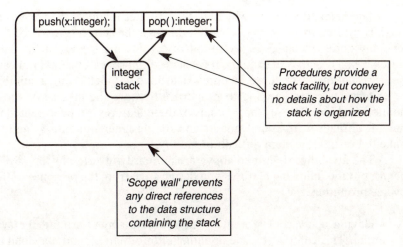

Figure 4.5   Example of information-hiding for an integer stack.

software components that may use the module. In many cases, a number of 'access procedures' may be provided to give controlled forms of access to the 'clients' of the module. The effect is to provide a 'scope wall' around information, preventing direct access to it.

As an example, this principle might be used in designing a module to provide an integer stack facility to support a set of reverse Polish calculations using integers. Using the principle of information hiding, one would seek to conceal the form adopted for implementing the stack, and provide a set of procedures for accessing it, such as:

> push an integer onto the stack
> pop an integer from the stack
> test for an empty stack

as is shown schematically in Figure 4.5.

This interface then conceals the detailed design decisions about how the stack is to be implemented, which helps to ensure its integrity by preventing 'short-cut' access directly from other program units. It also makes it possible to change the detailed form of implementation without requiring changes in any of the units that make use of this stack.

Powerful though the concept is, it is difficult to make use of it in any procedural practices for design, and equally difficult to devise a set of tests to identify its use. In terms of system quality factors it is clearly related to both reliability and maintainability. In terms of processor time and memory use, it is apt to conflict with ideas of efficiency on occasion, since the use of a hierarchy of access procedures may lead to reduced run-time performance.

The detailed forms in which these attributes manifest themselves in software sytems are somewhat elusive, although the concepts involved are generally quite tractable. A useful aid to considering the extent of their presence in a design is to examine it for signs of those features that indicate that a design may lack these qualities. This involves identifying a suitable set of features corresponding to properties that are the inverse of those mentioned above. The presence of any of these features can be expected to make it difficult to read and understand the designer's intentions and to make the resulting system difficult to modify.

The attributes described above are not easily inverted by any direct means, but the following features of a design stem from the presence of the inverse properties.

- Having many copies of 'state' information spread around the system. This complicates the updating of information, and may lead to inconsistencies in system behaviour.

- Using interfaces that are too complex. In programming terms these are usually characterized by procedures that have too many parameters, some of which may not even be necessary. In design terms, they are more likely to be identified by the degree of information flow associated with them.

- The use of excessively complex control structures. This may indicate design modules where the designer has chosen unsuitable interfaces and data structures.

- Needless replication of information. This can also be reflected in module interfaces: for example, procedures may pass a complete record as a parameter, when only one field of the record is relevant to their operation.

- Using modules that lack 'functional strength'. Program units of this type are not well focused in terms of their purpose, and may well be parametrized for use on different tasks.

These characteristics have been expressed largely in terms of implementation features, since these are more familiar and are more readily quantified. However, they can equally well be assessed for design descriptions, although extracting the information is less easily achieved through any form of automatic analysis.

4.3.2 Assessing design quality

A technique that has proved itself useful in assessing design structure and likely behaviour is the review, or walkthrough. The use of reviews for this purpose is quite well established, and a set of basic rules has been assembled from experience (Yourdon, 1979; Weinberg and Freedman,

1984; Parnas and Weiss, 1987). In using such a technique, though, it is essential to distinguish between the **technical review**, which is concerned with assessing the quality of a design, and the **management review**, which is concerned with issues such as project deadlines and schedule. This section and the next are concerned only with the role performed by the first of these forms of review.

Technical reviews can include the use of forms of 'mental execution' of the design model, and so can help with assessing dynamic attributes as well as static ones. The references cited above provide some valuable guidelines on how such reviews need to be conducted in order to meet their aims and not to become diverted to issues that are more properly the province of the management review. It is also essential that the review does not become an assessment of the design team, rather than of the design itself.

While a design review cannot provide any well-quantified measures of 'quality' (if such a thing is even possible), it can help to identify weaknesses in a design, or potential weaknesses that might arise as details are elaborated. It therefore provides a means of answering the first question posed at the start of this section: 'How can information about these attributes be extracted from design documents?' In the present state of the art, the technical design review probably offers the best means of both extracting and assessing information relating to the quality of a design. In particular, if carefully planned and organized, it brings together those people who have both the domain knowledge and the technical knowledge that is needed to make realistic projections from the available design information.

This section ends with a summary of those properties of a design that Parnas and Weiss (1987) believe should be the designer's goals and hence should be studied in a technical design review. Most of them are properties that we have met already in this book, but they bear repeating at this point.

The eight requirements that they identify for a good design are that it should be:

- well structured: consistent with chosen properties such as information hiding;
- simple: to the extent of being 'as simple as possible, but no simpler';
- efficient: providing functions that can be computed using the available resources;
- adequate: meeting the stated requirements;
- flexible: able to accommodate likely changes in the requirements, however these might arise;
- practical: module interfaces should provide the required facilities, neither more nor less;

- implementable: using current and available software and hardware technology;
- standardized: using well-defined and familiar notation for any documentation.

The last point obviously has special significance in the context of a review, since the reviewers must be able to capture and comprehend the 'mental models' developed by the designers. They are likely to find this much harder if the notation used is unfamiliar and itself undocumented.

4.4 Assessing the design process

Any design product emerges as a result of some form of design process, however structured or unstructured this might be. So while no degree of quality in the process can actually ensure some particular degree of quality in the product, the quality of the design process is obviously an important factor that needs to be considered when seeking to understand design quality issues.

Our study of the nature of the design process so far has shown that it typically involves the designer in building a 'model' of the end system, and then exploring ways of realizing that model (Jones, 1970). We have also seen that opportunistic design techniques are widely used for these tasks (Visser and Hoc, 1990), even where structured design practices are also in use. So we might reasonably expect that the creative nature of this phase in the process of software development does not readily lend itself to any rigorous measures of quality.

Experience seems to suggest that this is so, and that even for the more quantifiable tasks involved in software development, such as coding and testing, the existing measures of productivity and of quality are rather limited. In his book *Managing the Software Process* (Humphrey, 1991), Watts Humphrey has drawn together a valuable survey of quality issues applied to software development processes. In particular, within his 'Software Process Maturity Model', he identifies five levels of maturity that occur in the processes that an organization uses for producing software systems:

- Initial: The software process is characterized as *ad hoc*, and occasionally even chaotic. Few processes are defined, and success in a project depends upon individual effort.
- Repeatable: Basic project management processes are established and used to track cost, schedule and functionality. The necessary process discipline is in place to repeat earlier successes on projects with similar applications.

- Defined: The software process for both management and engineering activities is documented, standardized and integrated into an organization-wide software process. All projects use a documented and approved version of the organization's process for developing and maintaining software.

- Managed: Detailed measures of the software process and product quality are collected. Both the software process and the products are quantitatively understood and controlled using detailed measures.

- Optimising: Continuous process improvement is enabled by quantitative feedback from the process and from testing innovative ideas and technologies.

As of 1991, no organizations had been identified as attaining maturity levels 4 or 5, although some projects had managed to reach these levels.

The material of the preceding sections and chapters will have made it clear why the design solution developed for a system will be much more strongly problem-oriented than (say) the structuring practices that might be adopted for coding, or the testing strategies that might be used. This is most certainly not an argument against seeking to find quality measures for the design process, but it does indicate why, regardless of the levels that may be achieved by the overall development process, it is hard to get the design phase even to the point of being repeatable.

To improve the quality of the design process it is particularly necessary to find ways of including input to design activities that can provide:

- domain knowledge about the type of problem involved, and about important aspects of any implementation features;

- method knowledge that helps with understanding any design techniques being used;

- experience from similar projects, wherever available.

There are three widely adopted ways of providing these inputs to the design process.

Technical reviews were outlined in the previous section; their use allows the design team to gain knowledge from the experiences of others, and particularly from any domain and method knowledge that they might possess. While this form of input is largely aimed at improving the design product, it can also have a significant impact upon the design process by identifying useful techniques or notations that might be applicable to a particular problem.

Management reviews are primarily concerned with developing and refining estimates of effort and deadlines for the project as a whole, and with gathering any data that might be needed for such estimates. The task of estimation is one that draws heavily upon both domain knowledge and experience, since it requires the use of these to make the projections needed.

Prototyping provides the means of gaining both domain knowledge and some forms of experience about a particular problem. (In this context, prototyping may be considered to play what Floyd (1984) has termed the 'exploratory' or 'experimental' role.) By constructing suitable prototypes, it may therefore be possible to supplement the knowledge and experience available to both management and the design team.

Of these three, it is the management review that is most likely to involve making some form of assessment of the way that a design is being developed, and which may provide a framework for using the other two forms. The use of reporting and tracking mechanisms will play an important role in monitoring quality issues, and with ensuring that these issues are actually addressed during a review.

Once again the quality of design documentation (and in larger projects the quality of any configuration and control procedures used for organizing this documentation) plays an important role in establishing a high-quality process by reusing experience.

While the use of standard notations for design, and of specific forms of 'design method', cannot *ensure* quality in either the design product or the design process, it should be clear by now that their use is likely to be highly influential. We are therefore now in a good position, in the next chapter, to begin examining their roles in terms of the more technical issues affecting software design.

SUMMARY

In examining ideas about 'good' design, the following points are particularly significant:

- Software quality concepts are concerned with assessing both the static structure and the dynamic behaviour of the eventual system.

- The ultimate goal of quality must be that of fitness for purpose, although the criteria for determining whether this is achieved will be both problem-dependent and domain-dependent.

- While the use of abstraction is an important tool for the designer, it makes it difficult to make any direct product measurements during the design process.

- Technical design reviews can provide a valuable means of obtaining and using domain knowledge to aid with assessing the design product as well as method knowledge to aid with assessing the design process.

FURTHER READING

Parnas D.L. and Weiss D.M. (1987). Active design reviews: Principles and practices. *J. Systems and Software*, **7**, 259–65

A short paper that focuses on the use of reviews in the design process and identifies (from experience) some rules to assist with making design reviews as effective as possible.

Humphrey W.S. (1989). *Managing the Software Process*. Oxford: Addison-Wesley

One of the very few books to examine the context within which software is produced, and to study the nature of the development process.

Fenton N.E. (1991). *Software Metrics: A Rigorous Approach*. London: Chapman & Hall

Provides a 'measurement' view of how well quality attributes can be derived from descriptions of software. While the book is mainly concerned with measurement of code structures, it contains many useful ideas that can be equally well related to design.

EXERCISES

4.1 Given the four 'ilities' *reliability*, *usability*, *maintainability*, *reusability*, consider how you would rank them in order of importance for each of the following systems:

    (a)   a process control system for a chemical plant that produces toxic insecticides;

    (b)   a bank autoteller network used to issue cash and short statements describing accounts;

    (c)   an interactive database used for stock control at each branch of a chain of stores that sell electrical goods.

4.2 A computer program uses a number of resources, including processor time, memory, devices and system facilities (such as windows). Consider how you would measure *efficiency* in terms of these and identify your priorities for the two programs that you have written most recently.

4.3 List the criteria that you would expect to be used in planning a design review in your own organization and suggest some basic rules that might help to ensure that these are met.

5 Expressing Ideas about a Design

5.1 Representing abstract ideas   5.3 Forms of notation
5.2 Design viewpoints for software

Much of the discussion of the book has so far concentrated on examining the actions that are involved in the process of design, and the constraints that affect these. The preceding chapter began to consider the attributes possessed by the particular design medium of software; now this chapter starts to examine some of the ways in which these different attributes can be described and modelled by the designer.

5.1 Representing abstract ideas

Abstraction performs an essential role in the design process, by allowing the designer to concentrate on those features of a problem or its solution that are the most important at any particular stage in the development of the design. Therefore the designer needs ways to represent abstract ideas about problem and design objects, and about the various relationships that will exist between these. While this is a general design requirement, and not specific to software design, the abstract nature of software adds some problems of its own.

A **representation** is used to provide a particular abstraction of a system, and is typically needed for a purpose such as:

- capturing the designer's ideas for a solution;
- explaining the designer's ideas to others (such as customers, fellow designers, implementors, managers);
- checking for consistency and completeness in a solution.

A major use for representations is to provide support for particular steps in a design method: each design method makes use of a particular set of representations to form the inputs and outputs for the various transformations it uses.

However, this should not constrain one's thinking about how design representations should be used. Although design methods use representations, so can any form of design activity, whether it be graced with the name of a 'method' or not. Indeed, it is likely that at the present time most software is designed without the use of a particular defined 'method', but that is not to imply that designers do not use any form of representation to describe their ideas. Representations can be associated with problem models and solution (program) forms, quite independently of any particular form of design process.

Nor should the association between methods and representations be regarded as particularly rigid, so that the adoption of a method precludes in some way the use of any representation that is not normally associated with it. The objective of design is to solve problems, not to be 'politically correct' in its use of a form! (To some extent this association of method with representation forms is a natural enough consequence of using a design method, since the method guides the designer into considering particular issues in sequence, and so into using particular notations to support these.) For that reason the discussions of representations and methods have been separated in this book, so that the power of abstraction provided by different representations can be seen in a wider context than that of a particular method.

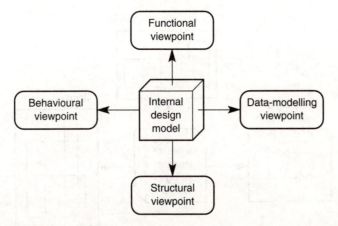

Figure 5.1 The four principal viewpoints as projections from the design model.

Because representations provide particular abstractions of a system, they are closely linked to the concept of a **viewpoint**. Many of us are familiar with the type of plan drawing that is used for describing buildings and other physical objects. Such a drawing can be considered as describing the 'physical' appearance of the object. However, the wiring plan will also provide an abstract representation of the building, although it may look very different from the physical plan. While these viewpoints are very different in many ways, they need to be kept consistent at the points where they 'intersect' through references to common attributes of design objects.

The notion of a viewpoint puts a particular emphasis upon the role of a representation. A representation is the means that we use to capture certain attributes of a design, and it should not be regarded as being the design itself. This concept of the viewpoint as a projection of a design model is illustrated in Figure 5.1, and is explored in some detail in Brough (1992). When using this conceptual framework, we can regard the different viewpoints as encompassing particular sets of attributes of the design model, and the representations are then the means that are used to describe these attributes. (There may, of course, be more than one representation that can be used to describe the attributes of a particular viewpoint, a point that will be examined further later in this chapter.)

Returning for a moment to the description of a building that was used in the earlier example, we can now see that:

- 'plan' diagrams capture the attributes that are concerned with spatial dimensions, accessibility, and the like;
- a wiring diagram captures the attributes that are concerned with the logical organization of the distribution of electrical power and its control.

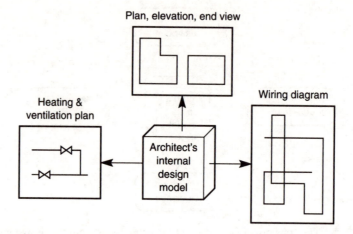

Plan, elevation, end view

Heating & ventilation plan

Wiring diagram

Architect's internal design model

Figure 5.2 Examples of representations as realizations of viewpoints.

However, both are particular projections of the architect's (mental) design model for the building. Indeed, such representations are the only real means that the architect can use to convey ideas about the design to others. Even so, the representations are not the design model, they are only projections from it, as is illustrated in Figure 5.2.

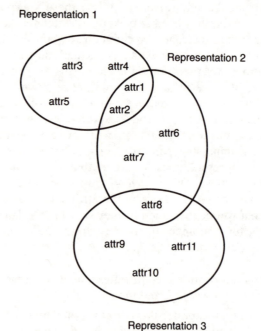

Representation 1

attr3 attr4

attr1

attr5

attr2

Representation 2

attr6

attr7

attr8

attr9 attr11

attr10

Representation 3

Figure 5.3 Intersecting attributes for different representations.

Of course, these projections need to be kept consistent with one another, in order to maintain a consistent design model. Since each representation describes a set of design attributes, there is frequently some intersection between the different sets of attributes, and hence some means of checking for consistency between the corresponding forms of representation. Figure 5.3 shows this concept in a symbolic manner. Unfortunately, since the design model is captured only through the representations, we can only check for consistency between forms, and so cannot use the model itself to check that the representations are 'correct' in any absolute sense.

The next section examines more closely the ways in which these concepts can be used in the domain of software design. In particular, it considers the principal features that distinguish software systems, and the ways in which design representations can be used to describe the attributes that reflect these features.

5.2 Design viewpoints for software

Perhaps the most distinctive property of software is its dynamic nature. Software is not only an abstraction (which adds to the complications of describing it with abstract forms), it is also the description of a process. So in order to formulate and explore the design model, a designer needs to use a set of description forms that are able to describe both the static and the dynamic properties of a system.

In order to describe *system-oriented* properties, the designer usually needs forms that describe the dynamic behaviour of the system. Such forms tend to emphasize features such as the flow of data or information around a system, or the sequencing of operations. For more detailed *solution-oriented* design needs, which are often concerned with describing program structures such as packaging, procedure hierarchy, and data forms, the chosen forms will generally focus on static design attributes. This change of emphasis during design is illustrated in Figure 5.4.

The nature of software and the many paradigms that exist for developing software systems, based on different structuring criteria, has led to the use of a large number of design representations (Webster, 1988; Harel, 1992). These can be broadly classified as follows:

- structural forms, in which the viewpoint is concerned with essentially static aspects of the system;
- behavioural forms, a set of viewpoints that seek to describe the causal links between events and system responses during execution;
- functional forms, viewpoints that seek to describe what the system does in terms of its tasks;

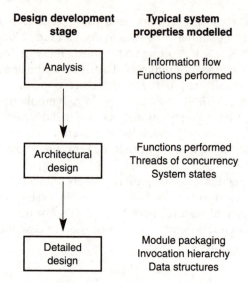

Figure 5.4   Changes of viewpoint with evolution of the overall design model.

- data-modelling forms, concerned with the data objects used within the system, and the relationships between these.

Within each of these broad classes, there are a number of forms in general use, partly because the many possible relationships require different sets of attributes for their description, and partly because no representation ever quite captures all of the attributes that a designer needs to consider.

These representations can all be classified as 'direct' viewpoints, in that they are created directly by the designer. A further class of viewpoints can be described as 'derived' viewpoints (Budgen and Friel, 1992), shown in Figure 5.5; in these some transformation is applied to the design model in order to generate a 'new' representation form. An example of such a derived viewpoint is that produced by the use of some form of interpreter in order to 'execute' a design (Friel and Budgen, 1991); here the output from the interpreter forms the derived viewpoint in terms of some sequence of states or diagrams. (This particular example is based on the observed behaviour of designers in 'mentally executing' a design in order to assess its behavioural aspects (Adelson and Soloway, 1985).) While observation suggests that designers make use of a number of such viewpoints in an informal way, they do not form part of any currently formalized design practices and they will not be explored further in this book.

The rest of this section looks briefly at some of the characteristics of the four classes of direct viewpoints. The following section considers how these can best be described in terms of the use of text, diagrams and mathematical forms.

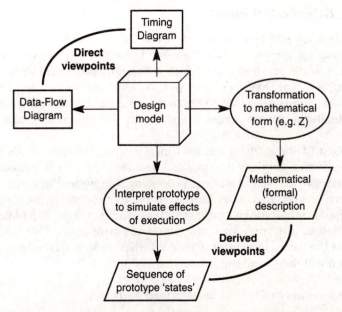

Figure 5.5 Examples of the use of derived viewpoints within the viewpoints model.

5.2.1 Structural forms

These are generally used to model the static relationships between the objects identified in the designer's models. At the abstract (architectural) modelling level these model objects generally correspond closely to the objects in the real-world problem, whatever the design strategy adopted. At this stage in the development of the design model, the type of dependency that links the objects is likely to involve forms such as data flow and data dependency. These are likely to be identified by considering system functions, and issues such as data rate and causality are unlikely to be particularly significant.

At the detailed design level, the objects being modelled are likely to be program entities such as compilation units (for example, the Ada package) or subprogram units (procedures) and the relationships that exist between these. These relationships may include the 'uses' hierarchy for compilation units (Parnas, 1979) and the 'invocation' hierarchy for procedures. Both are viewpoints that are concerned with modelling static structures rather than with any form of run-time behaviour. (An attempt was made to combine structural form and behavioural features in a development of the structure chart that was proposed in Yourdon and Constantine (1979), but this does not appear ever to have been used to any significant degree.)

5.2.2 Behavioural forms

These are essentially concerned with causal issues, connecting an 'event' to a 'response' via any necessary conditions. These forms tend to be far more abstract than the previous class, which are usually concerned with compilable entities that have definite syntax and semantics. In contrast, behavioural forms are more likely to be concerned with operations that may actually be spread across a number of the physical elements in a system.

Most of these forms can be considered as examples of *finite-state machines*, being concerned with the transitions that occur between different states of a system (waiting, processing, output and so on), and the conditions (events) that are required to make them occur. Being concerned with dynamic relationships (causality), these forms require to handle some of the design attributes that are concerned with time. Our ability to represent the varied influences of time is rather uneven, as the examples of Chapter 6 will show, and can be summarized thus:

- *sequencing* aspects can be described fairly well;
- *fixed-interval* descriptions are also fairly tractable, although their use is mainly restricted to particular features of real-time systems;
- *constraint* effects are very difficult to capture and describe using existing forms of description.

5.2.3 Functional forms

One of the hardest tasks for the designer is to describe exactly what it is that a system does. This is essentially a problem-driven issue and hence is difficult to describe in any general form. However, in exchange, this may well be one of the better-defined aspects of the initial problem specification, and the algorithmic aspects in particular may be better specified than other features.

At the detailed design level such forms are generally needed to describe the run-time behaviour of program elements such as subprograms.

5.2.4 Data-modelling forms

While the description of data structures need not be a very significant issue in architectural design terms, it is often a critical aspect of a detailed design. Again, there are a number of relationships that may need to be captured. These include such dependencies as: *type* (both in compounding types to create new ones, and in such mechanisms as inheritance, used to create new 'classes'); *sequence* (in terms of structures such as trees and lists); and *form*.

For some classes of problem, the choice of data structures is a central one, and cannot easily be divorced from the functional issues. Because the viewpoints describing data structures are essentially static in nature, and hence more easily handled, there are a number of well-established representations that are widely used for modelling these forms.

5.3   Forms of notation

This section examines how the different forms of notation for constructing representations are used. The three basic components that can be used in a representation are:

- text
- diagrams
- mathematical expressions

Of course, these are not mutually exclusive in any sense: indeed, neither of the latter two forms is likely to be of very much use without a textual component (try removing all of the text from *any* diagram and see what sense it makes!). Their use during the design process also need not be mutually exclusive.

5.3.1   Textual description forms

Text is very widely used as a means of summarizing information, not just for design. In particular, 'structured' forms such as ordered lists and tables provide a ready means of referring to information – many examples of 'bullet' lists and numbered lists appear in this book. Since a summary is a form of abstraction, such mechanisms are therefore useful to the designer too.

The main problems with using text alone are that:

- Any structure that is implicit in the information can easily be obscured, unless it is in a form that maps easily onto lists and tables. Indentation can help with providing structure, but its usefulness is limited, owing to the difficulty of recognizing alignments over long blocks of text.
- Natural-language forms are prone to ambiguity, and resolving this can lead to the use of long and complex sequences of text.

This shows that text is often most effective in conveying information when it is used in small blocks or tables. The use of **bold** or *italic* fonts (when available) can help to highlight items, but the effect of this is rapidly lost if used to excess. (In handwritten material, underlining acts as an adequate substitute.)

So textual forms are rarely used as the sole means of providing information about design ideas, although they can play a supplementary role. A good example of text in this role is the use of standard 'forms' in the SSADM method (see Chapter 13) in order to capture information about certain design decisions. The use of a standard form provides the structure needed to overcome the problems of producing and reading free text.

5.3.2 Diagrammatical description forms

Diagrams have been extensively used in the first four chapters of this book to illustrate concepts about hierarchy, position, flow of information and other forms of relationship between abstract objects. As with text, diagrams also benefit from simplicity of form, and there is probably a 'natural limit' to the number of items of information that can be easily assimilated when reading a diagram. (Miller's 'magic number', 7 plus or minus 2, is much quoted in this context of handling information within the human brain (Miller, 1957); but it is misused here, since it referred to handling 'events' rather than abstractions.)

Diagrammatical notations are very widely used in software design, as in many forms of design activity. Indeed, most of the forms that will be discussed in this book are diagrammatical, and so their properties will be discussed only very briefly at this point.

Historically, the earliest form of diagram associated with software design is probably the flowchart. Figure 5.6 shows some of the main symbols that are used in drawing flowcharts, together with a very simple example of the form. As sometimes happens with pioneering ideas, it has not stood the test of time very well and is now used for specialist purposes.

A major criticism of the flowchart is that it chiefly describes a solution in terms of the operations of the underlying machine, rather than in terms of the problem and its structures. As a part of this, it also places great emphasis upon forms for sequencing operations, a feature of detailed design that is now made much more explicit by modern programming structures. Perhaps the most significant reason is that the flowchart describes structural forms that are not much more abstract than the final program code, and so offers little benefit. (Some years ago now, we experimented in a small way with documenting the development of a system by using both flowcharts and pseudocode. After a few months, we decided to drop the flowcharts as we found that our information was always extracted from the pseudocode.)

The use of flowcharts for general software development is certainly not recommended, and they are now rarely taught or used except for specialist purposes. However, very many other forms of diagram are now

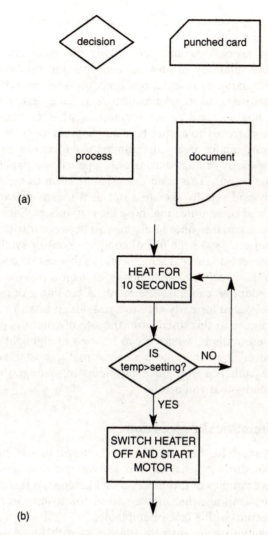

(a)

(b)

Figure 5.6 The traditional flowchart notations: (a) Some of the symbols used; (b) A simple example of a flowchart.

used in software design, with properties that more closely reflect the forms of abstraction required in the design process.

It is interesting to look at the number of symbols that are used in the more successful diagrammatical forms. (By 'successful' is meant those that continue to be used over a period.) Many of them have no more than four or five symbols, which in itself is a measure of the degree of abstraction involved in their use. As a general rule, the forms with the larger numbers of symbols tend to be at lower levels of abstraction (the flowchart is a good example), and one problem with their use is that of remembering all the nuances of the notation.

For most users, diagrams are usually the most effective way of providing a clear summary of abstract concepts and relationships. However, this is not guaranteed, and a bad diagram is no more helpful than a heap of unstructured and ungrammatical text. Like text, diagrams have both a syntax ('how we say it') and a semantics ('what it means'), and these need to be used correctly to ensure that the diagram meets its purpose.

A necessary quality in any diagrammatical form of representation is that it should be easily produced using only a pencil and paper (or pen and whiteboard, and so on). This is an essential criterion to meet if diagrams are to be easily and rapidly sketched out as a means of exploring ideas about a design and communicating those ideas to others. Such conventions as the use of thick and thin lines to distinguish between attributes are ruled out by this criterion, as are the use of complex icons or symbols. (Unfortunately some object-oriented design forms fail this test, and when they are combined with the widely available powerful diagramming tools on workstations, their adoption can have the effect of binding a designer into the use of these tools even for early architectural design tasks.)

As a footnote to this discussion: the use of colour is probably best restricted to presentations, where it can be used to highlight features of a diagram. However, even then, do remember that a substantial percentage of the average audience may have problems in distinguishing between many of the colours that you use.

5.3.3 Mathematical expressions

In recent years there has been an increased interest in using mathematical forms to provide abstract descriptions of software designs, and we will look briefly at some examples of this in Chapter 14. Much of this interest stems from the great advantage that mathematical forms have in being able to combine abstraction with a lack of ambiguity.

Since computers are discrete machines, with finite word size and many states, the form of mathematics most appropriate for the needs of software design is that which describes discrete structures. Unfortunately, discrete mathematics is still less likely to be part of the engineer's armoury than more classical forms, and so one of the disadvantages of using mathematical forms is the need for additional staff training and education, often at quite advanced levels. However, this problem should not be exaggerated, since the concepts involved are frequently familiar enough to programmers.

Mathematical forms have particular strengths in describing system behaviour, and in handling some of the issues of time dependency. Major limitations include the complexity of the notation in terms of using a range of unfamiliar symbols (together with a certain lack of standards for these on occasion) and difficulties with handling descriptions of large-scale systems.

SUMMARY

This chapter has examined the issues involved in providing descriptions of a designer's ideas. Some key points and terms that were identified in this were:

- the roles of representations in capturing, explaining, and checking design information;

- the concept of a viewpoint of a design model, as a means of capturing a particular set of design attributes, and as projected through the use of a representation;

- the principal classes of direct design viewpoint – the structural, behavioural, functional, and data-modelling forms;

- the use of text, diagrams, and mathematical expressions as the three basic forms in constructing design representations.

FURTHER READING

Webster D.E. (1988). Mapping the design information representation terrain. *IEEE Computer*, **21**(12), 8–23

A paper that surveys the use and roles of a wide range of representations. Some of these are not design representations as discussed in this book (being nearer to what we might consider high-level implementation forms), but the comparisons remain valuable.

Brough M. (1992). Methods for CASE: A generic framework. In *Advanced Information Systems Engineering* (Loucopoulos P., ed.), pp. 524–45. Lecture Notes in Computer Science No. 593. Berlin: Springer-Verlag

This paper explores the concept of representations providing 'views into the model' and the roles of representations within the development of a design model.

Harel D. (1992). Biting the silver bullet. *IEEE Computer*, **25**(1), 8–20

This paper was written in answer to an earlier paper by Fred Brooks Jr (Brooks, 1987). It is mainly concerned with the problems of describing reactive systems and discusses the use of what I have termed 'derived viewpoints' for design model execution as well as representation forms in general.

EXERCISES

5.1 For the example of building design that was used in this chapter, suggest any other viewpoints that might be needed in order to provide a full design description, and the representations that could be used for these.

5.2 Write down:

(a) a list of reasons *in favour* of standardizing any particular form of design description;

(b) a list of reasons *against* standardizing the same form of description.

5.3 Consider the (much-maligned) example of the flowchart. What design attributes does it capture, and hence what viewpoint on the design model does it provide?

5.4 Suggest how you might represent the following viewpoints using in turn: text on its own; a diagram; a mathematical form:

(a) the hierarchy of procedures in a program (that is, which procedures are called by each procedure);

(b) the program units (procedures) that make use of a particular data type in a program.

6 Some Design Representations

6.1 A problem of selection

6.2 The Data-Flow Diagram (DFD)

6.3 The Entity–Relationship Diagram (ERD)

6.4 The Structure Chart

6.5 The Structure Graph

6.6 The Jackson Structure Diagram

6.7 Pseudocode

6.8 The State Transition Diagram (STD)

6.9 The Statechart

6.10 The Petri Net

This chapter provides a set of examples of design representations that covers a wide spectrum of the roles and forms that were discussed in Chapter 5. In the first section the reasons behind the choice of examples is explained. Then each example is discussed, identifying its form and the role it plays in the design process.

6.1 A problem of selection

This chapter examines a selection from the many design representation forms that are used in software design methods. There are very many such representation forms, as well as variants on some of the more popular forms, and rather than producing a 'laundry list' of these, this chapter focuses upon a fairly small sample, chosen to give as wide a spectrum as possible.

Chapter 5 provided a framework for describing the roles and forms of representations, and gave some general classifications for these. For this chapter, which looks at specific examples, the selection from these forms has been made so as to range across the spectrum of:

- *form*, including textual, diagrammatical and mathematical forms of notation;

- *viewpoint*, in terms of the ideas described in Chapter 5, where we considered structural, behavioural, functional and data-modelling viewpoints;

- *use*, in terms of the form's role during the phases of design, the type of problem domain in which it might be appropriate, and the extent to which it is used.

(Remember too that some notations used for software design may well have originated with quite different purposes – in some cases, even before the invention of computers!)

The selection is not exhaustive, nor is it likely to meet with universal agreement. As emphasized throughout this book, the activity of design is a creative process, and hence the forms that go with it are also subject to personal preference when it comes to a question of use.

The ordering of the discussion is somewhat arbitrary, since it is virtually impossible to impose any sequence on such a selection – not least because some of the forms play multiple roles. All the forms also meet the criterion of being easily produced with the aid of pencil and paper alone, as described in the last chapter.

These are not the only forms of representation that will be met in this book, since further examples will be encountered when specific methods are looked at. (In particular, the examples of mathematical forms have been deferred until they can be shown in the context of the associated methods.) However, the ones discussed in this chapter are considered to be of enough significance to be introduced in advance of the description of the techniques for their use. Table 6.1 provides a summary of the viewpoints on the design model that each of these forms can provide, and lists the attributes of the design that can be captured through its use.

Table 6.1   Summary of design representations and viewpoints.

Representation form	Viewpoints	Design attributes
Data-Flow Diagram	Functional	Information flow, dependency of operations on other operations, relation with data stores
Entity–Relationship Diagram	Data modelling	Static relationships between design entities
Structure Chart	Functional and structural	Invocation hierarchy between procedures, decomposition into procedures
Structure Graph	Structural	Packaging (information-hiding), uses relationship, concurrency
Structure Diagram	Functional, data modelling, behavioural	Algorithm form Sequencing of data components Sequencing of actions
Pseudocode	Functional	Algorithm form
State Transition Diagram	Behavioural	State-machine model of an entity
Statechart	Behavioural	System-wide state model, including parallelism (orthogonality), hierarchy and abstraction
Petri Net Graph	Behavioural	Interaction between parallel threads

A final point that follows on the one that was made in the previous paragraph: the level of detail in the following sections is not intended to be consistent. In particular, those notations that will be used in the later chapters on design methods are not normally described in such complete detail as others, since further examples of their use will be provided in the relevant chapters.

6.2   The Data-Flow Diagram (DFD)

The Data-Flow Diagram (usually termed a DFD) is mainly used for describing a very problem-oriented view of the workings of a system. It provides a description based on modelling the flow of information around a network of operational elements, with each element making use of or modifying the information flowing into that element.

The use of some form of Data-Flow Diagram for describing the operation of complex systems almost certainly predates the computer era, and Page-Jones (1988) has suggested that it is likely to have originated in a number of places and times, all quite independently. The earliest reference that he can find (although admittedly this one is largely folklore) dates from the 1920s.

The general nature of the Data-Flow Diagram concept has been shown very effectively through an example used by Tom De Marco (1978). In the introduction to his book *Structured Analysis and System Specification*, he gives an example of an informal flow diagram being used to clarify the assembly instructions for a kayak. While obviously the 'data flow' in this case is physical (consisting of subassemblies), the principle is the same as for software, and the example provides an excellent demonstration of the effectiveness of such a form when it is used to describe a *process*. In the same spirit, the simple flow diagram in Figure 6.1 shows how this form can be used to describe the assembly of a garden shed.

Even this simple example is sufficient to show one of the strengths of the DFD when used to describe a sequence of operations, namely that one can readily see the prerequisites for any operation at a glance. For example, if we take operation 5, 'fit door to walls', we can see that it is dependent upon having the completed results of operations 3 and 4 available, and we can see why. Sequential lists of actions may be able to convey the same information, but the dependency aspect, which is so easily visualized through the use of a DFD, is generally less clear in such forms. The benefits of this ready visualization become even more important for operations that involve much greater complexity than this simple example.

The DFD has been widely used for software design purposes over many years, and a number of variations in the exact forms of the symbols used for drawing DFDs are to be found in the literature. This chapter will concentrate on describing the form that has been popularized through the work of De Marco (1978) and others, since Chapter 10 will be making use of this. Another form, which uses a more 'formal' notation and performs a somewhat different role in the design process, will be examined when the SSADM method is described in Chapter 13.

6.2.1 The form of the DFD

The DFD is a graphical representation, and it makes use of only four basic symbols. Because of its highly abstract nature, in terms of the level of description provided, it is chiefly used during the early design stages that are often termed 'analysis' – at a time when the designer is likely to be making major architectural design decisions.

Figure 6.2 shows an example of the use of a DFD to describe the operation of a bank autoteller (cashpoint) system. The four basic elements that are used in the diagram are:

- the circle (or, as it is popularly termed, the bubble), which is used to denote an operation, and is labelled with a brief description of the operation;

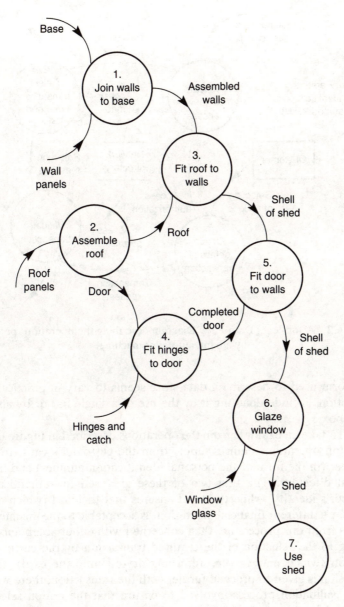

Figure 6.1   A flow diagram providing instructions for the assembly of a simple garden shed.

- the box, used to denote an external source or sink of information;
- the parallel bars, used to denote a data store or file;
- the arc, used to denote the flow of information between the other three components.

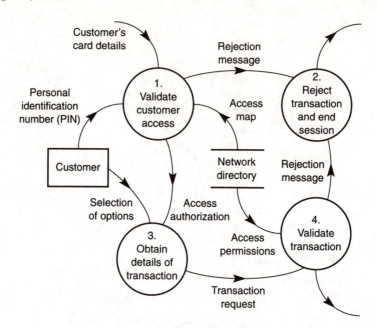

Figure 6.2 A top-level Data-Flow Diagram describing the operations performed by a bank autoteller machine.

(The form used to describe a data store seems to vary in practice; other conventions include denoting it by the use of a single bar or by an open-ended box.)

To take an example from the operations described in Figure 6.2; the validation operation requires inputs from the customer's card, from the customer (in the form of the personal identification number) and from an internal directory. The first two of these are used to authenticate the customer's identity, while the third ensures that the card (which may be issued by a different financial institution) is acceptable to the machine. The outputs from this process are then concerned with either acceptance (proceeding to the selection of the required transaction by the customer) or rejection (which may involve returning or retaining the card). Even if permission is given to proceed further with the transaction, there will be a further validation process involved to ensure that the option selected is permitted for this customer.

So essentially this DFD provides a top-level 'model' of how the designer intends the autoteller to operate. It is expressed in terms that are part of the *problem* domain (customer, PIN, transaction), rather than of the *solution*, and as such it identifies the main architectural tasks for the autoteller system.

An important characteristic of the DFD is that it can be expanded in a hierarchical fashion, with the operation of any bubble being described by

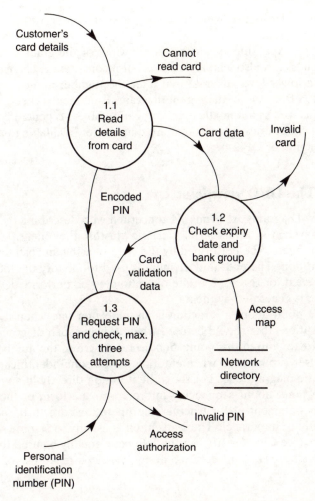

Figure 6.3   An expansion of one of the 'bubbles' from the top-level Data-Flow
Diagram for the bank autoteller machine.

means of a further DFD. As an example of this, Figure 6.3 shows an
expansion of bubble 1 of Figure 6.2, using the same symbols. This also
emphasizes the significance of the numbering scheme used for identifying
the bubbles, since the identity number indicates the 'level' of a bubble, its
position within an expanded description of the system.

In this example, the designer has elaborated on his or her ideas for
the operation 'Validate customer access'. Note particularly that in the
operation represented by bubble 1.3, there is no attempt to show the
structure of the *control* flow that is associated with the possible iteration
required to permit the customer three attempts at entering the PIN. The
DFD is not concerned with the control logic involved in performing this

operation, and its details will need to be elaborated later, using other forms for its description.

While expansion is valuable in allowing for the gradual refinement of a design, it can also lead to problems of inconsistency: changes may be made to a lower-level diagram that alter the number and/or form of the information flow arcs in the parent diagram. Consistency checking of such changes (as well as automatic numbering of bubbles) is generally provided by the specialist drawing tools that are quite widely available to assist with the production of DFDs.

6.2.2   The DFD viewpoint

Data-Flow Diagrams are primarily concerned with describing the architecture of a system in terms of its *functions*, in that they identify the operations that need to be performed by the system, using an abstract level for the description. The data-flow element is used to identify the information that is needed for the appropriate operations to be performed, as well as that which is generated by them.

The point about abstraction is an important one when it comes to the conventions that should be used when drawing such diagrams. Figure 6.3 has already raised this point: bubble 1.3 describes the number of tries that the user is permitted when entering the personal identification number, but the diagram does not show the iteration directly in any way. On this same point about sequencing information, the form of the diagram makes no statement about whether the operations are to be performed sequentially or in parallel. The convention is usually to assume sequential operations (see Chapter 10), but the DFD can equally be used to describe parallel operations. Indeed, some design methods make use of it in this way.

6.2.3   Using the DFD

Because of its abstract nature and ability to describe function, the DFD is widely used for the initial modelling of systems (often termed 'analysis'). It is a major component of the widely used SSA/SD (Structured Systems Analysis and Structured Design) approach, which is described in Chapter 10, and it is also used in the various derivatives of this method.

In this role, one of its benefits is that it can fairly easily be understood by the user, since it is used to model the *problem* rather than a computer-oriented solution. De Marco makes a distinction here between 'logical' and 'physical' DFDs, which is useful to consider.

The **physical** DFD is used to model a system in terms of the physical entities concerned, rather than their functions. For example, Figure 6.4 shows a physical DFD that is used to model the workings of the booking

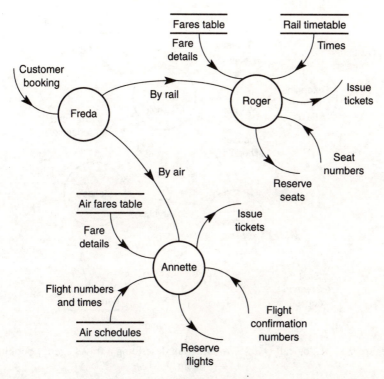

Figure 6.4   A 'physical' Data-Flow Diagram describing a travel agency booking system.

system in a travel office. The labels on the bubbles in this diagram indicate who does a job, rather than describing the job in any detail. (For example, Roger clearly handles all arrangements concerning rail travel, although we can only conclude this by examining the data-flow arcs.)

Figure 6.5 shows the equivalent logical DFD, in which the bubbles are now labelled to show what is being done to the data, rather than who is doing it. This is a more abstract and more structured view of the system described in Figure 6.4, but is clearly derived from it. Both of these forms are important: the physical DFD helps with initial modelling tasks and with communication with the customer, while the logical DFD is necessary when the designer begins to build up the architectural model required in order to build the system. (In this case, the system will presumably be some sort of automated reservation system.)

As mentioned earlier, other forms of DFD are used to help with more detailed modelling of a design, a point that emphasizes the general usefulness of this tool. This in turn reflects the fact that it is often relatively easy to think in terms of actions (as is demonstrated by the emphasis that older programming languages place on providing forms that describe

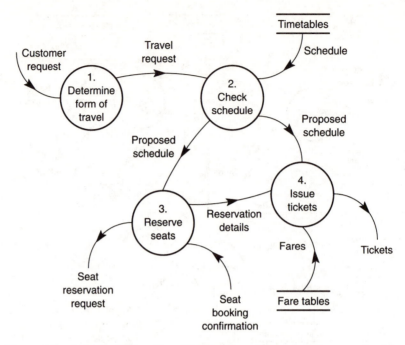

Figure 6.5 A 'logical' Data-Flow Diagram describing a travel agency booking system.

actions rather than data structures). There is therefore a strong intuitive appeal to the DFD: it can be understood relatively easily, and can often be developed more easily than could many other forms of description.

6.3   The Entity–Relationship Diagram (ERD)

This form of diagram is principally used to capture the relationships that exist between static data objects in a problem model or a design model. In particular, the *Entity–Relationship Model* has provided an essential foundation for the development of the relational models that are used in many database systems (Batini *et al.*, 1992; Stevens, 1991).

However, Entity–Relationship Diagrams (ERDs) can play other roles apart from their use in database design. For example, they are sometimes used to model the detailed form of the data stored in a system (Page-Jones, 1988; Stevens, 1991), while on a larger scale they can be used to model the relationships that occur between more complex and abstract design 'objects' (Booch, 1991).

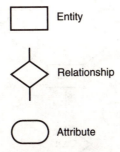

Figure 6.6   The basic Entity–Relationship notation.

6.3.1   The Entity–Relationship notation

In their detailed form, many ERD notations exhibit 'local' variations, but most of the widely used forms seem to have been derived from the notation devised by Peter Chen (1976). This section will seek to concentrate on the more 'generic' elements of the notation, and will not explore the more detailed nuances of the form.

Figure 6.6 shows the three principal symbols that are used in these diagrams, together with their meanings. (The symbols for entities and relationships are fairly standard, but beyond that the representations of attributes and other qualities are apt to differ in detail.) These basic elements are defined as follows:

- *entities* are real-world objects with common properties;
- a *relationship* is a class of elementary facts relating two or more entities;
- *attributes* are classes of values that represent atomic properties of either entities or relationships (attributes of entities are often the more recognizable, as can be seen from the examples).

The nature of an entity will, of course, vary with the level of abstraction involved, and so, therefore, will the form of its attributes and the nature of the relationships between them. Entities may be connected by more than one type of relationship, and attributes may be composite, with higher-level attributes being decomposed into lower-level attributes. (For example, the attributes student and teacher might be connected by the relationships attends-class-of and examines, while the attribute position might later be decomposed into range, bearing, and height.)

Relationships are also classified by their '*n*-ary' properties. Binary relationships link two entities, such as the relationship 'married to' occurring between the entities 'husband' and 'wife'. Relationships may also be 'one to many' (1 to *n*) and 'many to many' (*m* to *n*). Examples of these are:

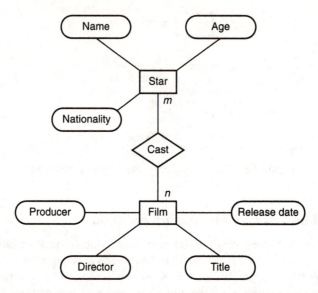

Figure 6.7 An ERD showing a simple relationship between two classes of entity.

- books (entity of order n) held in library (of order 1)
- authors (n) having written books (m)

(In the latter case, an author may have written many books, and a book may have multiple authors.) The effect of the n-ary property is to set bounds upon the cardinality of the values that are permitted by the relationship.

The development of an ERD typically involves performing an analysis of specification or design documents, classifying the terms in these as entities, relationships or attributes. The resulting list provides the basis for developing an ERD. Figure 6.7 shows an example of the ERD form being used for describing information about some fairly recognizable entities, and so describes the data structures that might be used in some form of indexing system.

In contrast to this, Figure 6.8 offers an example of a more system- and design-related use of the ERD form to model the entities that might be involved in a basic air traffic control system. This figure also provides a simple illustration of a point that was made earlier, concerning the possible existence of multiple relationships between two entities.

6.3.2 The ERD viewpoint

ERDs are purely and simply concerned with providing a data-modelling viewpoint of a system. As with many notations, they can be used both

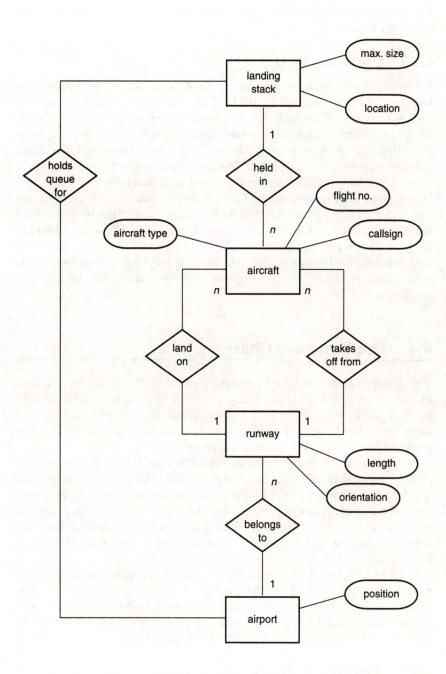

Figure 6.8   An ERD relating some of the major entities in an air traffic control system.

during the analysis of the problem and during the development of the solution (design).

6.3.3 Use of the ERD

ERDs are widely used for developing the schema used in relational database modelling (Batini *et al.*, 1992). This is a rather specialized area of system design, and as such has not been addressed in this book. (The design of databases probably fits somewhere between the 'template' form of design that is widely used for producing compilers, and the more general-purpose systematic forms described later in this book.)

The data-modelling viewpoint is also used as a subsidiary viewpoint in a number of design methods. One example in which it occupies such a role is the SSA/SD (Structured Systems Analysis and Structured Design) method described in Chapter 10: other examples are the object-oriented forms of Chapter 12 and SSADM (Chapter 13), which uses a variant of the notation described in this section. However, it plays a relatively minor role in all these methods, when compared with its central role in database design and development.

6.4 The Structure Chart

The program Structure Chart provides a visual 'index' to the hierarchy of procedures within a program, using a treelike format. It is therefore very much a solution-oriented form of description and, when allied with an algorithmic form such as pseudocode, can be used to provide a fairly comprehensive blueprint for the programmer.

Its origins lie in the research performed at IBM to understand the problems encountered with the design of the OS/360 operating system, which in many ways was the first real example of an attempt at programming in the large. A major problem that the researchers identified was that of complexity, and the Structure Chart was one of the means suggested for helping to resolve and understand the structuring of a program (Stevens *et al.*, 1974).

The Structure Chart provides a means of recording the details of a program's structure in a form that is of great value to anyone who is trying to understand its operation. It is particularly useful to the maintainer, who needs to understand the general architecture of someone else's design, in order to make changes that are consistent with its form.

6.4.1 The form of the Structure Chart

The Structure Chart uses a treelike notation to describe the hierarchy of procedures (subprograms) in terms of the invocation relationship between

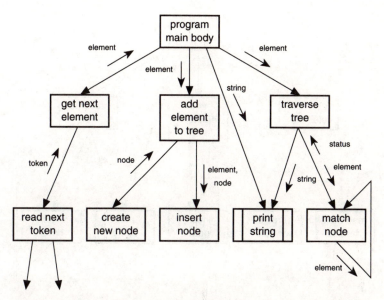

Figure 6.9   A Structure Chart describing a small program (first form).

them. It therefore highlights the dependence of a procedure on the lower-level procedures that it invokes. Figure 6.9 shows an example of a Structure Chart, in which the three main components are:

- the *box*, which denotes a procedure (subprogram);
- the *arc*, which denotes invocation;
- the *side-arrows*, which provide information about data flow in terms of parameter-passing.

There are a number of conventions that can be identified from this example. Three in particular are as follows:

- Procedures are drawn below the level of the lowest calling unit – in Figure 6.9, the procedure PrintString is drawn at the lowest level, because it is called by procedures in both the top (first) and second levels.
- Double side-lines (again using PrintString as the example) are used to indicate where the designer expects to be able to use a standard 'library' unit. There will therefore be no further design details for such a unit.
- The use of recursion can be indicated in a fairly simple manner. For example, in the procedure MatchNode, the recursive calling is indicated by the closed invocation arc.

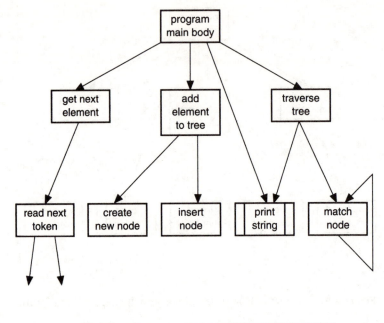

subprogram	in	out
AddElementToTree	e:element	s:status
PrintString	s:string	
MatchNode	n:node	m:match status

Figure 6.10 A Structure Chart describing a small program (second form).

The form of the Structure Chart is also hierarchical, in the sense that any box on the diagram can itself be expanded using the same form, although normally this would only apply to a box drawn at the lowest level. In the example of Figure 6.9, the procedure ReadNextToken is an obvious candidate for such treatment, since it is likely to call a number of other procedures in performing its task.

An alternative notation that is sometimes used for drawing Structure Charts is shown in Figure 6.10, and this is more akin to that which was originally proposed in Stevens *et al*. (1974). Instead of annotating the diagram with text describing the parameter flow, which can rapidly become cumbersome, this form uses a separate table to indicate the parameters for each procedure.

One of the benefits of this latter form is that it can easily be extended for use with programming languages that support local permanent data structures, such as Ada and Modula-2. In using a Structure Chart to record the design of a program written in such a language, a third column can be added to the table, in which to record the details of any local variables that are used by the procedure. In designing for such programming languages, the use of direct references to such structures can be an important practice, and one that supports the use of information-hiding. It is important to record the details of such a direct access form in order to clarify the use of such practices.

6.4.2 The Structure Chart viewpoint

The principal role of the Structure Chart is to describe the way in which a program is assembled from a set of procedures. Its primary features are the description of procedure function and of connectivity with other procedures through invocation, although only the presence of the latter is recorded, with no attempt to indicate anything about frequency or sequencing of calls. While the transfer of data via parameters is recorded, it is not a primary feature of the diagram.

The Structure Chart contains some information about the construction of a program, and can therefore be regarded as also providing a certain amount of structural information.

6.4.3 The use of the Structure Chart

The Structure Chart provides a relatively low degree of abstraction from the final implementation of a solution and, as was observed earlier, it can form a useful index to the structure of a program. (Some tools exist for 'reverse engineering' program code in order to construct the details of the Structure Chart.) For this reason, it not only provides a blueprint for the programmer during design, but also gives information that will be useful to the maintainer of a program (or to the marker of student programs!).

Chapter 10 provides an example of a widely used design method in which the output from the design transformations consists mainly of Structure Charts. When combined with pseudocode to describe the algorithmic portion of the design, they form a quite detailed set of outputs from the design process.

6.5 The Structure Graph

This notation was devised by Ray Buhr (1984) to assist with the design and description of Ada programs. It is not completely Ada-specific, for it can also be used to describe programs that are to be constructed in any programming language that has similar constructs for packaging and concurrent threads of execution, such as Modula-2 (Budgen, 1989).

As a representation, it involves capturing relatively low-level design attributes concerned with packaging and with the detailed form of task

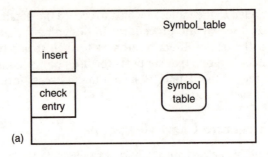

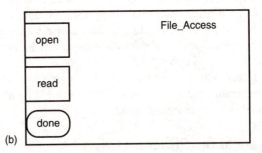

Figure 6.11 Packaging of data structures and procedures described using Structure Graphs. (a) Package with concealed data structure and externally visible procedures (insert, check_entry). (b) Package with an externally visible data object (the Boolean variable done).

interactions. As a means of describing program structure it can form a useful complement to the Structure Chart described in Section 6.4, since the two provide a description of a system in terms of some common entities (such as procedures) and attributes (such as invocation) from different viewpoints. Both of these forms provide much detail about constructional issues.

6.5.1 The Structure Graph notation

The complete notation used for the Structure Graph is quite extensive. This reflects the relatively low level of abstraction that is involved. This section will describe only a subset of the complete notation, and will use Ada terminology to describe the program constructs involved.

The Ada 'package' provides a compilation unit that is used to define 'scope' boundaries that limit the extent of references to data items and procedures, and it is denoted by an oblong box. The symbols for objects, such as procedures and variables, that are to be declared so as to be visible to other objects that lie outside the scope defined by the package are drawn inside the box and against its boundary. Symbols for those objects that are to be private to the package – not visible outside it – are drawn as totally

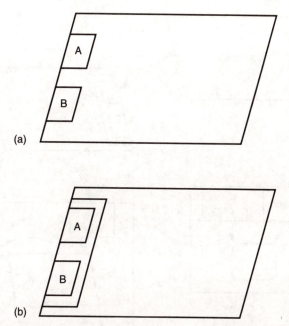

(a)

(b)

Figure 6.12   Parallel structures in a Structure Graph: the task notation. (a) Task with two 'accept' entry points A and B which are normally used to receive alternate calls. (b) Task with two 'accept' entry points that can be called in any ordering.

enclosed within it. Procedures are denoted by smaller boxes, while data objects are described using smaller boxes that have rounded corners. Figures 6.11(a) and 6.11(b) show examples of packages with procedures that can be called from outside ('sockets') and examples of both internal and visible variables.

The Ada 'task' acts as the thread of concurrent execution; it is denoted by a parallelogram, with its interface operations (basically those provided by the 'accept' mechanism) denoted by smaller parallelograms on the surface. Again the positioning of subordinate objects, either on the surface or internally, denotes their visibility. Figure 6.12 shows an example of an Ada task.

These basic structures can be linked in various ways, reflecting the possibilities provided by the Ada language. Thus packages can be embedded in other packages or in tasks, and tasks can be embedded within packages. Arcs are used to denote control flow via procedure calls (invocation) or task-to-task links via the Ada rendezvous mechanism (call–accept). A simple example of a system described with these forms is shown in Figure 6.13.

There are a number of further conventions used in the Structure Graph. As an example of one of these, the extra lines drawn around the entry points of task producer in Figure 6.13 indicate that there is a selection mechanism to determine which accept entry point is to be used during a

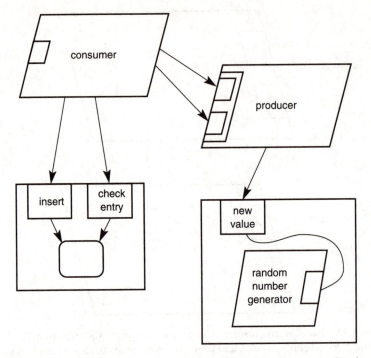

Figure 6.13   A Structure Graph showing the use of packages and tasks.

rendezvous – the entry points are not to be used in sequence, which would be the default. As can be seen from this example, the level of description provided through the Structure Graph is concerned with quite detailed design issues, although it is still considerably more abstract than the actual program code.

6.5.2   The Structure Graph viewpoint

The basic viewpoint provided by the Structure Graph is a structural one, being concerned with how the program units are linked at compilation. The arcs on the diagram describe the 'uses' relations (see Chapter 12) between the entities (Parnas, 1979), and the positioning of symbols indicates information about their external visibility. There are also some additional elements in the notation that can be used to provide further information. These are typically concerned with providing details about invocation and sequencing, and so provide a behavioural element to the viewpoint.

When designing for a programming language such as Modula-2 we can still make use of this notation. Although the language does not support the parallel tasking mechanisms of Ada, the packaging element is still present, and so the notation can be used to indicate the 'uses' hierarchy of the modules, in the same way that it is used with Ada packages.

6.5.3   Use of the notation

In Buhr (1984) the notation is used extensively through the basic design cycle. (An additional symbol that is used there is the 'cloud', which describes an object that has yet to be resolved!)

In Chapter 5 it was observed that design representations can be regarded as essentially independent entities, and that their use should not be considered as being tied exclusively to specific design methods. The Structure Graph provides a good example of this point, and indeed, while Buhr's associated design strategy is not widely adopted, at least one well-established CASE tool provides an essentially method-independent graphical editor for constructing Structure Graphs.

Part of the reason for this is that this viewpoint is increasingly important, and needs to be considered when designing for implementation in languages such as Ada, Modula-2 and C++, where concepts such as information-hiding can be realized through the implementation features. While various 'object-oriented' notations have been devised to describe these structural attributes (see Chapter 12), most are really much inferior to the Structure Graph. (In addition, many fail the basic test of practicality – that of requiring that they can be readily drawn using just a pencil!)

6.6   The Jackson Structure Diagram

Although similar in appearance to the Structure Chart notation described in Section 6.4, the Structure Diagram describes a very different set of attributes, and performs a very different set of roles. It is basically concerned with describing the sequential structure of an object, in terms of the three 'classical' structuring forms:

- sequence
- selection
- iteration

As a notation it is particularly important in that it can describe both the form of data structures (sequencing of items), and the form of operations (sequencing of actions, as performed by a program or a 'real-world' object that is being modelled).

Since this notation will be used extensively in the later chapters of this book (albeit under a variety of names), this section will concentrate on the basic 'rules of form' involved, leaving the main examples of its use until later.

6.6.1 The form of the Structure Diagram

The Structure Diagram takes the form of a 'tree', constructed from a set of boxes and arcs. Each set of 'child' boxes provides an elaboration of the description contained in the parent box, and hence the full description of a complete sequence is described by the lowest boxes on each branch. (In

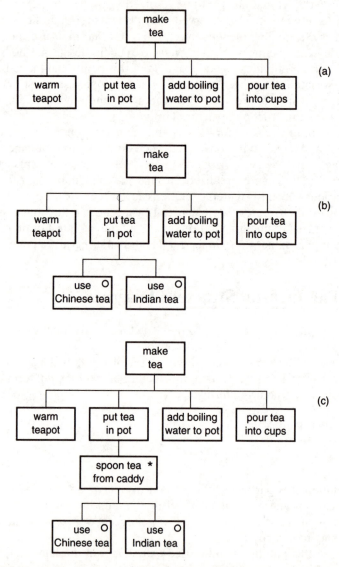

Figure 6.14 A Jackson Structure Diagram describing the operation of making tea. (a) A simple sequence of actions. (b) Adding a choice. (c) Adding iteration and choice.

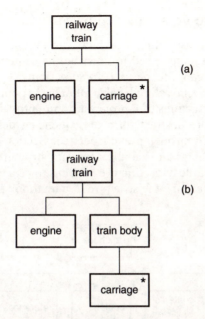

Figure 6.15 An example of an incorrect Structure Diagram. (a) The sequence and iteration forms are wrongly mixed on a single level. (b) How this can be resolved by adding a further level of abstraction in the description.

that sense, the parent boxes are themselves abstractions of the lower boxes.)

The basic notation is very simple, and is based upon three forms of box:

- A simple box denotes a component of a sequence – so in Figure 6.14(a) the action of making tea is described as a series of actions.
- A box with a circle in the upper right corner denotes selection from an option, and so in Figure 6.14(b) the previous description of tea-making is extended to include the possibility of using either China tea or Indian tea.
- A box with an asterisk in the upper right corner denotes an iteration, and so in Figure 6.14(c) the description is further extended by including the possibility that we might put more than one spoonful of tea into the pot.

There are a number of rules used in constructing these diagrams, but the most important is: 'forms cannot be mixed within a sequence'. Applying this rule shows that Figure 6.15(a) is incorrect. To correct it, it may be necessary to add an additional abstraction of 'carriages' above the iteration box, as shown in Figure 6.15(b), in order to keep the first level of abstraction as a pure sequence.

6.6.2   The viewpoints provided by Structure Diagrams

As already indicated, Structure Diagrams can be used to provide a *data modelling* viewpoint, when used to describe the sequential structuring of data objects. They can also be used for describing a viewpoint that has elements of both *functional* and *behavioural* viewpoints, when they are used to describe the actions of a program or an entity. In particular, they provide a much more abstract form of sequencing description than can normally be provided through pseudocode (see Section 6.7).

Figure 6.16 shows an example of a data structure described in this manner. In this case, the data structure happens to be a physical one, as the diagram is used to describe the structure of a textbook such as this one. A

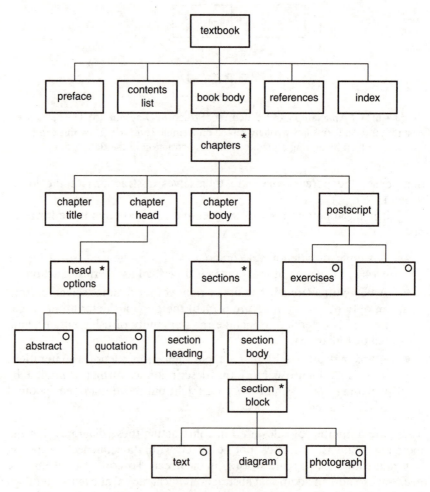

Figure 6.16   A Jackson Structure Diagram describing a static object (the structure of a textbook).

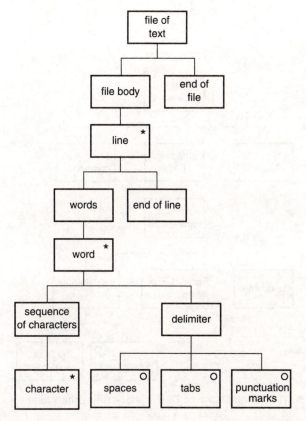

Figure 6.17   A Jackson Structure Diagram describing a simple file containing text.

more conventional programming data structure is shown in Figure 6.17, where a simple file of text is described using this form.

In Figure 6.18 an example of this form is used to describe the dynamic form of a program. In this example, the task of the program is to print out a page of a monthly bank statement. Clearly this is closely related to the appearance of the statement on the page.

6.6.3   Uses for the Structure Diagram

As it turns out, this form is ubiquitous. In examining the JSP design method (described in Chapter 9), it will be used to describe the structures of the input and output data streams. In both the JSD (Chapter 12) and SSADM (Chapter 13) design methods it is used to describe the 'evolution' of entities over time. The title of the form might vary, but the basic notation does not.

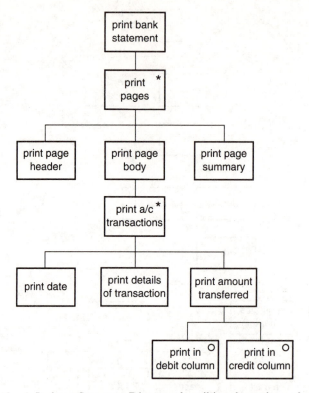

Figure 6.18 A Jackson Structure Diagram describing the actions of a program (printing a bank statement).

Since this form will occur so often later in the book, these roles will not be outlined any further at this point, and fuller descriptions will be left to the appropriate chapters.

6.7 Pseudocode

Pseudocode is, of course, used very widely indeed. It sometimes appears under other (more imposing) titles such as PDL (program description language), but it is easily recognized, even when concealed behind such grander titles.

If anything, pseudocode is used rather too much, as the low level of abstraction that it provides tends to conceal the wood within the trees as far as design abstraction is concerned. Perhaps some of its attraction lies in the ease with which it can be maintained using an ordinary computer terminal and keyboard.

```
boil water;
pour some water into teapot;
empty teapot;
REPEAT
    place spoonful of tea in pot
UNTIL enough tea for no. of drinkers;
REPEAT
    pour water into pot
UNTIL enough water for no. of drinkers;
```

Figure 6.19   The use of pseudocode to describe an algorithm.

That said, the level of abstraction that it provides is an important one, in that it permits one to think about the detailed sequencing of a solution while still remaining distant from the detailed forms of the solution. However, in order to do this effectively, it is necessary to ensure that pseudocode does not become too much like the programming language!

6.7.1   Pseudocode form

Like the Structure Diagram that was described in Section 6.6, pseudocode is concerned with describing a solution in terms of sequence, although it is restricted to describing the sequencing of operations alone. Figure 6.19 shows a typical example of this role, and expands upon the tea-making example of the previous section. Figure 6.20 shows a more typical example of the use of pseudocode for program design.

To be effective, there are some useful rules of thumb for writing pseudocode. The principal ones (as illustrated in the example of Figure 6.20) are:

- Use indentation to emphasize structure (it aids the eye in following the form of a sequence and finding other nodes in a branch).

- Pull out 'language keywords' in some manner, perhaps by typing them in upper case or underlined.

- Try to 'bracket' executable blocks such as the body of a loop, or a branch in a conditional structure, by using such paired keywords as LOOP and ENDLOOP or IF and ENDIF.

- Avoid referring to the identifiers of program variables or the values of constants. For example, the line 'check for the end-of-line character' is more abstract and much more easily comprehended than 'check for #15', which requires a knowledge of the significance of '#15'.

```
INITIALIZE line buffer;
READ first character from keyboard;
WHILE not the end of line DO
    IF character is terminator of a word
    THEN
        mark end of word in buffer;
        SKIP any trailing word separators
    ELSE
        copy character to buffer
    END IF;
    READ next character;
END WHILE;
```

Figure 6.20 The use of pseudocode to describe the structure of a program unit.

While these practices cannot guarantee better levels of abstraction, they can certainly help to avoid writing pseudocode that is little better than poorly documented code!

6.7.2   The pseudocode viewpoint

As already mentioned, this is basically a functional one, based upon the sequencing of operations, expressed at quite a detailed level. There is also a small structural element, but this is relatively minor in terms of importance.

6.7.3   Uses for pseudocode

Pseudocode is widely used to complement and augment other forms of description used in the later stages of design. It is hard to develop a design using pseudocode alone (one hesitates to say 'impossible'), but it is certainly undesirable, not least because of the restricted viewpoint it provides when making design choices.

Pseudocode can be used to complement the Structure Chart by providing the details and sequencing information that elaborates on the boxes in the diagram. It can similarly be used with the Structure Graph, and can of course be generated directly from a Structure Diagram. Indeed, almost all forms of diagram can usefully be augmented with a textual description of this form, since its disciplined format can help to maintain the relevant levels of abstraction.

Pseudocode will rarely appear in the examples of this book, since we will not be taking any segments of our larger examples down to quite this level of detail. However, its use for detailed design should be taken as assumed, even if it is not mentioned explicitly in the context of a particular design method.

6.8   The State Transition Diagram (STD)

Some classes of problem (and solution) can usefully be described by considering them as 'finite-state automata'. Such a system can be considered as existing in a finite set of possible 'states', with external events being the triggers that can lead to transitions between the states.

A process executing in a computer fits this model quite well. Its 'state' at any point in time can be described fully in terms of the contents of its variables and the values of any associated registers in the CPU, most notably the program counter register, whose contents determine which instruction will be executed next. While we might not wish to model the complete behaviour of a process in terms of all its possible states, there might be some useful supersets that can be considered.

As an example, the standard UNIX screen editor **vi** (pronounced 'vee eye') has two basic states of operation, which are termed its current 'modes'. These are:

- **command mode**, in which keystrokes are interpreted as commands to the editor to perform such operations as opening a file, moving the position of the screen cursor, or beginning to insert text at some point;
- **insert mode**, in which any keystrokes are interpreted as data to be stored in the editor's buffer.

Transitions occur between these modes according to certain forms of 'escape' command. There are many commands that can be used to make the transition between command mode and insert mode, but only one that can be used for the reverse transition (namely, pressing the Escape key). Figure 6.21 shows a simple diagrammatical description of this model of the **vi** editor, in which the bubbles represent the states (modes), and the arcs correspond to the transitions, labelled by the events (commands) that cause these to occur. (Not all the commands that cause the editor to enter insert mode are shown, in order to maintain clarity, as **vi** has a rich set of commands for this purpose.)

Figure 6.21 is a simple example of a form of State Transition Diagram (several conventions for these are in use), and it provides a convenient means for modelling many other systems too. Indeed, the general class of real-time (or 'reactive') systems can often be usefully modelled in this way, since their event-driven nature leads readily to the use of such a form.

6.8.1   The form of the STD

In Chapter 10, when we come to consider the extensions to SSA/SD, the Structured Systems Analysis and Structured Design Method, we will

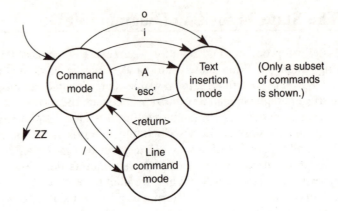

Figure 6.21   A simple state-transitional description of the UNIX **vi** text editor.

encounter a number of extended methods that are aimed at real-time systems. In the extension devised by Ward and Mellor (1985), they introduced a form of State Transition Diagram (STD) that will now be considered in a little more detail.

The form of this is a little more structured than that which was used in our first example. There are four principal components to this representation of an STD:

- The **state** represents an externally observable mode of behaviour, and is represented by a box, with a text label that describes its behaviour.

- The **transition** is described by an arrow, and identifies a 'legal' change of state that can occur within the system.

- The **transition condition** identifies the condition that will cause the transition to occur – usually in terms of the event that causes the transition – but is not concerned with the actual mechanism. It is written next to the transition arrow, *above* a horizontal line.

- The **transition action** describes the actions that arise as a result of the transition (there may be several, and they might occur simultaneously, or in a specific sequence). These are written *below* the horizontal line and the details of the transition conditions.

To complete the diagram, we also need to identify a default **initial state** (which has an arrow pointing in to it, with no source state attached), and may (possibly) need to identify a **final state** (which will have transitions into it, but none out from it).

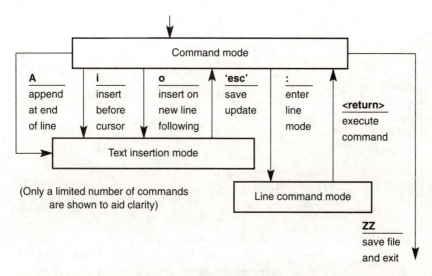

Figure 6.22 A description of the UNIX **vi** text editor using a State Transition Diagram (Ward and Mellor).

Figure 6.22 shows how the earlier example of the **vi** text editor can be modelled using this form of STD. Note that multiple transitions are still permitted between a given pair of states. (Once again, not all possible transitions are shown, in order to avoid too complex a diagram.) A state has also been added that is entered when the editor terminates, and command mode has been identified as the initial state when the editor begins operation.

Figure 6.23 shows a rather more complicated system modelled in this way (complicated in the sense of having many more states). In this case, the system described is the behaviour of an aeroplane modelled as a component of an air traffic control system. The event that causes the initial state to be entered is the primary radar detecting the aircraft as it enters the airspace. The complexity of the transitions involved in this example arises because of the sheer number of actions that the aircraft might take, from simply flying through the airspace, to being stacked before landing, and of combinations of such events.

6.8.2 The STD viewpoint

The STD is our first example of a representation that is used to capture a behavioural viewpoint of a system, and so it is concerned with modelling dynamic attributes of the system in terms of entities such as states, events and conditions. It only identifies the possibility that particular transitions will occur, with no indication as to how these will be sequenced.

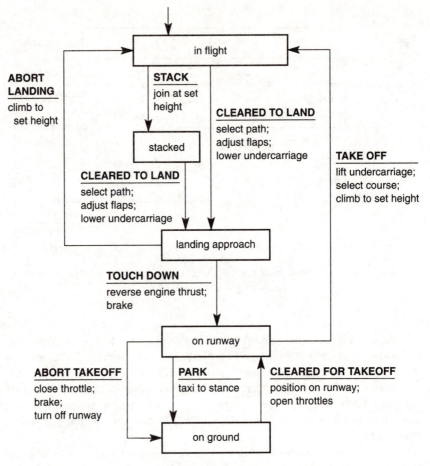

Figure 6.23 A State Transition Diagram describing the behaviour of an aircraft in an air traffic control zone.

6.8.3 Use of the STD

A major role for the STD is in modelling problem entities: although it can have a role in building models of solutions, this is less significant. It is also particularly useful in modelling some of the real-time needs of a system, hence its popularity in real-time variants of design methods.

The STD is a useful modelling tool, but as with all diagrammatical forms, it has limitations. As the example of the **vi** editor has shown, if there are a lot of transitions between a small number of states, the diagram can become very tangled. Similarly, large and complex systems lead to large and complex diagrams, as the form does not lead directly to any form of hierarchical layering of diagrams. In the next section we describe another state-oriented form of description that overcomes the problem of layering by adding a hierarchy to the states themselves.

6.9   The Statechart

Like the State Transition Diagram that was described in the preceding section, the Statechart is concerned with describing the behaviour of a system as a form of finite-state automaton, or finite-state machine. Like the STD, it is a form that is particularly well suited for use in describing reactive systems, in which the main functions arise in response to particular events.

The Statechart was devised by David Harel (1987; 1988) and he has observed that it is based on the more general concept of the 'higraph', which in turn has a range of applications. (We should perhaps discount his claim that 'this rather mundane name was chosen, for lack of a better one, simply as the one unused combination of "flow" or "state" with "diagram" or "chart".') It provides a rather more abstract form of description than the STD, and in particular it adds to the state-oriented viewpoint the ability to create a hierarchy of abstraction in the description, as well as permitting the designer to describe transitions that are 'orthogonal' in that they are completely independent of each other – so making it possible for the transitions to occur in parallel.

The Statechart shares a generality of role with the STD too. Both of these forms can be used for describing the structure of a problem, as well as the functioning of a solution. (However, the better examples generally come from the former.)

By far the best tutorial on Statecharts and their powers of description is provided in Harel (1987), where the author uses the functions of the Citizen Quartz Multi-Alarm III watch as the basis for his examples. The examples below are rather less inspired, but should at least provide some basic ideas about the scope of this particular form of description.

6.9.1   The form of the Statechart

In this notation, a state is denoted by a box with rounded corners, labelled in the upper left corner. Hierarchy is represented by encapsulation, and directed arcs are used to denote a transformation between states. The arcs are also labelled with a description of the event and, optionally, with a parenthesized condition. (Conditions are quite common in real systems. For example, it might not be possible to engage a cruise control mechanism in a car while either accelerating or braking.)

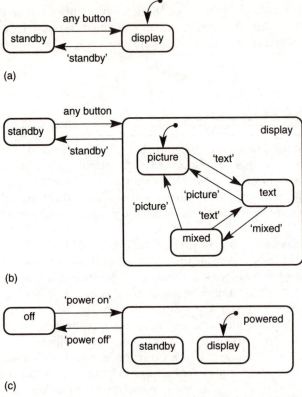

Figure 6.24   A Statechart describing a teletext television set. (a) The two main states of the television set. (b) An expanded description of the states shown in (a). (c) A more abstract description of (a).

Figure 6.24 shows an example of the use of this notation, to describe the operation of a teletext television set. Figure 6.24(a) shows that the set has two states, 'standby' and 'display'. The transition between 'display' and 'standby' occurs in response to the operation of the 'standby' button on the remote control. The reverse transition will occur when any button on the control is pressed. In Figure 6.24(b) the description of the state 'display' is expanded further, and it is now elaborated into the three encapsulated states, which are labelled as 'picture', 'text' and 'mixed'. The small arrow above 'picture' shows that this will be the default state, which will be entered when the set is switched to 'display' (an extension of this particular convention can be used to indicate when selection is made by means of some 'history' mechanism that remembers the previous use of these states). Note also that the state 'mixed' can only be entered from 'text'.

The elaboration of the description of a state is similar to the form used in the Jackson Structure Diagram, in that the state 'display' is an abstraction of the three states 'picture', 'text' and 'mixed', so that selecting 'display' must result in selecting one of these three states. In the Jackson Structure Diagram abstraction was denoted by the levels of a tree, while in the Statechart it is denoted by encapsulation. One benefit of this latter form is that it makes it relatively simple to denote any transitions that apply equally to all the encapsulated states, by showing them as applied to the outer box.

Figure 6.24(c) shows the first diagram expanded in a bottom-up rather than top-down fashion. The two initial states are now shown to be within a superstate 'powered'. (There are no specific limits about how many levels of a hierarchy can be shown in a diagram, but obviously there are practical issues of notational complexity that limit this. About two or three levels seem to be as many as can fit easily on a single diagram and be readily comprehended. Of course, the diagrams themselves can also be layered in a hierarchical fashion.)

6.9.2 The Statechart viewpoint

Like the STD, the Statechart is concerned with providing a behavioural description of a system. However, there are some significant differences between them in terms of the attributes that they each capture.

Watches and television sets have the advantage that the events that cause state changes are directly identifiable in terms of button presses, and hence are readily described. Figure 6.25 reworks the example of Figure 6.23 into this form, and shows a description of an aircraft in an air traffic control system, this time using the Statechart.

When comparing this with the STD form used in Figure 6.23, we can see that while the descriptions of state, event and transition are common to both, the STD provides a more detailed description in terms of the actions that occur, while the Statechart has more refined mechanisms for describing abstraction, defaults, history, and, of course, scale. The STD's lack of

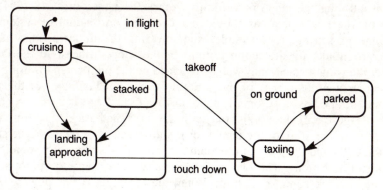

Figure 6.25 Statechart describing the actions of an aircraft in an air traffic control system.

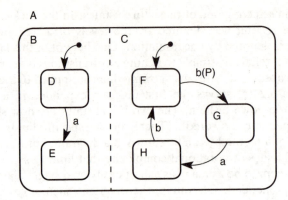

Figure 6.26   Describing orthogonality in the Statechart notation.

hierarchy also limits it largely to describing the behaviour of individual design elements, whereas the Statechart can describe whole systems through a hierarchy of diagrams and states. In that sense they are largely complementary, with the STD perhaps being more suited to modelling problems, and the Statechart being better suited for modelling detailed solutions.

The remaining major feature of the Statechart that ought to be described here is **orthogonality**. Figure 6.26 shows an example of a state A that can be described as a superstate of two orthogonal states B and C. B and C can in turn be described in terms of further states, but these are essentially independent groupings. Events may be common, as can be seen from the description of the transformations due to event a. Also, in describing A, note that we need to identify the default entry to states B and C, shown here as being the inner states D and F.

Orthogonality is important in reactive systems, where we expect to observe a suitable separation of concerns between groups of parallel functions, although all might be working towards the same objective. (Switching on the lights of a car should not cause its cruise-control system to change its setting, for example, and lowering the undercarriage of an aircraft should not affect the settings of the wing surfaces. In the latter case, the wing surfaces may well be changed by the pilot when lowering the undercarriage, as a part of the general routine for landing, but the two should not be linked automatically in any way.)

Figure 6.27 shows this concept in terms of the basic architecture of a computer. The state of the computer is shown as a compound of the state of the CPU and the state of the main memory (this is obviously something of a simplification). The two have various substates, and there are some events that are common to both. When the computer is first powered up, they each assume a default state that is expressed in terms of their internal operations. While there is communication via some memory bus, and

Computer system

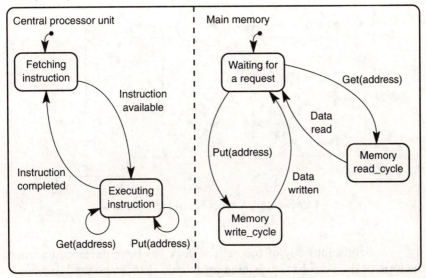

Figure 6.27 A Statechart describing the architecture of a computer.

hence some synchronization, the memory might also be accessed by device controllers or the like, and so its operations are suitably separated from those of the CPU.

6.9.3 Use of the Statechart

The Statechart is clearly a powerful and useful tool, and like the STD it has an important role in modelling reactive systems. Both forms are generally used to support other design viewpoints such as data flow. (To reinforce this point: Harel's 'STATEMATE' system uses two other viewpoints of a system, in addition to this form (Harel *et al.*, 1990).)

6.10 The Petri Net

Like the State Transition Diagram and the Statechart, the Petri Net notation can be considered as capturing those design attributes that are concerned with behavioural features of a system. However, the Petri Net can be considered to address a more restricted set of attributes than the Statechart, in order to provide more detailed cover of the interaction between parallel components within a system. As such it is generally used as an auxiliary design notation rather than as a primary form.

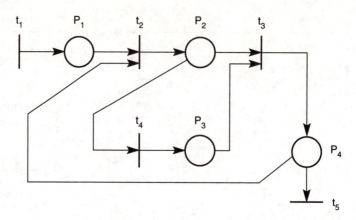

Figure 6.28   A simple Petri Net Graph.

A significant body of theoretical work has been developed around the form of the Petri Net, providing techniques that can be used to analyse the properties of nets and to identify particular weaknesses. A good summary of the role that Petri Nets can play in software design is provided in Birrell and Ould (1985) and in Stevens (1991), where the authors provide examples of the use of Petri Net Graphs for software design. In the latter reference, the author also discusses how the theoretical developments relate to the use of these nets for software design.

6.10.1   The Petri Net notation

The diagrammatic form of Petri Net notation uses four components (once again, note that a relative simplicity of form is sufficient to provide considerable descriptive power). These are:

- **places**, which represent system states and are denoted by labelled circles;
- **transitions**, which correspond to events, and are denoted by bars;
- **preconditions**, which are the input requirements necessary for a transition to occur;
- **postconditions**, describing the outputs resulting from the occurrence of a transition.

Both of the last two components are denoted by directed arcs, so providing the notation with even greater simplicity of form.

Figure 6.28 shows a very simple example of a Petri Net Graph in which there are four states and six events connecting them. (The diagrammatical form is generally referred to as a Petri Net Graph, or PNG, since

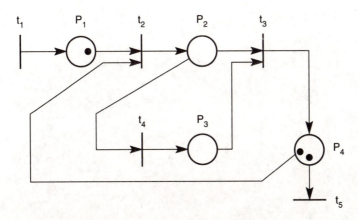

Figure 6.29   A marked Petri Net Graph.

there are alternative algebraic forms that can also be used to describe the form of a Petri Net.)

As described so far, the static form of this notation may appear to offer little that we did not find in data-flow notations such as the DFD, other than an added degree of formality about the nature of the interactions. What distinguishes the Petri Net, however, is that it can be used to model the behaviour of a system by 'executing' it using the notion of the 'token'.

The **token** is a small dot that is placed in a circle representing a place; a Petri Net with tokens is said to be 'marked', with the distribution of the tokens being referred to as the 'marking'. Figure 6.29 shows a marked version of the previous simple example.

The execution of a Petri Net is performed by 'firing' the transitions. A transition can be fired if there is at least one token at each of its input places (signifying that its preconditions are satisfied), and the act of firing the transition consists of removing a token from each of its input places and putting one at each of its output places. (The use of Petri Net Graphs is clearly assisted greatly if the designer has access to a photocopier!) Figure 6.30 shows the example of Figure 6.29 after transition t_2 has been fired, showing that both t_4 and t_5 are now eligible to be fired. (Interaction with the 'real world' is managed through the introduction and removal of tokens at the boundaries.)

Indeed, because more than one transition may be eligible to be fired at any given time, the Petri Net can provide a means of modelling the asynchronous behaviour of a system in a nondeterministic manner. It is this property, combined with the availability of analysis techniques, that can be used to explore such system properties as boundedness, reachability and equivalence, and which makes the Petri Net so valuable when modelling complex parallel interactions.

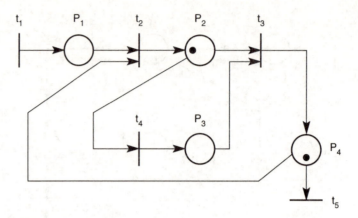

Figure 6.30 The marked Petri Net Graph after firing transition t_2.

As a final example of the use of this form, Figure 6.31 shows a very simple Petri Net modelling the operations of a Bank Autoteller Machine (ATM) used for dispensing cash. The customer's insertion of a card creates a token by satisfying the precondition that a customer is available, and so begins the dispenser cycle. (While this example has little inherent parallelism, it does show a more realistic example of the actual appearance of a Petri Net Graph.) Note too that the object of the form is to model interaction and dependency rather than conditional information flow (as in the case of the DFD used for a similar example in Section 6.2).

6.10.2 The Petri Net viewpoint

The Petri Net Graph is primarily concerned with modelling the behaviour of a number of independent but cooperating processes. The particular attributes that it captures are those concerned with the asynchronous relationships that exist between these processes. (The STD is purely concerned with modelling the behaviour of a single thread of execution, and the Statechart models parallelism only in terms of states and transitions, with no attempt to model the interactions between the parallel threads.)

6.10.3 The use of Petri Net Graphs

Because the notation is inherently executable, it can be used to explore detailed behavioural features of a system. The analysis techniques developed for use with Petri Nets can then be used to help with considering system-critical issues such as the potential for system deadlock; the possibility that certain system states may not actually be reachable through any set of transitions; and points where the possible outcome of any

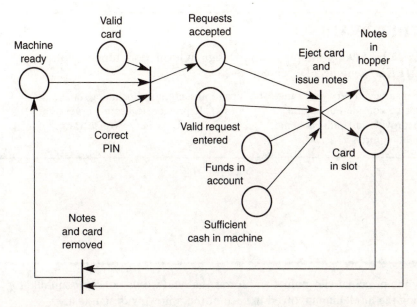

Figure 6.31 A Petri Net describing the actions of a Bank Autoteller Machine.

nondeterministic behaviour may require to be resolved by the designer in order to ensure some desired behaviour.

The Petri Net Graph therefore provides a notation that is somewhat different from all of our previous examples, and which like the Statechart is more closely allied to the power of mathematical modelling techniques than is common for diagrammatical forms.

SUMMARY

This chapter has examined a wide range of notations that are used to support and document the processes that are involved in the design of software systems. In particular, the selection of design representations has included examples from the four principal viewpoint forms, which are:

- structural features
- functional (algorithmic) forms
- behavioural aspects
- data-modelling features

The relative values of each of these will, of course, differ, according to the particular problem domain being addressed for any given design problem.

FURTHER READING

Webster D.E. (1988). Mapping the design information representation terrain. *IEEE Computer*, December, 8–23

This paper surveys a very wide range of design representations (including some that might not be considered general design forms). It provides a useful survey that seeks to provide an initial scheme of classification for a very diverse range of representation forms.

EXERCISES

6.1 Identify the principal viewpoints and forms that you would consider suitable for describing the modelling involved in each of the following design tasks:

   (a) the top-level design for an Ada compiler;
   (b) the detailed design for a program that will be used in a microprocessor-controlled washing machine;
   (c) the design of a payroll-processing program.

6.2 Why are the diagrams in Figure 6.32 wrong? Redraw them using the correct forms.

6.3 Complete the Statechart in Figure 6.33 by adding the internal transitions and any further external ones.

6.4 Draw a Statechart that describes the operation of a simple electric cooking ring. (Remember, even if the ring is switched on, it will not need current whenever its temperature is higher than the selected level.)

6.5 Choose a set of representations that you consider suitable for the most recent program that you have written, and use them to describe (or document) its structure.

6.6 Draw a Data-Flow Diagram that represents the processes involved in cooking and serving a three-course dinner, including all such associated tasks as laying out the table. Seek to ensure that your solution does not impose any unnecessary assumptions about the sequencing of actions.

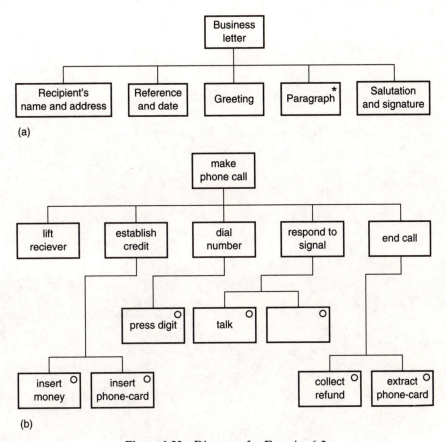

(a)

(b)

Figure 6.32   Diagrams for Exercise 6.2.

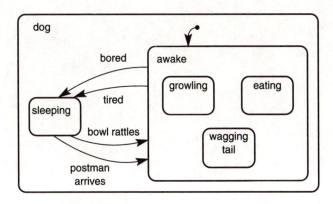

Figure 6.33   Diagram for Exercise 6.3.

Part II

Design Practices

Chapter 7   **The Rationale for Method**   141
Chapter 8   **Design Strategies**   159
Chapter 9   **Jackson Structured Programming**
             (JSP)   177
Chapter 10   **Structured Systems Analysis and**
             Structured Design   205
Chapter 11   **Jackson System Development**
             (JSD)   239
Chapter 12   **Object-Oriented and Object-Based**
             Design   265
Chapter 13   **Some Other Systematic Approaches**
             to Design   305
Chapter 14   **A Formal Approach to Design**   337
Chapter 15   **The Evolution of Software Design**
             Practices   363

7 The Rationale for Method

7.1 What is a software design method?

7.2 Why design methods are needed

7.3 Why methods don't work miracles

7.4 Problem domains and their influence

This chapter introduces the initial steps in the study of design methods. It considers the nature of a design method, its component parts, and some of the reasons why design methods are used. As well as identifying the benefits that can be obtained from the use of a design method, it also reviews the limitations on what they can provide for the user, and examines the extent to which particular classes of problem may be suited to the use of specific design methods.

7.1 What is a software design method?

Chapters 1 and 2 examined the nature of the design process in general, as well as its role in the development of software. They particularly emphasized the nonanalytical nature of the design process: it is highly unlikely that different designers will come up with exactly the same solution to a problem, and there are no clear criteria that allow us to select one of these as being *the* solution.

Based upon this observation, one view that can be taken of the design process is that it corresponds to a process of 'navigation through a solution space'. Each step in design may provide the designer with many options, and it is a part of the design task to identify these and to choose among them. One of the major roles of a design method is therefore to assist the designer by providing some guidance as to how the choices should be made, and how to assess the likely consequences of a particular decision in terms of the constraints it may impose on subsequent structures and choices.

This chapter examines the nature and form of software design methods; considers the reasons why they are used (and why they sometimes are not used); lists their strengths; and identifies the factors that limit their usefulness. When taken together with the material of the next chapter, these topics provide a framework for an understanding of the structure, strengths, and limitations of the various design methods that will form the subject of the remainder of this book.

However, before we can begin to examine the structure of a design method, we need to have a better understanding of what a method is, and hence how it can fulfil the roles identified above. A typical dictionary definition of the word 'method' is couched in such terms as the following: 'a way of doing things, especially a regular, orderly procedure'. It is this view that will form the main theme for the remainder of this book. (As we have previously observed, it is unfortunate that, in software development at least, a habit has arisen of using the rather grander-sounding term 'methodology' as if it were a synonym for 'method'. The correct meaning of 'methodology' is: 'the science of method or orderly arrangement'. This term describes what this book is seeking to do, by trying to analyse the forms of design methods and to classify them in some way.)

The idea of a method as a structured way of doing things is one that should be familiar enough. 'Methods' are used to structure the way that we perform many routine tasks, such as making a pot of tea:

Boil the kettle; warm the pot; add the tea; pour on water; wait a number of minutes; pour the tea.

Like most methods, this puts a strong emphasis on the ordering of actions (if you don't think so, try changing the order of any of the operations in the above example, and see what results!). However, it provides little or no guidance on those issues that are more a matter of taste, such as:

- how much tea to add

- how long to wait for the tea to brew

since these are personal preferences of the tea-maker. Since they are also essential to the success of the tea-making process, we can reasonably conclude that 'method' guidance alone is insufficient for this purpose, and that some 'domain knowledge' is also required.

We can devise methods for organizing many other activities, from driving a car to constructing kitchen units, model aircraft and so on. However, such methods are rarely *creative* in quite the same sense that we consider the act of design to be creative. Rather, these methods are *recipes* for doing something that we have learned to do through 'experiment' or 'theory' (or some combination of both). We might be able to adapt a method like that in the example above for other tasks (for making coffee instead of tea, perhaps), but we cannot easily change its basic domain (that of making hot drinks).

A design method is generally much less prescriptive than the kind of method that we might use for making tea, or for assembling a new garden shed. Indeed, in some ways a software design method can almost be considered as a 'meta-method', in that it is used to develop new processes, which in turn are ways of doing things – where the 'doing' that is involved will be the task of the computer. Returning to the tea-making example the analogy in this case would be using a design method to design the form of the tea-making process itself.

So we can reasonably expect that a design method should identify a general strategy to be used by the designer, and provide some rather general guidelines on its use, based upon experience. However, a method cannot be expected to be very prescriptive about how the ultimate solution to a problem is to be attained, since the specific design decisions required will be determined by the nature of the problem, rather than by the method. (Think of all the different processes that are used for making coffee!)

Returning to the need to find ways of designing software: in Chapter 2, the following three main components of a software design method were identified, as shown in Figure 7.1:

- The *representation* part consists of one or more forms of notation that can be used to describe (or model) both the structure of the initial problem and that of the intended solution, using one or more viewpoints and differing levels of abstraction.

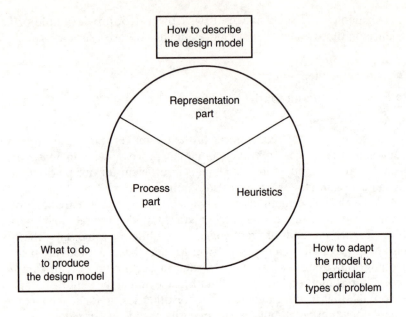

Figure 7.1 The three components of a design method.

- The *process* part describes the procedures to follow in developing the solution and the strategies to adopt in making choices. This generally involves the designer in making a series of transformations on the different forms that comprise the representation part.

- A set of *heuristics* or *clichés* provide guidelines on the ways in which the activities defined in the process part can be organized for specific classes of problem. These are generally based on experience of past use of the method with a particular problem domain, or for a particular form of structure.

This description will be elaborated further in the next chapter; for the moment these terms will provide a very general descriptive framework.

Software design methods fall into two very broad and general categories. These are essentially distinguished by the forms of representation that are used, although in turn the representation forms have some influence upon the forms of process that can be used within them. This division is illustrated in Figure 7.2.

Formal methods largely depend on the use of mathematical notations for the representation parts. These notations permit a degree of consistency checking between the descriptions used in the different stages of design, as well as more rigorous design transformations. However, while the representation parts for such methods have been the subject of

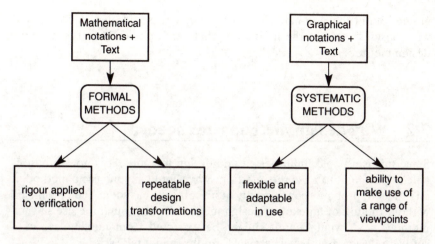

Figure 7.2 Some properties of formal and systematic software design methods.

considerable research and development, the process parts are less well refined and are apt to be developments of the 'top-down' strategy (this strategy is discussed more fully in Section 8.2).

Systematic methods are generally less mathematically rigorous in form, both in terms of the representation part – which normally consists of one or more forms of diagram – and also of the process part. This is true even for those methods that are generally considered to be more prescriptive in their form, such as JSP and SSADM. As a consequence, there is far more scope to use 'mix and match' techniques with systematic methods, in which ideas or representation forms from one method can be used to help resolve a particular issue, even though the design is being developed using the strategy of another method.

The third component of a design method, the *heuristics* (or *clichés*) usually consist of a set of techniques that are recommended for use in handling particular situations that may be encountered across a wide variety of problems. These heuristics are generally built up over a period of time, as experience is gained with using the method in a wider problem domain, and so they are essentially experiential in origin, although they may be highly systematic in form. We will encounter a number of examples of these in later chapters, and they play an important role in allowing a designer to reuse the experience of others. Examples of heuristics can be found in both systematic and formal methods.

The majority of the methods discussed in this book are systematic in their form, although we will also examine some of the formal methods. This bias partly reflects the relative preponderance of systematic methods in current industrial practices, and partly the wider variety of design models that they tend to provide. The rest of this chapter will examine in greater detail the rationale for using any method to design software, and will consider some of the limitations that generally apply to the use of a design method.

7.2 Why design methods are needed

Since this is a book about design and design methods, it is not unreasonable at this point to raise the question: why should anyone use a method at all? Indeed, probably considerably more software has so far been produced without the use of an explicit design method than through the use of such methods – so what benefits might be expected from making use of a software design method (whatever form this might take)?

One answer to this is simply that of scale. As the use of computers has expanded into more and more aspects of life, the size and complexity required of many systems has also increased. So while many problems involved in programming in the small can indeed be resolved by one individual working from experience, those encountered in programming in the large (where the eventual system may be implemented using thousands, and possibly millions, of high-level statements) require a more structured approach to their development. Other factors that encourage the use of 'standard' methods include the long service life of many systems, with the consequent need for updates and modifications to be made while preserving the integrity and structure of the system; and the safety-critical nature of many of the roles that software may be called upon to perform.

There are really two aspects of the software development process (and of the subsequent maintenance task that normally goes with software systems) that can be expected to benefit from using a method to provide a structured and systematic approach to the development process. These are:

- *technical* issues
- *management* issues

and so both of these are considered in this section.

'Technical issues' consist of the problem-related aspects of design. There are a number of these to consider, with the relative importance of each one being somewhat dependent upon a range of external factors such as the structure of the development organization (Curtis *et al.*, 1988), as well as the nature of the design problem itself. So the following points should not be considered as ranked in any particular order:

- The use of a method provides the designer(s) with a set of guidelines to use, both in producing the design and in verifying it against the original requirement. Studies of designers suggest that experienced designers may often work in an opportunistic manner, but that this practice may be less well-formed and reliable when the designer is less familiar with a problem or its domain (Adelson and Soloway, 1985; Guindon and Curtis, 1988; Visser and Hoc, 1990). So for the inexperienced designer, or the designer who is working in an unfamiliar domain, the use of a design method may assist with the formulation and exploration of the mental models used to capture the essential features of the design. In this way, therefore, *method knowledge* may provide a substitute for *domain knowledge*, where the latter is inadequate or lacking.

- The use of a design method should help the designer to produce a system that is structured in a consistent way, which may be particularly important if the design is being produced by a team of designers who will need to ensure that their contributions fit together correctly. In such a case, the use of a design method establishes a set of common standards, criteria and goals for use by the team.

- The use of a method should lead to the production of records and representations in standard form that can be used by a maintenance team to capture and understand the intentions of the original designer(s) (Littman *et al.*, 1987). This allows the system maintainers to make changes consistent with the overall structuring of the system, as originally planned, and so to help preserve its integrity. (However, as Parnas and Clements (1986) have observed, for this to occur it is important that the documentation should reflect the idealized design process rather than the actual one used!)

- The use of a method should reduce the likelihood of errors in the logical structuring of the system, and should ensure that all of the factors involved in a problem are properly weighed and considered by the designer(s).

While each of these points is particularly significant for large systems, they are valid for smaller ones too. The lifetime of an item of software, and the extent to which it is subsequently modified in maintenance, are not directly related to its size. (The only advantage of working with a smaller system is that if it proves impossible to understand its structure, the maintenance team can choose to recreate all or part of it from scratch – an option that is quite impossible to consider for medium or large systems.)

Each design method provides a particular form of 'Design Virtual Machine' (DVM), which in turn supplies the framework needed by the designer to develop his or her model of a solution. (One reason why

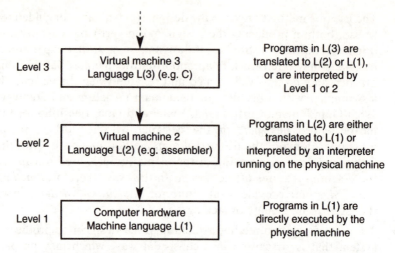

Figure 7.3 The use of virtual machines in the design process.

experienced designers may be able to work in an opportunistic manner is that they have developed their own Design Virtual Machines for particular classes of problem.)

The concept of a virtual machine is not a new one, although it is not usually applied to design methods. In computing terms, a virtual machine provides a layer of abstraction above that of the physical machine. An operating system provides a number of virtual machines, to allow programmers to access the resources of a computer at different levels of abstraction. (For example, a file may be treated as a sequence of characters, a sequence of records, or a sequence of blocks on a disk.) Programming languages also provide virtual machines: the programmer works with what is effectively a Modula-2 computer, or a C++ computer, without needing to understand the underlying architecture of registers, buses and processors. Figure 7.3 illustrates the basic ideas behind this.

The user of such a virtual machine structures his or her ideas around the behavioural model that it provides. It is then the job of some 'interpreter' to translate this into the form of a machine of lower level, and ultimately to that of the bare computer architecture itself. For example, when using Modula-2, programmers are concerned only with making decisions such as determining that they need the features of (say) a REPEAT UNTIL loop, and not with how that is to be achieved in terms of skip instructions and registers. They are therefore using a Modula-2 machine.

Each programming language therefore provides a virtual machine, whose architecture and form are determined by the features and semantics of the programming language. In the same way, a design method provides the user with a virtual machine that can be used to express ideas about program forms at a very high level indeed; although unfortunately, owing

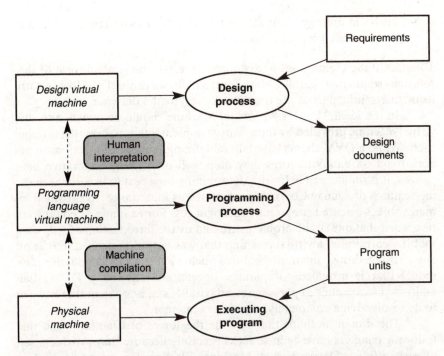

Figure 7.4 The link between the design virtual machine and the virtual machine levels used on a computer. (Each method has a design virtual machine embodied within it, helping to determine such aspects as the set of viewpoints used, the strategy, etc.)

to the imprecise semantics of current representations, the resulting design model has to be translated into a lower level of abstraction by the designer and the programmer together.

This is performed by following the process part of the method: as Figure 7.4 shows, the task really involves two levels of Design Virtual Machine. One is used for architectural design (often termed 'logical' design or 'analysis'). The model produced is then translated into the 'design blueprint' (physical design), which is effectively another level of DVM with more precise characteristics than the initial DVM, and with structures that are much closer to the eventual implementation form. A further process is required to translate this into a programming language, which can then be translated by machine and eventually leads to the execution of the system on the physical machine.

The Design Virtual Machine that is embodied in a particular design method is characterized by such factors as:

- the viewpoints used in the various phases of the modelling process;
- the relationships between these that are established by the form of the design process;

- the basic strategy of the method itself, since this determines how the design models will be elaborated.

Together these create a set of assumptions about the general form of the solution (sequential, parallel, data-centred, object-centred...) that in turn form an essential part of the framework used by the designer.

In the ideal, the Design Virtual Machine should be matched to the virtual machine provided by the eventual implementation form that is to be used. While a DVM that is based upon defining sequences of actions to be performed on data structures may map well onto many imperative languages, it is unlikely to help with determining how best to use the packaging features of a language, or a feature such as inheritance, as provided in many object-oriented programming languages. For example, it could well be argued that one of the problems created by the introduction of Ada was that it incorporated a virtual machine that was not well matched to that of any existing design method. Features such as the *package* and the *task* model that is provided for parallel operations required a DVM that addressed such issues as packaging and parallelism, a problem that has yet to be resolved in a completely satisfactory manner.

The design methods that provide the topics of Chapter 9 and the following chapters have been selected precisely because they provide a set of very different Design Virtual Machines. Perhaps the main feature that they possess in common is that they all assume that the final system will be implemented using imperative programming forms.

The management benefits of using design methods are (not surprisingly) linked to many of the same issues as the technical benefits. In particular, the documentation of a system is important both for the development of the system and for its maintenance.

So from a management viewpoint, using a recognized design method will provide:

- a framework for recording decisions and reasons in a systematic manner;
- a set of procedures that should ensure consistency in the structure of a design, and in the structure of the interfaces between design components, so making it easier to use a team of designers on a large project;
- a framework that helps with identifying important progress milestones.

In particular, the use of a design method helps with structuring the design *process* as well as the design *product*.

All of the above issues become even more important when we consider the extent to which designers spend their time modifying existing systems, rather than developing new ones. For much of the time, a designer is likely to be performing tasks that can be regarded as 'perfective maintenance' rather than undertaking original design work. Even for a totally new system, the designer is unlikely to be completely unconstrained in terms of the available choices, and so much of the work is likely to involve adaptation of existing structures. In this context, one of the strongest benefits that a design method can offer is that it encourages the designer to plan for change, and to think ahead in terms of subsequent developments and extensions. Some methods do this explicitly, others less so, but, whatever the method, they encourage the designer to explore the solution in a structured manner that is likely to encourage consideration of later modifications.

The need to design for change was strikingly demonstrated when the British government changed the rate of Value-Added Tax (VAT) in 1991. The billing software used by British Telecom to issue telephone bills could not cope with a split rate of VAT – one rate applying until a given date, and a new rate after that. So all bills covering that period were issued with VAT charges set at the new rate, with refunds to follow! Whereas software designed to cope with income tax rates will normally allow for such changes, because they tend to occur annually, VAT rates change only very infrequently – with embarrassing consequences for some hapless design team.

7.3 Why methods don't work miracles

The preceding sections have explored some of the major reasons for using design methods to help with solving software design problems. However, it is important to appreciate that a design method does not offer a panacea that will automatically remove all problems. In the first two chapters, we examined the nature of the design process, and the reasons why it is so difficult to impose any structure on its form, and the points that were made there need to be kept in mind in assessing the usefulness or otherwise of specific software design methods.

A design method provides the designer with a framework within which to organize the development of a design. It provides a set of recommended representation forms that can be used to give insight into the issues that are significant for that Design Virtual Machine. It provides guidance on the steps that the design process should follow, and advice on the criteria that should be considered when making design choices. However, none of this guidance can be problem-specific, and hence the emphasis must very much be on the notion of providing guidance. For an actual design task, the designer's choices and decisions will need to be resolved solely on the basis of the needs of the particular problem that requires to be solved.

One analogy that it may be helpful to repeat here concerns the use of a recipe for cooking. A recipe is a process that determines how a particular dish will be produced – much as a computer program is a process that determines how a graph will be drawn, or how tax rebates will be calculated. Designing software is therefore rather like designing a recipe – it requires the designer to possess insight into the problem domain, to be aware of the potential that is present in the basic materials, and to know the capabilities of the system that will execute the process (whether this be a cook or a computer!).

A design method intended for producing recipes might be able to provide some guidance as to how a recipe should be organized, presented and described, and would be able to provide advice on:

- how to lay out the instructions to the cook (for example, terms to use and/or appropriate forms of measure);
- the best use of photographs, tables and so on;
- making suggestions about possible variants.

But it cannot be more specific than this. Decisions about detailed issues – such as the choice of ingredients and the amounts of each to be used, the length of time in the oven, the oven temperature to be used – must all depend upon the nature of the dish and the materials, not upon the format used for developing the recipe.

Because a software design method provides a form of 'process' that is used to design another process, it is all too easy for the inexperienced to fall into the trap of believing that a design process is itself a recipe – but that is not so at all, as the above example demonstrates. Instead, a recipe is something that is output from the design process, rather than being the model for the design process itself.

One way in which it is possible to increase the amount of guidance from a method slightly is to focus it upon a particular domain of problems. By concentrating upon (say) data-processing problems, or information-retrieval systems, it is possible to give somewhat tighter guidance for some of the decisions that the designer needs to make. However, even this will be limited in the extent to which it can be usefully carried out. (In the ultimate, of course, we could narrow down the problem domain until the method would be only suited to one problem!) In practice, most methods are aimed at reasonably wide domains so as to try to optimize their use: hence the benefits of familiarity with the method.

To make their forms as prescriptive as possible, design methods are based on defining a set of carefully itemized sequences of actions that should be performed by a designer. However, observed design practices suggest that experienced software designers may work on several different threads of action in parallel, and that these may also be at different levels of abstraction (Guindon and Curtis, 1988; Visser and Hoc, 1990). So a design method that recommends only sequential actions can provide only a very inadequate approximation to expert behaviour, although this might be partly offset by the iterations that are necessary in design activity. (A further factor that may offset this disadvantage is that, as designers gain expertise, they may be better able to adapt a method to their needs, and so employ parallel activities where their use would be appropriate.)

The purpose of this section is not to encourage the idea that design methods should not be used, but rather to point out that they have limitations and that these need to be recognized. Unfortunately the purveyors of courses and textbooks on methods are sometimes guilty of encouraging exaggerated expectations about their wares, and it is important to be able to keep these in perspective.

7.4   Problem domains and their influence

The concept of a problem domain figured in the preceding section, and this section elaborates a little the implications of the concept as applied to the design process.

Almost all software design methods expect the designer to begin the design process by building some form of model of the real-world problem that is to be solved. The form of this model is essentially based on the underlying Design Virtual Machine, and hence is highly method-specific. Ultimately, therefore, the chosen method will strongly influence the form of the solution that is derived from it.

The basis for model-building can vary quite considerably, but usually involves projecting the original problem into one or more of the following viewpoints:

- function
- information flow
- data structure
- actions
- data objects
- time ordering of actions

(Of course, some of these descriptions may be realized in different ways.) The form of this initial model is a major factor in determining how well the method will map onto particular problem domains. For example, real-time problems will normally require that the initial model incorporate timing issues in some way; while data-processing problems will be likely to incorporate models of data structures or information flow.

Sometimes a method may be very specialized. An example is the design of compilers. For imperative programming languages there are some very well-established techniques (with supporting software tools) that can be used for constructing compilers. However, this is a relatively unusual situation, and most problem domains are much more general in form. In addition, domains are not necessarily mutually exclusive, so that a design method that is targeted largely at one class of problems might still prove useful with other problems that can be considered as belonging to quite a different class. An example of such a design method, and one that we will be meeting later, is JSP. This method is essentially intended for use with data-processing problems, but it can sometimes be used to help solve other types of problem too.

An important point arises from this concept of the problem domain that is relevant to the remaining chapters of this book. Because the domains of application for software design methods are essentially ill-defined, it is generally impractical to seek any form of 'comparative methods' evaluation of design methods, along similar lines to those performed for programming languages, which have a well-defined syntax and semantics.

Any attempt to classify problem domains in other than a very general way will usually lead to difficulties, because real problems are rarely easily categorized in a simple manner. However, some rather general domains can be identified, and there are three in particular that are useful:

- **In batch systems** the main feature is that all the operating characteristics of the system are essentially determined when it begins processing one or more data streams. Any changes in these characteristics arise because of the contents of the streams, when considered as sequential flows of data. Such a system should therefore perform operations that are *deterministic* and *repeatable*. An example of a batch system is a compiler, all the actions of which are determined by the nature of the input source program. It goes without saying that compilation should be deterministic!

- The principal characteristic of **reactive systems** is that they are event-driven. For such systems, the events are almost always asynchronous and nondeterministic. An obvious example of such a system is a screen editor, for which the operations of the process depend upon the events that are generated externally, by the user. A commonly encountered subsidiary characteristic of such systems is that the specifications of the required responses to events will often include explicit requirements about timing.

- **Concurrent systems** are characterized by the use of multiple threads of execution within the problem, so that a solution might utilize one or more processors. For such systems, the process of design may need to consider such issues as the overheads of process scheduling, as well as the need for mutual exclusion and synchronization between processes.

These classifications should not be considered as mutually exclusive: while a system is unlikely to have both batch and reactive aspects, either of these forms could well have concurrent features.

A somewhat different approach to classifying problem domains is to consider how these influence the designer's goals. To illustrate this, consider the distinction between the following two classes of design problem:

- Problems where the *form* and content of the data guide the designer's actions. Examples occur in such applications as transaction-processing systems, in which the key criterion is to process the data correctly (where the data may be financial information, hotel bookings, and so on), and there is no time constraint beyond that of processing the necessary volume of transactions within a particular time interval.

- Problems where the *existence* and content of data will guide the designer's actions. This is more typical of the domain of real-time systems, where the occurrence of the event will be highly significant (this may be the detection of a gas leak, or an approaching missile, or an aircraft that is too close), together with the need to process the data within a time interval determined by the nature of the data itself and before it is replaced by new data.

In the former case, the important thing is for the system to generate a correct response (it will not be disastrous if some small delay in processing is involved on occasion, but debiting the wrong bank account by several million pounds may well be considered catastrophic!). In the second case the important thing is to generate a response within a critical time interval. The response needs to be a correct one, but an approximation may suffice: disaster *will* occur if an approaching missile is ignored for too long, while an 'incorrect' response that fires two counter-missiles, because there is not time to ensure that one will be accurate enough, may not be too critical.

In the first case a design method is required that allows the designer to check thoroughly for correct behaviour, and to verify this in some way. The second case also has these needs, but adds the requirement that correct performance of the eventual system must be guaranteed. Each of these domains will require design practices that help to focus attention on the aspects that are most critical, as illustrated in Figure 7.5. The next chapter begins to examine what forms these might take.

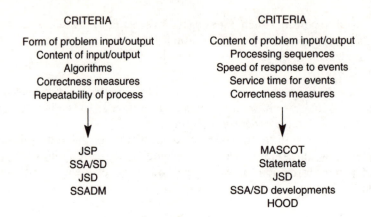

Figure 7.5 Some design criteria and related design methods.

SUMMARY

This chapter has considered the nature of the software design process in terms of its components and of the potential for providing these with a structure.

In the design process itself, the following three principal components have been identified:

- a *representation* part
- a *process* part
- a set of *heuristics*, or *clichés*

and their roles have been discussed. The rationale for using a design method has also been considered, and how 'method knowledge' may provide a substitute for 'domain knowledge' when necessary. By looking at the nature of the design process in this way, it has tried to determine what the limitations of *any* software design method are likely to be.

As a final step before a fuller consideration of the structure of design methods, the nature of problem domains was considered. In particular, the characteristics of the

- batch
- reactive
- concurrent

problem domains were identified.

FURTHER READING

Parnas D.L. and Clements P.C. (1986). A rational design process: How and why to fake it. *IEEE Trans. Software Engineering*, **SE-12**(2), 251–7

This paper starts from a recognition that software design is not a precise and systematic process, and argues that we should, however, seek to document a design as though it had been produced by such an ideal process. The paper provides a valuable discussion of the issues of the documentation of design features.

Visser W. and Hoc J.-M. (1990). Expert software design strategies. In *Psychology of Programming* (Hoc J.-M., Green T.R.G., Samurçay R. and Gilmore D.J., eds.). London: Academic Press

This is a review of research involving observations of expert designers of software and the strategies that they use when designing systems. While it does not examine the relationship of these actions to specific design methods, it does identify the design practices that should be approximated through the use of a design method.

EXERCISES

7.1   How would you classify each of the following systems in terms of one or more of the domains batch, reactive or concurrent?

   (a)   A bank autoteller machine.
   (b)   A system utility program used to list the contents of a user's directory (such as the UNIX **ls**).
   (c)   A BASIC interpreter.
   (d)   A multi-user operating system.
   (e)   An airline seat reservation system with terminals in travel agents' offices.

7.2   Making tea (or coffee) is a process executed in a manner influenced by the conditions that apply at the time of execution (the preferences of the drinker, the amount of tea or coffee available, and so on). Find examples of similar everyday processes that are not based on the kitchen and related operations.

7.3   Faced with the need to understand and modify a simple interactive text editor that was originally written by another person, list five forms of information about its design that you would like to have available to you, and rank these in descending order of importance.

Design Strategies

8.1 Strategy and method
8.2 Top-down strategies for design
8.3 Design by composition

8.4 Organizational methods of design
8.5 Design by template and design reuse

Design methods embody design strategies, which give a sense of direction to the procedures of the methods and reflect their basic philosophies. This chapter examines some of the more widely adopted strategies, together with the principles that underpin them. Strategies are not necessarily wholly technical, and so we examine the extent to which they can also be influenced by the needs of the organization developing the software.

8.1   Strategy and method

Chapter 7 examined the nature of design methods in a rather general way, and identified the major components that a design method might be expected to possess. In this chapter, this thinking is developed a bit further, and it begins to examine the principal strategies encapsulated in the process parts of some major software design methods. This completes the groundwork needed to undertake the more detailed study of specific software design methods in the remaining chapters of this book.

We begin with a reminder of the form used for describing the structure of a design method, as developed in Chapter 7. There it was suggested that a software design method could be described in terms of the following principal components:

- *representation* part
- *process* part
- set of *heuristics*, or *clichés*

The properties of some widely used forms of representation have already been described in Chapters 5 and 6. In Chapter 7 it was further observed that the set of these used in a method are important in defining the Design Virtual Machine that is embodied in a method, since they determine the type and form of design model(s) that a designer is encouraged to produce when using the method.

The process part of a method is closely entwined with the representation part, since it provides guidelines on how the models should be developed and transformed. We now look more closely at the nature and form of the process part, while in the following chapters the three components are brought together when we look at examples of design methods and examine the specific forms of heuristic that are associated with them.

Figure 8.1 shows this transformational model of the software design process in a symbolic fashion, and we will be making use of it throughout the rest of this book. The basic symbols it uses to describe a design method are:

- an oblong to denote a representation form;
- an oval to denote a transformation step;
- an arc to denote the sequence of transformation.

These can be seen more fully in Figure 8.2, which shows a slightly expanded form of Figure 8.1. (Note that our notation possesses the important property of being hierarchical, as discussed in Chapter 5, in that the description of any transformation step can be expanded further using the same three components.) The iterations that occur between phases of the

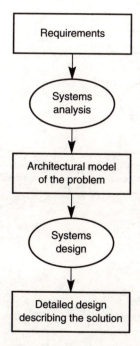

Figure 8.1 General transformational model of the software design process.

design process are not shown explicitly: the model is concerned with describing overall strategy rather than the detailed sequencing of actions, since these will be driven by the needs of a specific problem and the experience of the designer.

This notation will be used to describe a number of different design methods in the following chapters. It is by no means the only form that we can use to help with this task. The form that has been used by Potts and Bruns takes a rather different viewpoint on the process (Potts and Bruns, 1988; Potts, 1989; Lee, 1991); it can be considered as complementing our own basic transformation model. Figure 8.3 shows the use of this viewpoint to describe a typical design step.

The model developed by Potts and Bruns can be used for looking at the factors that are involved in making design decisions in more detail. The example of Figure 8.3 demonstrates how this is based on the use of five entity types (the boxes) and eight binary relationships (the arcs). The relationships operate as follows (Potts, 1989):

- Steps *modify* artifacts. In 'derivation', a new artifact is created. In 'revision', a new version of an existing artifact is created.

- Steps *raise* issues. This may occur automatically, but the issue may not have to be addressed immediately.

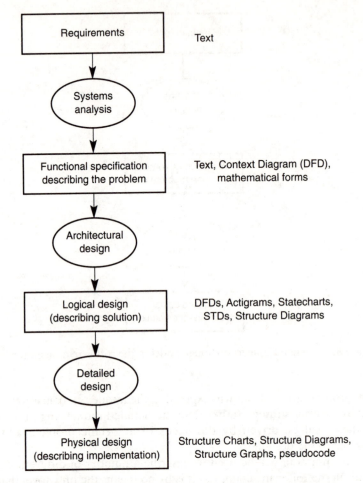

Figure 8.2 Expanded view of the transformational model of the software design process.

- Issues *review* artifacts. An issue may be raised to review the property of an artifact.
- Positions *respond to* issues.
- Arguments *support* positions.
- Arguments *object to* positions. Arguments are often paired, with one supporting a position, and the other opposed to it.
- Arguments *cite* artifacts. The artifact provides evidence for the argument.
- Positions *contribute* to steps. A step is performed because a set of commitments has been made.

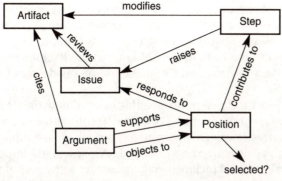

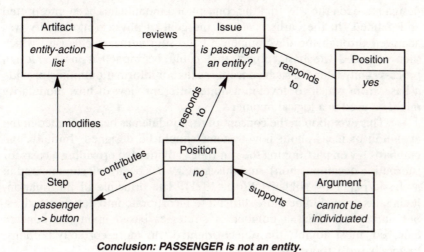

Figure 8.3 A Potts and Bruns model of the processes involved in design steps. (a) The generic form. (b) An example from the JSD method (applied to a passenger lift). (© 1988 IEEE.)

In Potts (1989) this model has been used to analyse the initial stages of the JSD method, and to model the processes involved. This form therefore provides a useful supplement to our basic process model, since it can be used to elaborate on the form of specific components from the process model.

The design transformation steps in a method can be considered as embodying local tactical decisions, which are in turn guided by the strategy that is adopted by a particular method. Strategic issues, for their part, are generally concerned with large-scale factors such as the domain of a particular problem, specific structural and behavioural characteristics and likely forms of implementation.

Where strategy does play a particularly important part is in determining the form of the initial model that a designer will create in order to describe the problem. While almost all design methods claim to begin by modelling the 'real world', the form of the Design Virtual Machine that is used for this can vary very widely, and can make use of a wide variety of viewpoints.

There is also a historical perspective to this issue of how the design process is performed. David J. Koepke (1990) has recorded his research into the evolution of software design ideas and has described how thinking about software design has developed and evolved. A particularly important element of this work is that it included making contact with some of the pioneers of the field, in order to obtain their impressions and recollections.

A major factor in the development of thinking about software design has been the way that the concept of a module has been interpreted and defined. In the earliest stages, the goal of physical modularity was achieved through the development of the subroutine mechanism, which then provided the basic object that could be modelled in the design process. Only later did such concepts as that of information-hiding provide a basis from which to develop a quite different view of how modularity might be used in a logical manner.

This evolution in the concept of the module has been reflected in the evolution of ideas about how systems should be designed. Initially, the emphasis lay on partitioning the run-time activities (so providing a basis for subroutine decomposition), and this strategy has been well summarized in a classic paper by Niklaus Wirth (1971). The principle of information-hiding has proved to be more difficult to incorporate into design practices, but during the 1980s a number of strategies based upon this concept emerged, most notably the object-oriented (or, more correctly perhaps, 'object-based') approaches to design.

Software design methods are not influenced by technical issues alone, of course. There are environmental, cultural, organizational and national influences, as well as the continually increasing scale of user expectations and need as systems have become ever larger and more complex (Curtis *et al.*, 1988).

Clearly, many factors have influenced the development of design methods, and for that reason design methods are difficult to classify in any very systematic manner. For the purposes of the rest of this chapter, though, we will use the following broad groupings in order to discuss how strategy is incorporated into a design method:

- *decompositional* methods, which generally take a 'top-down' view of the design process;

- *compositional* methods, whereby the basic design model is built up from the identification of 'entities' of some form;

- *organizational* methods, for which the structure of the design process is strongly influenced by the requirement that it should conform to nontechnical requirements that are based on the form of the organization;

- *template*-based methods, where a specific problem domain provides a class of problems that can be tackled using a fairly standard strategy.

The rest of this chapter examines the characteristics of each of these strategies, and makes an initial classification of methods in terms of them.

Before proceeding, however, one other point should be mentioned here: the relationship between strategy and such ancillary aspects as the design of the user interface and the design of error-handling strategies.

Design strategies (and associated methods) tend to encourage the designer to focus on fairly global attributes in building up a model of a problem. As a result, such issues as the organization of human–computer interactions (HCI), and the handling of error (exception) conditions, are generally deferred until a later stage in the design process, when the design model is being refined and elaborated.

This is generally a reasonable practice to adopt, particularly for such issues as exception-handling, since any attempt to include these in the initial model may lead to it becoming excessively complex. The designer is then faced with the following alternatives when determining how to incorporate these issues:

- to incorporate them into the later stages of design refinement, by which time architectural decisions may have been made that are inconsistent with their needs;

- to repeat the design process from a much earlier stage, using the experience gained from producing a design for the basic problem to help with the greater complexity of the fuller problem.

As always with design, there is no hard and fast rule about which of these strategies may be the most appropriate. Constraints such as project deadlines may push the designer towards the former choice, but where significant HCI elements are involved, or where error-handling is an important element, this may lead to considerable distortion of the design structure.

On the whole, existing design practices do not help greatly with either of these issues. HCI design is now becoming a rather specialized field in its own right, and designing for exceptions is a relatively unexplored field in design theory.

8.2 Top-down strategies for design

The top-down (decompositional) approach to the design of software has a long pedigree. Most of the earliest programming languages to become widely available, such as assembler and FORTRAN, provided quite powerful mechanisms for describing action-oriented structuring of a program through the use of subprograms, but rarely provided the means of creating and using complex data structures. With such an emphasis among the implementation forms, a natural design strategy was one in which the main task of a program was subdivided into smaller tasks, with this subdivision being continued until the resultant subtasks were considered sufficiently elemental to be implemented as subprograms. This strategy has been elegantly summarized in a paper by Wirth (1971), which suggested practical ways to implement this approach. Wirth used the term 'stepwise refinement' for this strategy; the phrase 'divide and conquer' has also sometimes been used.

In its most basic form, the success of this approach of finding a good solution will be highly dependent on the way in which the original problem is described, since this forms the model that is the basis for the designer's initial choice of subtasks. Indeed, it can be argued that this approach is therefore inherently unstable, in that small differences in the decomposition of a task can lead to solutions that are functionally equivalent, but structurally very different. Figure 8.4 provides just such an example of how we can easily find two ways to decompose a given problem. (It may be that these two decompositions will converge following further decomposition, but this cannot be guaranteed by the use of the strategy alone.)

This instability arises because, when following a top-down strategy, the important decisions about basic structures have to be made at the beginning of the design process, so that the effects of any wrong decisions will be propagated through the following steps. This in turn may lead to significant problems at a later stage of design, and even to the need to totally redesign a system. When using a top-down strategy, it is particularly important to explore the design options as fully as possible at each stage of decomposition.

The top-down strategy also illustrates one of the characteristic features of the design process itself. When discussing Rittel's definition of a 'wicked problem', we identified one of the characteristics of such a problem as being the lack of a 'stopping rule' that the designer can use to determine that the design process is complete. This feature of the design process is particularly evident in functional decomposition, since there are no generally applicable criteria that can be used to determine how small a task should be to be considered as suitably elemental.

One other consequence of using this strategy that should also be mentioned is the problem of duplication. Because the strategy consists of a sequence of (essentially divergent and disconnected) refinements, there is

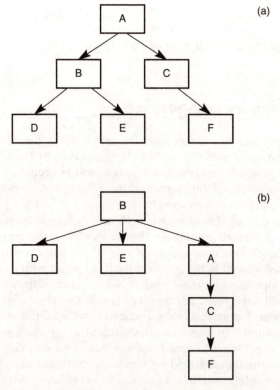

(a)

(b)

Figure 8.4   Decompositional solutions to a simple problem. (a) Solution 1.
(b) Solution 2.

potential for duplication when the low-level operations are defined. The
scope for this is, of course, even greater if the design is the responsibility of
more than one person. So the use of a refinement process implies the need
to explicitly check for, and resolve, any such duplications.

However, because of its long history and the relative ease with
which it can be applied, the top-down strategy has played quite an important role in the development of design methods, and ways of avoiding some
of its more undesirable features have been developed and used in the
methods that are based upon it. Indeed, even where other design strategies
are to be used for developing a system, it is not uncommon for the initial
design steps to consist of a functional decomposition, using a top-down
strategy to identify the major functional modules of the system, with the
design of these then being elaborated using a quite different strategy.

The SSA/SD (Structured Systems Analysis and Structured Design)
method, evolved by Yourdon and coworkers (Page-Jones, 1988; Gane and
Sarsen, 1979) is an example of a widely used method based on an enlarged
version of this strategy. Chapter 10 will show how the recommended

process steps incorporate ways of handling these major criticisms of top-down design. Even in more recently developed methods, such as SSADM (Chapter 13), there is still a significant top-down aspect to the process model itself.

8.3 Design by composition

In a top-down strategy for design, the emphasis is heavily focused on identifying the operations that need to be performed by the system. So the model of the problem that results is based almost entirely on consideration of the functional viewpoint, although the refinement of the model may make use of other viewpoints.

The reverse of this approach is to use a compositional strategy for building the designer's model. In this, a model of the problem is constructed by developing descriptions of a set of particular entities or objects that can be recognized in the problem itself, together with a description of the relationships that link these entities. The nature of the entities used in the model will vary with the method, as will the viewpoints chosen for describing them. Figure 8.5 shows a schematic view of this strategy.

In a method that uses a compositional strategy, such as JSD (Chapter 11), and the 'object-oriented' approaches (Chapter 12), the relevant entities are normally identified by analysing an initial description of the problem. A complete and detailed model of the solution is then developed by elaborating the descriptions of the entities and the interactions occurring between them. While the type and form of entity and interaction may differ considerably (as indeed they do in the two examples cited above), the overall strategy of composing the design model by grouping elements together is the same.

JSP (Chapter 9) is another design method that can be regarded as using a compositional strategy. In the case of JSP, however, the model of the problem is created using a data-modelling viewpoint, by assembling a set of descriptions of the structures of the input and output data streams. While these are rather less concrete forms of entity than those used in the two methods referred to above, the basic strategy involved in the design process is still a compositional one.

It is probably reasonable to consider the process of using a compositional strategy as rather less directly intuitive than the top-down strategy. However, it can also be argued that this 'intuition' is partly a matter of familiarity, since programmers are generally more experienced with function-oriented (imperative) programming languages, and therefore have acquired greater experience with a function-oriented view of systems. We can therefore expect that this bias can be offset by training in a compositional method, and this view seems to be borne out by experience.

If compositional methods are less directly intuitive than those

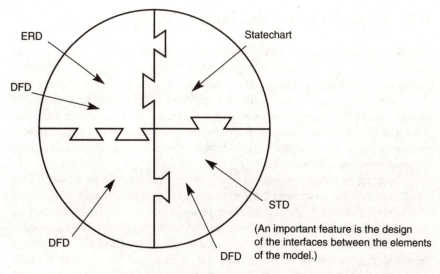

ERD

Statechart

DFD

STD

DFD

DFD

DFD

(An important feature is the design
of the interfaces between the elements
of the model.)

Figure 8.5   The compositional design strategy. An important feature is the design
of interfaces between the elements of the model.

methods that are based on a top-down approach, and so perhaps require
more discipline in their use, they are also:

- more *stable*, in that their use will tend to lead to the same solution
  for a problem, regardless of the user, since the design strategy
  makes use of more 'objective' aspects of the problem;

- more *even* in terms of the transformation steps involved, with a
  more gradual progression of design development than is common
  for top-down methods;

- better able to provide a good *verification* process between the design
  and the original specification, since solution objects correspond
  closely to problem objects.

A particular benefit of the compositional strategy is that it gives more
opportunity for using multiple viewpoints to exploit the use of such important design concepts as modularity and information-hiding (Parnas, 1972) in
the structuring of a designer's solution. This arises from the emphasis on
'grouping' that occurs in the elaboration of a design model, with scope to
group elements by considering different relations between them, including
shared data structures, shared data objects, function, and so on. This is a
process that is difficult to achieve (if not impossible) through the use of a
top-down strategy.

   These points will be examined as a part of the descriptions of specific
methods given in the following chapters, in order to show how well this
view of the compositional strategy is justified.

8.4 Organizational methods of design

For our purposes, an organizational design method can be considered as one in which the form of the process part of the method is strongly influenced by a set of nontechnical factors, arising from the nature and structure of the organization using the method. While these factors do not usually affect the representational part so directly, their influence may still have the effect of extending or formalizing it in some way. To understand the nature of such a method, the rationale that lies behind their adoption and use must be considered.

International agencies, as well as central and local government bodies, are major customers for software-based systems. These range from specialized defence real-time systems to applications for stock control or taxation. Many of these systems are very large; they are difficult to specify; the requirements may change with technology, legislation or internal re-organization; and they may be produced by in-house teams or by outside contracting agencies.

A significant feature of such organizations is that they are highly likely to provide their staff with career structures that are geared to overall organizational needs, and hence are not directly related to project needs. As a result, staff at all levels may be transferred in and out of a project team (and the project management) at times that are determined by factors largely or wholly independent of the state of the project.

The British Civil Service is an example of just such an organization, and it is mirrored by similar bodies in Britain as well as in other countries. During a civil servant's career, he or she may expect to progress through a series of grades, and may well be required to occupy a number of positions for fixed intervals of (say) two or three years. Each transition between grades or posts will therefore occur at an externally determined time, regardless of the state of any software-based project that they might be involved in. While this view is perhaps a little simplified, it does embody the main principles and practices that are used by such organizations.

To help with control of the increasing number of large software-based projects needed in such organizations, there has been a corresponding growth in emphasis upon the use of 'standard' methods for analysis and design. The use of a standard method within an organization (and preferably beyond it) has a number of benefits:

- there is minimum disruption of a project when staff changes occur;
- a change of project manager should not lead to a change of technical direction;
- standardization of documentation allows for better management of maintenance;

- there is scope for better planning, costing and control of projects, based on the use of past experience, which can be related directly to current practices.

There are, of course, some negative features of such methods to offset these positive ones. Perhaps the major negative aspect is that they tend to be overly bureaucratic, with the attendant risk that creative options may not be adequately explored, and also that the overall technical direction can be lost.

There are a number of methods that can be classified as having an organizational element. These include:

- SSADM (Structured Systems Analysis and Design Method), which has been produced for use with data-processing projects by central and local government agencies in the UK (Chapter 13);
- MERISE, which is a French equivalent to SSADM;
- HOOD (Hierarchical Object-Oriented Design), which has been developed on behalf of the European Space Agency for use in designing Ada-based systems;
- MASCOT (Modular Approach to Software Construction, Operation and Test) is intended for use in real-time systems, and originated in the UK defence sector. (Strictly, MASCOT is not a method as we have defined the term, having only a representation part and no well-defined process part.)

These are all examples from Europe, as the development and use of such methods has not yet become common in the USA, nor elsewhere, as far as can be ascertained.

At a technical level, in terms of the strategies involved in their use, these methods differ quite considerably, according to their domain of application. In that sense, therefore, we can regard the 'organizational' category as being essentially independent of strategy, so that a method can be both top-down and organizational, or compositional and organizational.

8.5   Design by template and design reuse

One of the problems for those concerned with the design of software is to find ways in which a designer can reuse the experience of other designers. Many software design methods provide a vehicle for this through the component we have previously termed 'heuristics' or 'clichés'. To a limited degree these act as 'pattern books', allowing a designer to see some examples of how a particular strategy can be applied to solving certain well-defined classes of problem.

This form of reuse is obviously limited in scope, although it can play a very important role in its own right. For the present, it is probably as close as we can get to finding a mechanism for sharing design experience in this field.

One other way of reusing design experience is by a design 'template'. Unfortunately, the opportunity for using such a form arises in only a few problem domains: the basic requirements for using a template are that the problem domain should:

- be very well-identified, well-defined and tightly constrained;
- contain a significant number of problems that each need a design solution;
- allow for the production of a syntactically and semantically complete requirements specification.

So far, the only really good example of such a problem domain is that of compiler-writing. This meets the above requirements in that:

- the domain is well-defined;
- there are plenty of problems within the domain, since there is a continual need to produce new compilers for use with new or extended programming languages and new 'target' machines;
- programming languages have well-defined syntax and semantics.

As a result, a number of well-explored standard techniques have been developed for structuring compilers; tools such as the UNIX operating systems' **lex** (lexical analyser) and **yacc** (yet another compiler constructor) have been developed; and no-one would now begin writing a new compiler by designing it from scratch using a general-purpose design method.

A more modern and hence less completely developed example is one touched on earlier in this chapter, in considering the problems that can arise when designing systems with a major HCI element. An important feature of a well-structured window system is that all the programs using it will have a consistent presentational interface, so that the various 'objects', such as pull-down menus and buttons, have a consistent appearance and are used in a consistent manner in the different programs. Window systems such as X achieve this through the use of libraries of standard objects (termed 'widgets' in X).

In this sense, therefore, the interface aspects of any programs can be constructed using a form of 'stylized' design, although the practices for using these window objects are far less well developed than in the case of compilers.

The production of compilers is perhaps unique as far as the use of 'stylized' design is concerned, since all the above conditions apply.

However, even where only two of them apply, there may be some scope for developing standard practices for design. This approach needs to be more fully explored for supporting future developments in software design technology and practice.

SUMMARY

This chapter has provided the basic material needed for the study of a number of design methods in greater detail. In particular, it has outlined the forms of the principal technical strategies that are currently used in software design methods, and has examined some additional ways in which the attributes of a design method can be classified.

From this, it can be seen that the major division in terms of design strategy lies between the

- top-down, or *decompositional* strategy; and the
- *compositional* strategy

and that design methods can further be classified according to whether they consider the effects of

- *organizational* structures and rationale;

and whether a design can be produced using

- a *template* for the design process.

Having examined the conditions for classifying software design methods in this manner, the following chapters are concerned with describing and assessing a number of widely used design methods, relating them to these issues in each case.

FURTHER READING

Wirth N. (1971). Program development by stepwise refinement. *Comm. ACM*, **14**(4), 221–7

This can be considered one of the classic papers in the area of software design. It is primarily concerned with the use of the top-down strategy for detailed program design, and is based around a worked example.

Parnas D.L. (1972). On the criteria to be used in decomposing systems into modules. *Comm. ACM*, **15**(12), 1053–8

This too is considered a classic paper in terms of its influence on software design (and the design of programming languages). It introduces the concept of information-hiding through the use of a worked example, before proceeding to discuss the consequences of such a strategy for design practices.

EXERCISES

8.1 Consider the task of designing the organization and layout of the garden for a new house. (For the purpose of this exercise, assume that the space for the garden is a rectangle 20 metres by 25 metres.) How would you set about this task using a top-down strategy, and what would be the criteria to use? (As a suggestion, the first-level decomposition might be into *lawn*, *vegetable plot* and *flower-beds*.) Would a compositional approach be better? If so, why, and how would you expect this to proceed?

8.2 Identify an example of the use of 'stylized' design in each of the following areas:

(a) software development (not compilers or HCI);
(b) designing buildings;
(c) designing bridges;
(d) designing washing-machines.

On the basis of your answers, would you consider this approach to design to be much more characteristic of 'traditional' engineering practice? If so, why is software so different?

8.3 When anyone moves house, do the removal men organize their work on a top-down basis or a compositional one? What criteria do they use in selecting objects to pack into boxes, and in organizing the packing of the van in a particular order?

8.4 List in order the factors that you think might influence the software design practices that are likely to be used in each of the following organizations:

(a) a large petrochemical company;
(b) a Local Government Authority;
(c) a small (three-person) software developer producing business packages for personal computers.

Why would the order of the common factors be likely to change between these?

A Brief Interlude

Chapters 1 to 8 have reviewed the background necessary for an appreciation and understanding of the forms and limitations of software design methods. In the next few chapters we now proceed to describe and analyse the features and practices of some of the more widely used and better-documented software design methods that are currently available.

Each chapter or section describing a specific design method has been organized around the following structure:

- an introduction outlining the history and background of the method, identifying its principal application domains, and describing some of the ways in which it may have evolved through use;
- a review of the representation forms that are used in the method, and the roles that they perform;
- an outline of the activities that form the process part of the method in terms of its basic strategy, major transformation steps and so on;
- details of any major heuristics or clichés that are associated with the method;
- a short review of any extensions to the method that might be in reasonably widespread use;
- a concluding summary, identifying supporting literature and other relevant material.

At the start of each major method description, there is also a simple viewpoints diagram that summarizes the representational forms used in the basic method and the viewpoints that they provide. (For some methods, the popular derivatives may involve the use of some additional forms of representation, but these have been omitted from the summary diagrams in order to maintain clarity.)

As a final proviso: the material of the following chapters is intended to provide a description and an analysis of the selected design methods, rather than detailed guidance about how to *use* them. For more details about any particular method, it will be necessary to consult a more specialized text that has the scope to describe the form and use of the method in greater detail. Although examples have been included wherever these can be contained within limits of the chosen structure, they are principally provided for the purpose of illustration, rather than tuition.

9 Jackson Structured Programming (JSP)

9.1 Some background to JSP
9.2 JSP representation forms

9.3 The JSP process
9.4 Some JSP heuristics

This chapter introduces our first study of a systematic design method, using the insight into method form that has been gained from the preceding chapters. The well-defined and well-constrained objectives of JSP make it a suitable candidate for a quite detailed study, and it provides a set of examples for all the components of the framework that we have developed. This chapter therefore aims to provide an introduction not only to JSP, but also to the form and structure of the descriptions of the methods in the following chapters.

9.1   Some background to JSP

JSP is one of the two design methods described in this book that have emerged from ideas and experiences of Michael Jackson (the second is JSD, Chapter 11). It has been chosen as the first detailed example of a software design method for the following reasons:

- It has limited and well-defined applications, which make it possible to describe it more concisely yet fully than most other design methods. It is therefore a good choice for the first method in the book.
- Ever since its development in the early 1970s it has been widely used, and therefore has a historical claim to be discussed in depth.
- It is an excellent example of the use of a compositional design strategy.
- It is well documented and widely used.

However, some of the attributes that make JSP so valuable for developing ideas about design also have the potential to mislead. Because of its limited domain of application, JSP provides more *prescriptive* forms of design transformation than almost any other systematic design method, and this makes it possible to incorporate a greater degree of verification than is generally practicable with other methods. So, while JSP forms an excellent introduction to the form and structure of software design methods, one should be cautious about extrapolating this initial lesson to design methods as a whole.

JSP is essentially a *program* design method. It is concerned with the design of systems that

- are realizable as a single sequential process;
- have well-defined input and output data streams.

While historically it has often been viewed as primarily of interest to the data-processing community, its use is by no means restricted to such problems, as will be illustrated here by examples and in the discussion in the final section. Indeed, because it is a program design method, there is scope to employ it in larger system design practices, as we will find when describing some other design methods.

Because of the well-rounded nature of JSP, significant extensions to further domains have not been developed. So the method that will be described here is essentially the only form that is in widespread use.

In Chapter 7 it was suggested that all software design methods begin by building some form of 'model' of the problem that is to be solved. In the case of JSP, this model is constructed by modelling the sequencing of the components in the input and output data streams; so the next section briefly reviews the forms of representation that are used for this purpose.

9.2   JSP representation forms

Since the forms of representation that are used in JSP have already been
described in considerable detail in Chapter 6, the discussion of this section
will be kept to a minimum.

JSP is unusual as a design method, in that it uses only a single
diagrammatical form in its transformations. This is the Structure Diagram
introduced in Section 6.6, where its use for describing the sequences
involved in both static data structures and dynamic program behaviour was
demonstrated. It is used in JSP for modelling both the structures of the
data objects of interest, and the forms of the program(s) that manipulate
them. Figures 9.1 and 9.2 reproduce Figures 6.16 and 6.18, as examples of

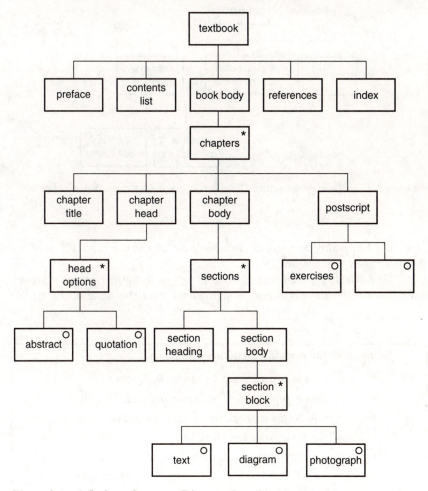

Figure 9.1   A Jackson Structure Diagram describing a static data structure (the
structure of a textbook).

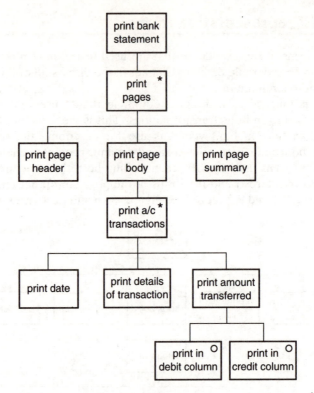

Figure 9.2 A Jackson Structure Diagram describing a program that prints out bank statements.

Structure Diagrams being used in both these roles; the rules for drawing them are shown in the box below.

Because JSP is concerned with program design, it places a strong emphasis on the development of algorithms, and the detailed forms for

---

Some rules for drawing Structure Diagrams

- sequence is represented by unmarked boxes
- selection is represented by boxes marked with circles
- iteration is represented by an asterisked box
- sequencing is from left to right
- the three forms may not be mixed in a sequence
- the last selection part should always be conditionless (the ELSE clause)

these are usually better described through the use of text. So JSP also makes use of pseudocode forms for the later stages of design, with these being derived from the diagrammatical forms as a part of the design transformation process.

9.3 The JSP process

The process part of JSP consists of five principal steps that are performed in sequence (although of course, as with all design problems, there will be iterations between these). The tasks performed in these steps can be summarized as follows:

(1) Draw a Structure Diagram that describes each of the input and output data streams.

(2) Merge these to form the program Structure Diagram.

(3) List the operations that need to be performed by the program, and allocate each operation to an element in the program Structure Diagram.

(4) Convert the program to text without specific conditions for any of the decision points.

(5) Add the conditions used for each iteration and selection operation.

As this shows, the JSP design method is based on a strategy of producing a program structure that reflects the structure of the task itself. This structure is therefore based largely on consideration of algorithmic forms, and the JSP design process does not address issues of modularity, such as procedural decomposition.

The first two steps are major ones, and may well require about half of the total design effort. While step 1 may seem relatively mechanical in nature, it is not necessarily so, and step 2 is far from simple. As a check on the results of step 2, experts generally consider that any problems encountered in performing the tasks of step 3 (allocation of operations) are likely to indicate that the structure produced by step 2 is not correct. JSP also incorporates a useful verification process that can be used to check that the structures generated by step 2 are consistent with those produced by step 1.

As already mentioned, JSP is unusual in that it uses only a single diagrammatical form of description. However, the transformation diagram in Figure 9.3 shows that this is perhaps misleading, since while the *form* of diagram used remains the same, the *interpretation* of it changes as a result of the transformation performed in step 2. Indeed, part of the complexity of step 2 is that it involves a transformation from a static model of data sequencing to a dynamic model of time-ordered sequencing of program actions.

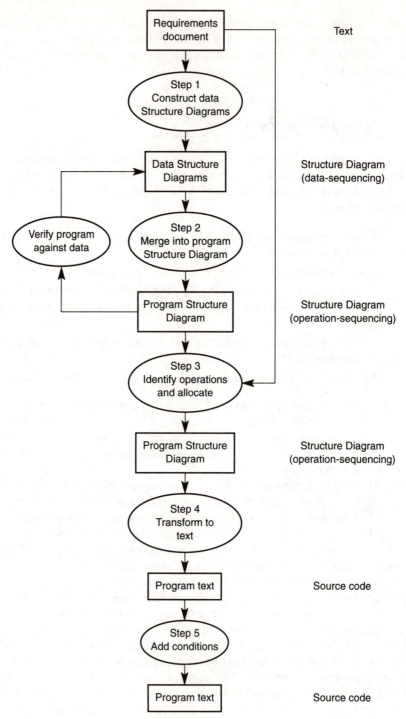

Figure 9.3 The JSP design process.

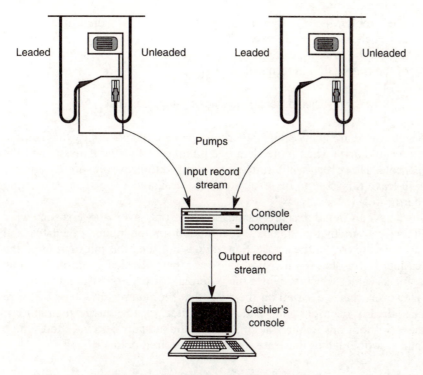

Figure 9.4 Schematic of a filling station.

To illustrate the basic design process more fully, we will work through a short example of the use of JSP, concentrating on steps 1 to 3 of the design process, since it is these that form the major components of the method.

Since JSP is often (unfairly) associated only with 'classical' data-processing problems based on handling files, with the final structures expressed in COBOL, the example problem has been chosen to look as unlike this as possible. The basic system requirement is as follows:

A petrol filling station (shown schematically in Figure 9.4) has a number of self-service pumps, each of which can be used to dispense both leaded petrol and unleaded petrol. There is a small local computer in each pump that maintains the display of price and volume on the pump; when the customer returns the pump nozzle to its socket, this computer sends a record to the cashier's console computer, containing the details of the current transaction as the sequence:

pump identity; grade of petrol; volume of petrol

The problem is to design the software that receives these messages. For each message it receives, the program is required to generate a line on the printer positioned in front of the cashier, giving the details of the transaction in terms of

pump identity; volume of petrol; total cost

(Since there are many pumps, there is of course the possibility that contention could arise when more than one pump tries to send a message to the console. However, in the time-hallowed tradition of software design, we will leave this issue to be resolved by the designers of the communication hardware!)

As an initial design specification, the one given above is somewhat imperfect, in that although the computer in the pump calculates and displays the cost of the transaction, it does not send this information to the cashier's console. We therefore have a repeated calculation of the same 'object' value, which provides the potential for an inconsistency to occur. However, this is excused on the basis that the pump computer's software has already been designed and implemented (a not untypical situation); also, without this feature the problem would actually be a little too simple and so would fail to illustrate some of the desired points!

9.3.1   Step 1: Draw the input/output Structure Diagrams

On this occasion, this task is a fairly undemanding one, since the system has just one input data stream and one output data stream. The Structure Diagram for the input data stream is shown in Figure 9.5, and the levels of abstraction for this can be interpreted as follows:

- the *Pump record stream* consists of many instances of a *record*;
- a record consists of the sequence:

  pump identity
  grade of petrol
  volume of petrol

- the grade of petrol field can specify the grade as either:

  leaded
  unleaded

  petrol.

In this case, the structure of this record has been determined previously by the pump designers, and hence it is assumed that it cannot be modified as a part of the design process.

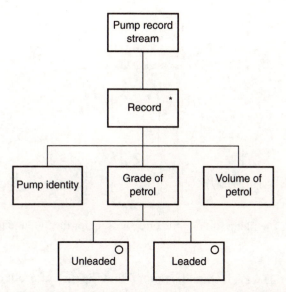

Figure 9.5 The filling-station Structure Diagram for the input data stream.

The form of the output data stream is shown in Figure 9.6, and again this can be interpreted as meaning that:

- the *sales record stream* consists of many instances of a *record*;
- a *record* consists of the sequence:

  pump identity
  volume of petrol
  total cost

There is obviously some scope to improve on this. One such improvement would be to add some degree of page-handling, which would print headings on a page and begin a new page after printing the details of a set number of transactions. However, this is not fundamental to the problem and hence it would be better to add this feature after the basic structures have been established. Redesigning the system to include this feature is therefore left as an exercise for the reader!

Note that at this level of design the designer is solely concerned with handling abstractions such as pump identity and total cost. There is no attempt to consider how these are to be realized in terms of strings of text, number of digits and so on.

The apparent simplicity of this first step as demonstrated in our example risks being misleading. While many real problems can be

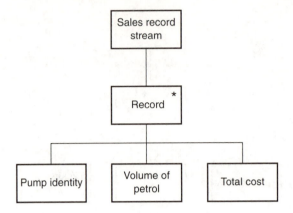

Figure 9.6 The filling-station Structure Diagram for the output data stream.

described in this way, it should be noted that the task of producing correct descriptions in the form of Structure Diagrams can form a significant proportion of the overall design effort required.

9.3.2 Step 2: Create the program Structure Diagram

Without a doubt, this can be the hardest part of the JSP process, although for this example it happens to be relatively easy, as there are no contentions of structure to resolve. The resulting program structure is shown in Figure 9.7. The letters 'C' and 'P' have been added to the labels of the boxes in order to emphasize whether data is being 'consumed' or 'produced' in the given operation. (Much of the simplicity of this step as applied to the example comes from the relatively direct match between the input and output data forms. As a result, there is no need to introduce any new structures or extra levels of abstraction, which might occur with a less tractable problem.)

It is this step that leads to the conclusion that JSP should be classified as a method that uses a compositional design strategy, since the program structure is very much one that is 'composed' by bringing together the input/output data structures.

Using the same process of step-by-step elaboration of the diagrammatical description as before, the operations of the program shown in Figure 9.7 can be described thus:

- repeatedly consuming a new input record and generating a new output record;
- consuming and producing new records involves the following sequence of actions:

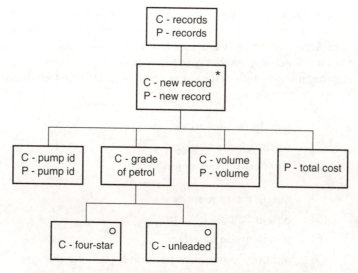

Figure 9.7 The filling-station program Structure Diagram.

      consuming and producing the pump identity
      consuming the grade of petrol
      consuming and producing the volume of petrol
      producing the total cost of the transaction

- consuming the grade of petrol involves consuming information to indicate whether it is
  four-star or
  unleaded

The basic verification process that forms a part of this design step can be easily performed in this instance. To check whether the program tree is consistent with the *input* data stream, erase all lines beginning with a P, and delete all empty boxes. To check whether the program tree is consistent with the *output* data stream, perform a similar exercise, erasing all lines beginning with C and then removing any empty boxes. (Try this as an exercise, and verify that each of these leaves the original input form.) Where the process of merging trees is more complex, then the verification process will, of course, be correspondingly more complicated.

9.3.3 Step 3: List the operations and allocate to program elements

Again, the nature of the chosen example is such that this is a relatively simple task to perform. Since most requirements place their emphasis on describing the outputs that are to be produced from a system, it may well be better to begin this task by considering the outputs first, and then using these to identify the necessary inputs and algorithmic operations. However, there seems to be no hard and fast rule about how this should be done, nor any direct way of checking for completeness.

For the filling-station system, the operations involved are the following:

Outputs   (1)   write pump identity

           (2)   write volume of petrol

           (3)   write cost to customer

Inputs   (4)   obtain pump identity

           (5)   obtain volume of petrol

           (6)   obtain grade of petrol

           (7)   multiply grade price per unit by volume dispensed

Once again, the exercise of adding page headers and pagination to the output is left for the reader to consider.

These operations are then allocated to the elements in the program Structure Diagram, as shown in Figure 9.8 (the operations are shown as small numbered boxes). Note that it is only meaningful to attach an

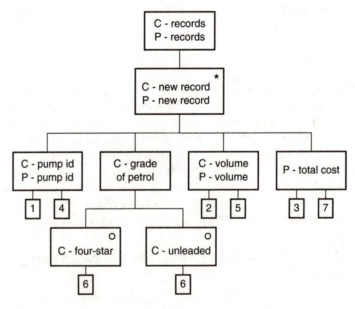

Figure 9.8 The filling-station program: allocation of operations to program elements.

(a) **Step 4:** Convert program
     to text without conditions

```
LOOP
    get pump identity
    get grade of petrol
    get volume of petrol
    calculate price
    print pump identity
    print volume of petrol
    print price
ENDLOOP
```

(b) **Step 5:** Add conditions

```
LOOP
    get pump identity
    get grade of petrol
    get volume of petrol
    CASE of grade
        unleaded: price calculation 1
        leaded:   price calculation 2
    ENDCASE
    print pump identity
    print volume of petrol
    print price
ENDLOOP
```

Figure 9.9   The last two steps of JSP.

operation to a box at the base of any branch of the Structure Diagram, since higher levels within the diagram 'tree' are essentially abstractions of the base levels.

9.3.4   Steps 4 and 5: Convert program to text and add conditions

These steps are relatively straightforward for this simple problem. Figure 9.9 shows the basic program structure that is generated by combining the operations from step 3 with the program structure produced in step 2 (which provides the sequencing information). Step 5 then requires a simple extension of this to incorporate the conditional expression used to select price according to grade. The remaining task is then to translate this into the chosen programming language in order to produce a usable program.

This simple example has provided an introduction to the process part of JSP, and to the design transformations that are involved. The next section considers some of the 'standard' ways in which this design process can be modified to handle some of the conflicts that can arise when using this approach.

9.4   Some JSP heuristics

With the extensive experience in the use of JSP that has accumulated since its development in the early 1970s, it is hardly surprising to find that some relatively systematic practices have been developed to provide guidelines for use in handling certain 'standard' types of problem that can arise.

These practices are needed in any design method, because assumptions that are made in its model-building process impose constraints on the form of solution produced. In the case of JSP, these constraints are chiefly placed on the forms of the input and output data streams (and they largely arise because no other viewpoints are used in composing the design model). Such constraints may not always map well onto some reasonably common situations and, as a remedy, the method developers evolve the ancillary strategies that we have termed 'heuristics' or 'clichés'.

This section will briefly describe three examples of such situations, together with outlines of the techniques for handling them. These examples respectively concern the use of the techniques of read-ahead, backtracking and program inversion. (For a more detailed account of how each of these is incorporated into JSP design practices, the reader is advised to consult one of the specialist texts identified at the end of this chapter.)

9.4.1   The use of read-ahead

JSP is essentially concerned with designing programs around algorithms that involve consuming and producing records, as the example of the preceding section showed. The algorithms for these programs may involve resolving particular conditions in order to make decisions about how data should be processed, and on occasion it may be necessary to know something about the next item of data to determine how the current item should be processed.

Programmers who are familiar with structured programming languages such as Pascal will be familiar enough with the nature of this problem. In such a language the use of a WHILE loop, containing an input statement that determines the termination conditions for the loop, will usually require an initial input statement to be included before the start of the loop, as shown in Figure 9.10. This statement is needed to ensure that when the conditional expression used for the WHILE statement is first evaluated, it will not cause the loop to terminate incorrectly before it has begun. Even if the logic within the loop is correct, incorrect initialization will lead to problems if one (say) attempts to perform input from an empty file by using a loop that terminates on finding the end-of-line mark.

The initial abstract level of design that is involved in the JSP design process simply identifies that iterations occur: the detailed form of the iteration structure is not determined until the conversion to text in steps 4 and 5. However, as we have just seen, if the loop construct eventually adopted is similar to that of the WHILE loop, it may be necessary to adjust the logic of the program structure in order to allow for correct initialization. On such an occasion, a restructuring of the program structure to include a single read-ahead operation may well be required in order to solve the problem.

In many ways this is a specific instance of a much more general design problem. Software design methods normally encourage a design structure that is concerned with meeting the requirements of the 'steady

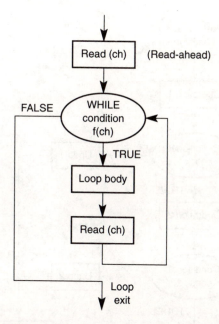

Figure 9.10   Read-ahead: the structure of a WHILE loop.

state' of a system, and this is then adjusted to incorporate the needs of initialization and termination, and of any error-handling facilities required. In general, this approach of solving the general problem and then adapting to the exceptions is probably the most practical one, since attempting to incorporate all of these factors from the outset is likely to destroy any chance of establishing a clear design structure.

9.4.2   Backtracking

It is not always possible to resolve a condition by using a single simple read-ahead operation; when this occurs we have an example of a 'recognition difficulty'.

It is sometimes possible to use multiple read-ahead in such cases, where a predictable sequence can be determined that will be needed to establish the condition. However, where this cannot be used, the more general technique of backtracking will need to be adopted during step 4 of the basic JSP design process.

The basic steps of backtracking are as follows:

- posit a default condition for use in all cases, this being assumed to hold until proved false;

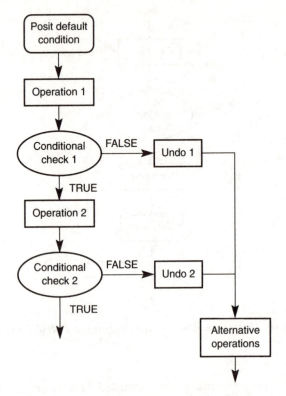

Figure 9.11 Backtracking: the basic strategy.

- at those points following which it is possible to test the hypothesis, insert 'quit' operations (where a 'quit' is effectively a constrained GOTO operation);
- provide for any necessary 'undo' operations to reverse the effect of actions performed before the path was proved to be the wrong one.

Figure 9.11 shows the resulting structure. The last step of this sequence can make life rather complicated, and as a general rule the use of temporary storage for intermediate results is suggested, with the main data structures being updated only when the transaction has been completed.

The use of backtracking leads to much more complicated program structures, possibly including large numbers of conditions. Its use can be considered as important when it is necessary to handle various forms of error in the input data streams.

9.4.3 Program inversion and structure clashes

Like the other two problems described in this section, structure clashes occur because of the assumptions that are made in the initial JSP model

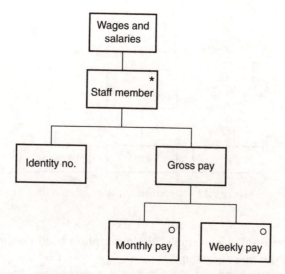

Figure 9.12   Structure of the finance file.

about the mappings used for the data structures. To explain the issue a bit more clearly, we will use a further example of the JSP design process.

The problem involves the Lotsalogs company encountered in Chapter 1. The company has a tradition of giving its complete workforce a long break over the Christmas and New Year period. However, its generosity does not run to providing them with their pay in advance, and so, in order to pay its workers during the holiday period, it is necessary for the company to mail cheques to their home addresses.

To complicate things a little further, the company employs people using two different types of contract. The more permanent employees enjoy monthly salaries, while others are paid on a weekly basis. Also, all employees have a unique staff identity number allocated to them when they first join the company.

The company's finance department maintains a 'payments file' for the company, which is structured in the form shown in Figure 9.12. By now, this should be so familiar that there is little difficulty in identifying the structure of the file:

- the salary file consists of many staff member records;
- the record for each staff member begins with the staff identity number, followed by details of gross pay;
- the details of gross pay are further structured according to whether the employee is paid on a monthly basis or a weekly one.

A full description of this file would obviously need to include further details about the structures used for monthly and weekly pay. However,

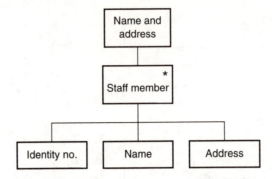

Figure 9.13 Structure of the personnel file.

for the purposes of this example, the description need not be elaborated further than this level of detail.

In order to send out the Christmas pay cheques, this information from the finance department needs to be combined with further information about such details as the name and home address for each employee. Fortunately, these are held by the personnel section, and Figure 9.13 shows the format of the file that they maintain for this purpose.

Since each of these files has one record per employee, we can reasonably assume that each file will contain the same number of records (assuming no fraudulent behaviour) and that they can therefore be combined to create a file giving the information needed for addressing the envelopes to be used for sending out the Christmas payments. Figure 9.14 shows the structure of the file required for this purpose.

Step 2 of the JSP design process is slightly more complicated than it was for the previous example; we now need to combine three structures in order to create the required program structure. However, as these data structures are not particularly complex ones, this can be done fairly easily,

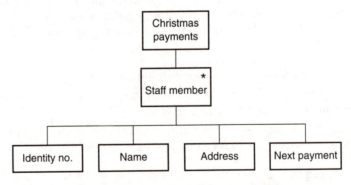

Figure 9.14 Structure of the output file.

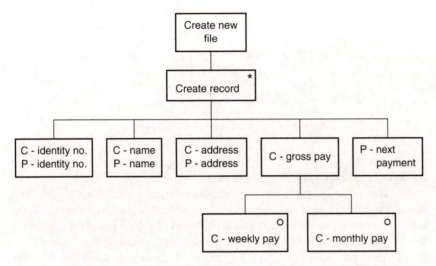

Figure 9.15 Structure of the Christmas payments program.

and the resulting program structure is shown in Figure 9.15. (This can again be verified against the data structures by the same process as before, although there are some slight extra complications involved in separating the inputs.)

So we now have a design for the required program, and the company should be able to proceed with generating the required output. Figures 9.16 and 9.17 show the first parts of the input files that are to be used for this purpose. Only at this point does it become evident that the design process has made a (flawed) assumption about the ordering of the records in the two files. The finance department likes to organize its files by using the staff identity numbers, while the personnel department prefers to use an alphabetical ordering based on the names of the employees. Unfortunately, unless the allocation of identity numbers is based on an alphabetical relationship – which is clearly not the case here – the records in the two files will be ordered quite differently. While Charlie Chips might be quite pleased to receive Sam Sawdust's salary payment, it isn't clear that Sam

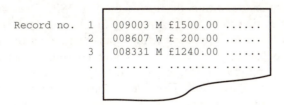

Figure 9.16 The finance department's file.

Record no.

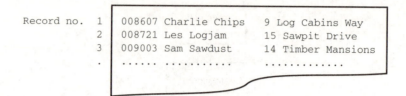

1	008607 Charlie Chips	9 Log Cabins Way
2	008721 Les Logjam	15 Sawpit Drive
3	009003 Sam Sawdust	14 Timber Mansions
.	....	....

Figure 9.17 The personnel department's file.

will be equally pleased with the size of his cheque, and so there obviously is a need to perform some form of remedial action.

This is an example of what Jackson terms a 'structure clash'. This particular form is an 'ordering clash', and occurs when one or more of the input streams are ordered using different keys. In the case of our example, the keys involved are the staff identity number and the name.

As it happens, this type of structure clash can often be resolved fairly easily, provided that the two files contain a common key. In this example, since both of the input files share a common key in the form of the identity number, the personnel data file can simply be reordered around this key by using an intermediate sorting program, so that the file corresponds to the ordering used in the finance data file. Following this reasonably simple operation, the Lotsalogs employees can look forward to receiving their correct Christmas and New Year pay.

The other two types of structure clash that Jackson identifies are the boundary clash, in which data is broken up using different criteria, although ordered by the same keys; and the multithreading clash, in which data elements overlap in the input file. The idea of a boundary clash can be clarified by considering the two views that can be taken when describing the structure of a text file stored on a disk. At the programming level, it is considered to consist of a sequence of variable-length *records*, made up of strings of characters. However, to the low-level software of the operating system, the file is organized as a sequence of *disk blocks* of standard size. Figure 9.18 shows the Structure Diagrams that represent these two quite different views of the same file – one record-based, the other block-based. It is the task of the file-handling routines of the operating system to resolve these and to transform between them as necessary.

Structure clashes essentially arise because of some implicit assumptions that are made within the forms used in JSP. They are based on inconsistencies that arise in the ordering of components when these are viewed at a lower level of abstraction than is provided by the Structure Diagram. To handle these clashes without continual recourse to extra sorting and merging routines, JSP has developed an associated technique known as 'program inversion'. However, as has been observed by Cameron (1988a), it is unfair to regard program inversion as simply a means of resolving structure clashes. It can be used to assist with the structuring of

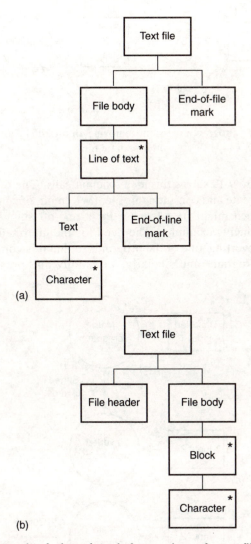

Figure 9.18 Example of a boundary clash: two views of a text file. (a) From the programmer's viewpoint. (b) From the operating system's viewpoint.

solutions to other types of problem, including interactive programs and interrupt-handling programs (Sanden, 1985).

There is not enough space to give a detailed account of program inversion in this chapter, but the basic idea behind it can be summarized fairly briefly. In order to use inversion, we adopt the form of solution that was originally identified as appropriate for the example of the Christmas payments, which is to design *two* programs that share a common data structure. In that example, this requires that one of the original files be sorted into an intermediate file, and that the sorted file be the input to the

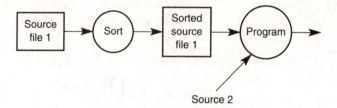

Figure 9.19 Program inversion: removing an ordering clash by a sorted intermediate file.

program. Figure 9.19 shows this idea schematically. The two programs are then used to create and consume this file. (We could, of course, just stop at this point, which might be adequate for a one-off situation such as the Christmas payments example.) The need for the intermediate file can be removed by 'inverting' one of the programs so that it becomes a subroutine of the other program (and similarly, we modify that program to call the

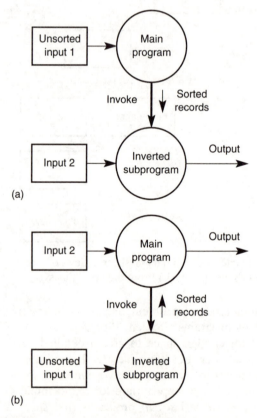

Figure 9.20 Program inversion: a schematic view. (a) Using the main program as the 'sort'. (b) Using the inverted subprogram as the 'sort'.

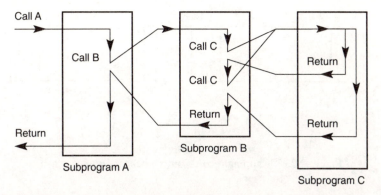

Figure 9.21   An example of the organization of flow of control for three subprograms.

inverted one). Figure 9.20 shows this form of solution schematically. In practice, as is shown in the diagram, either program can be inverted, for reasons now to be explained.

A more correct description of the process of program inversion is that it leads to a solution based on the use of two coroutines, rather than of a main program and a subroutine. Figures 9.21 and 9.22 show the difference between the two types of construct. As they show, coroutines resume execution from the point at which they last transferred control, whereas, whenever a subroutine is invoked, it always begins execution at its first instruction. (Coroutines are effectively 'equals', and this is why either program can be inverted.)

Very few programming languages support the coroutine mechanism – Modula-2 is an exception to this rule (Budgen, 1989). It is the need to

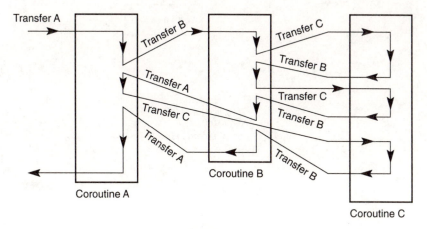

Figure 9.22   An example of the organization of flow of control for three coroutines.

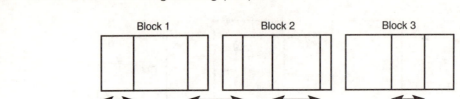

Figure 9.23 Mapping records onto blocks (boundary clash).

create an approximation to this construct that usually leads to the use of subroutines. This in turn produces much of the messy control flow that usually characterizes the examples of program inversion to be found in many textbooks.

The nature of program inversion can perhaps be seen most easily for the example used above to describe a boundary clash. Figure 9.23 shows an example of part of a file of records, stored in a sequence of disk blocks (for artistic convenience, records are always shown as shorter than a block, but this is not a real restriction). Figure 9.24 shows the structure of the library

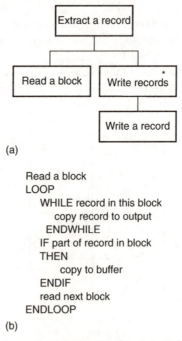

(a)

```
Read a block
LOOP
    WHILE record in this block
        copy record to output
    ENDWHILE
    IF part of record in block
    THEN
        copy to buffer
    ENDIF
    read next block
ENDLOOP
```

(b)

Figure 9.24 A simple program to extract records from blocks.
(a) Structure Diagram. (b) Pseudocode.

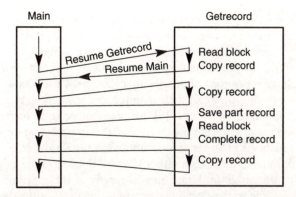

Figure 9.25 Execution sequence for inverted program.

routine that might be designed with JSP to extract records from the blocks and then pass them to a user program, one record at a time. Inversion of this program would then result in the construction of two coroutines: a section of their execution sequencing is shown in Figure 9.25.

So program inversion is a further example of a 'design heuristic', in the sense that it is a well-developed technique that can be used to overcome a problem that itself arises because of the needs and assumptions of the method. Because the method assumes the existence of certain ordering constraints upon the input streams, a technique is needed that can create these constraints whenever a particular problem does not fit the requirement.

SUMMARY

Because JSP provides a rather good and concise example of the major characteristics of all design methods, it has been given fairly comprehensive cover in this chapter. In some ways this probably exaggerates its importance in terms of current design technology. Indeed, because JSP explicitly builds on knowledge of the detailed structure of data in the formulation of a design solution, it cannot readily be used to build structures that incorporate such ideas as information-hiding. Similarly, it lacks any means of modelling data stores or events. However, JSP does have an important historical place in the development of design thinking, not least through its introduction of the notion of composition as a design strategy. But today its main role is more likely to be confined to assisting with detailed tasks of algorithm design rather than larger-scale design.

This is not to suggest that the only good reason for studying JSP is as an exemplar of design methods. One of the benefits of using JSP is that it encourages the designer to think about a form of model different from that which emerges from the event-driven or top-down views, and so it has an important educational role in its own right. Indeed, the value of the Structure Diagram as a modelling tool is widely recognized in many other methods, and we will be encountering it in other chapters. Also, as with COBOL, there is a large repository of designs that have been produced using JSP and related techniques, and their maintenance is likely to require that designers have some familiarity with JSP for many more years to come.

It is also important to reiterate the point that JSP is a *program* design method. Indeed, its main emphasis is on describing the time-ordered operations of the solution (sequencing), rather than on the derivation of any physical structure for the program, based on a hierarchy of subprograms. While it should be possible to develop this description relatively directly from the JSP solution, it is not explicitly included in any way.

As an aside, while JSP has spawned no real extensions or developments, there is an equivalent method in existence. This is Warnier's LCP method (Warnier, 1980), and while the notation is somewhat different, and LCP has some other restrictions when compared directly with JSP, it is much closer to it in philosophy than any other design method in use.

FURTHER READING

Jackson M. (1975). *Principles of Program Design*. New York: Academic Press

The original work by Michael Jackson. While it is well written and gives a clear exposition of the basic ideas, it is probably rather too COBOL-oriented in its philosophy for many modern tastes.

Ingevaldsson L. (1986). *JSP: A Practical Method of Program Design*. Bromley, Kent: Chartwell-Bratt

This short monograph provides a very concise introduction to JSP, and is not so heavily COBOL-oriented as Jackson's original work. It uses many illustrations and is permeated throughout with a very dry sense of humour.

King M.J. and Pardoe J.P. (1992). *Program Design Using JSP: A Practical Introduction*. 2nd edn. Basingstoke: Macmillan

Very clearly written, and has examples that are described using COBOL, Pascal – and BASIC! A good exposition of the method.

Cameron J.R. (1988). *JSP and JSD: The Jackson Approach to Software Development*. 2nd edn. Washington DC: IEEE Computer Society Press

This IEEE Tutorial provides something of a sourcebook for JSP, full of details, examples and associated information. While perhaps not so suitable for a first introduction as the other three books, it surpasses them as a reference text.

EXERCISES

9.1   For the example of the petrol filling station that was introduced in Section 9.3, extend the Structure Diagrams for the output data stream and the program to include:

(a)   a 'page throw' on the printer that occurs after every 50 lines of output, to be followed by the printing of a set of column headings at the top of the new page;

(b)   a total at the bottom of each page that shows the total value of the transactions on that page.

9.2   Taking your solutions to Exercise 9.1 above, identify the additional operations that will be involved, and allocate these to the program elements, as in step 3 of the JSP method.

9.3   Draw a Structure Diagram that describes the address of a person in the 'standard American' format of surname, forename, initials, number, street, city, state, zip code, elaborating on the details of each of these in turn. How would this model cope with Jim Smith, who lives in Blacksmith's Cottage with an address that has no street name?

9.4   The petrol pump example is a specific example of the general problem of producing a package for a point-of-sale system. Follow through the first three steps of the JSP method to design a program that will control a supermarket till: the program accepts input from a bar-code reader and the keys of the till in order to read the details of each item and the number of items. The till should print out the details of each transaction, and should also print out the final total price when the 'total' key is pressed.

10 Structured Systems Analysis and Structured Design

10.1 Origins, development and philosophy

10.2 Representation forms for SSA/SD

10.3 The SSA/SD process

10.4 The role of heuristics in SSA/SD

10.5 Extended forms of SSA/SD

10.6 SSA/SD: an outline example

SSA/SD, the design method examined in this chapter, has been subject to gradual refinement over a long period. Also, because it draws upon a wide range of viewpoints as well as addressing the needs of larger-scale problems, a number of versions and forms are in use, and are documented in the literature. So not only is its form much less prescriptive than that of the JSP method that was described in the preceding chapter, it is also suited to a very much wider range of application domains, and its basic design model is much more comprehensive than that of JSP.

This chapter does not attempt to identify or classify all of the variants that are in use, nor to provide comprehensive cover of the terminology. The purpose is rather to identify the main design themes and philosophies involved, and to draw these out and explain them within the terms of our general framework wherever possible.

10.1   Origins, development and philosophy

Although this method for software design was developed at much the same time as JSP, there are extensive differences between them, both in origins and strategy. Because of this, it is well suited to be the next method to be described, providing an example of a significantly different (and much broader) approach than that of JSP to the activities involved in software design. This contrast is of especial interest given the very wide use that has been made of both methods.

A number of people have been closely identified with developing the various forms of SSA/SD over the years. Much of the foundation for this approach to thinking about the structuring of programs and design was developed by Larry Constantine and Ed Yourdon, in association with their coworkers at IBM (Stevens *et al.*, 1974; Yourdon and Constantine, 1979). A further name that has been closely associated with the development of the analysis component of SSA/SD is that of Tom De Marco.

As a byproduct of this evolutionary development, there is a spectrum of variations in the details of the method. It is widely termed 'structured analysis and design', but to avoid confusion with other methods (the word 'structured' has been used rather liberally by method designers – presumably because of its positive connotations), throughout this book the longer description preferred by some users will be employed. The variations in the detailed form of the method and notation, and its evolution over the years, have also resulted in a range of textbooks that describe its use (for example, Gane, 1979; Page-Jones, 1988; Connor, 1985), but for the descriptions in this chapter the forms that are described by Meilir Page-Jones (1988) will be used.

As a design method, this one is really a composite of two separate but related techniques. The first is Structured Systems Analysis, which is concerned with the modelling of problem-related features of a system (often termed 'analysis'), making use of a set of descriptive forms that can also be used for architectural design. The second is Structured Design, which in turn is oriented towards the solution-related aspects (detailed design). Some texts concentrate almost entirely on the analysis stages alone (for example, De Marco, 1978), while others combine descriptions of the two in their presentation (for example, Page-Jones, 1988).

The earlier forms of the SSA/SD design process essentially made use of a refinement of the top-down strategy for design, with the choices that are usually involved in the functional decomposition process being moderated and constrained by considerations of information flow and, to a lesser degree, of data structure. Later variations have adopted a more compositional approach to the analysis stages, based upon such techniques as event partitioning. More recent developments have sought to combine the techniques of the method with object-oriented ideas of design (Henderson-Sellers and Constantine, 1991). For our purposes however, we will continue to regard this method as having a top-down philosophy.

The basic problem domain assumed for this method (and hence that which is normally assumed by most textbooks) is that of data processing. However, the basic strategy seems to be capable of quite wide application, and it has been extended in a number of different ways, mostly intended to enhance its usefulness for the real-time problem domain (Hatley and Pirbhai, 1988; Ward and Mellor, 1985; Ward, 1986; Gomaa, 1986).

Because of this background in the domain of data processing, most of the textbooks describing the method concern themselves with problems that involve the use of only a single sequential process for their solution. However, this is not a restriction imposed by the method (as it is with JSP), apart from the design transformation stages of the Structured Design process, and certainly Structured Systems Analysis is well able to cope with problems that involve concurrent processing of information.

As outlined above, the method has been extended and refined since it was first developed in the early 1970s. However, for the purposes of this chapter, which is concerned with providing an understanding of the general framework of the method, only the basic form will be considered. Having established a general model of the design process, it also provides a rather more abstract description of its procedures than was given for JSP in Chapter 9.

10.2   Representation forms for SSA/SD

10.2.1   Representations for Structured Systems Analysis

All of the many variants of this method make extensive use of two of the forms of diagrammatical representation encountered in Chapter 6. The Structured Systems Analysis techniques are centred on the use of the Data-Flow Diagram, or DFD (described in Section 6.2), while the Structured Design process makes use of the Structure Chart that was described in Section 6.4.

DFDs provide a problem-oriented and functional viewpoint that does not involve making any assumptions about 'hierarchy' (in the sense that all bubbles on the diagram are 'equal'). The techniques of Structured Systems Analysis guide the designer (or 'analyst') in building a model of the problem by using DFDs, elaborating this where necessary by using child DFDs in order to provide the necessary levels of detail. (This process of elaboration is rather confusingly termed 'levelling' of the DFD.) Figure 10.1 shows a simple example of a DFD, which we previously encountered as Figure 6.2.

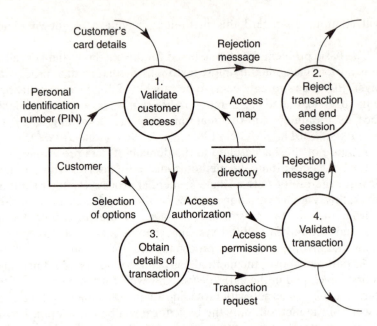

Figure 10.1   Example of a top-level Data-Flow Diagram.

The functional viewpoint provided through the use of DFDs is often augmented by means of more detailed descriptions in the form of 'process specifications', or 'P-Specs' (sometimes termed 'mini-specs'). A P-Spec is a textual description of the primitive process that is represented by a bubble in a DFD, and so can be regarded as a subsidiary functional viewpoint. A typical P-Spec will summarize the process in terms of its title, a description of the input/output data flow relating to the process, and the procedural tasks that it performs, couched in terms of the basic concepts of sequence, selection and iteration. An example of a simple P-Spec and its form is shown in Figure 10.2.

A data dictionary can also be used to record the information content of data flows. This typically includes descriptions of all of the data forms that are mentioned in the DFDs, P-Specs and any other forms of description that might be used. The initial description provided by the data dictionary should be highly abstract, and should not focus upon physical format (Page-Jones, 1988). (While the term 'data dictionary' may sound rather grand, it simply takes the form of a list of the data components, with their structure being described in a suitably abstract manner, as demonstrated in the example of Figure 10.3.)

More recent developments in design practice encourage the analyst to develop a set of Entity–Relationship Diagrams (ERDs) as a means of modelling the relationships between the data elements in a problem and determining their attributes in a suitably systematic manner. This

P-Spec number corresponds   P-Spec title
to bubble id-number

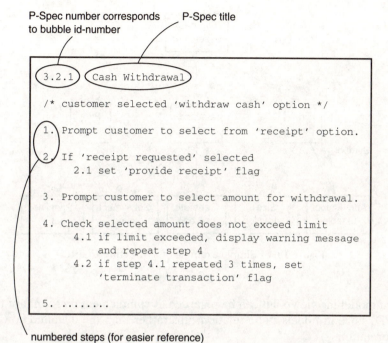

numbered steps (for easier reference)

Figure 10.2   A simple example of a P-Spec (mini-spec).

Conventions

For clarity, the use of the following operators is helpful:

= means 'is' or 'is equivalent to'

+ means AND

[ ] means either/OR, so that one of the enclosed options
will be selected

{ } means the components inside the braces are iterated

( ) means that the component is optional

A graphical equivalent is the Jackson Structure Diagram
(Section 6.6).

Examples

customer-id = bank code + sort code + account number

transaction-req = customer-id + [withdraw | withdraw with receipt |
account-summary | new chequebook req]
+ (withdrawal-amount)

account-summary = account number + {transaction log entries}
+ current total

Figure 10.3   Conventions for use with, and examples of, data dictionary entries.

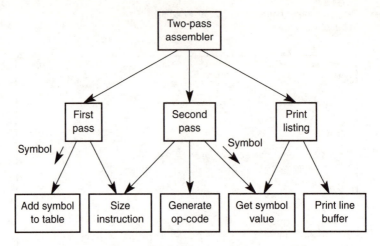

Figure 10.4 Simple example of a Structure Chart.

data-modelling viewpoint can be regarded as complementary to that of the DFD, since it models static relationships rather than the dynamic flow of information.

10.2.2   Representations used for Structured Design

In comparison with the wealth of forms that can be used for the task of analysing the structure of a problem, the Structured Design activities mostly make use of only one significant form of diagrammatical notation. As might be expected, the viewpoint adopted is a structural one, and it is provided by the Structure Chart.

Appropriately for a notation that is concerned with recording the details of 'physical design', as is shown by the example in Figure 10.4, the Structure Chart is very much a program-oriented form of description. It is chiefly concerned with describing the functions of the subprograms that make up a program, together with the run-time invocation hierarchy that links them. It is therefore the task of the Structured Design part of the method to bridge the gap between the very different viewpoints and forms that are used for Structured Systems Analysis and for Structured Design, and the next section provides an outline of the way in which this is achieved.

10.2.3   Other descriptive forms

While the forms just described are the principal diagrammatical tools used in this method, they can also be supplemented with other forms. Probably the most common of these is plain pseudocode, which provides a means of describing the algorithmic elements of the design and a more detailed description of the initial structure of the procedural units identified in the Structure Chart. Depending on the nature of the problem, designers may find it convenient to make use of further representations in order to help with resolving particular issues, including such forms as decision trees, decision tables and Entity–Relationship Diagrams (Page-Jones, 1988). While all of these can be useful, their prime role is to supplement the design transformations, which in turn are based on making use of the two main forms, and so the outline description here will not be concerned with the roles performed by these ancillary forms of design description.

Some of the ways in which the basic strategy of this method has been developed and enhanced were mentioned in the previous section. The real-time design methods based on the SSA/SD strategy have particularly developed the use of further diagrammatical forms, with these typically being used to capture the behavioural features of both the problem and the solution. These include such forms as the State Transition Diagram, as described in Section 6.9, and the Control Flow Diagram, a development of the DFD (Ward, 1986). These forms can assist the designer with modelling the time-dependent issues that predominate in a real-time system, as well as providing a means of describing the causal features that link external events to system reactions. Once again, though, these forms are not central to the present description of the basic strategy of SSA/SD, and so their use will not be explored in the description given in this chapter.

10.3   The SSA/SD process

As already mentioned in Section 10.1, in its original form the over-arching strategy adopted in this method can be regarded as a refinement of the classic top-down strategy of 'divide and conquer'. The designer begins by constructing a model of the top-level problem in terms of the operations that are performed by the system, and then this description of the problem is transformed into a plan for a program; this plan is in turn described in terms of the set of subprograms that are used to perform the relevant operations, together with the details of the interactions between the sub-programs.

The form of the design process is more subtle than that of the simple top-down design strategy, however: it extends the simple description of the system, expressed in terms of operations, by also considering the flow of information between the operations. The wider foundation that this provides assists the designer in producing a more consistent structure for the eventual design than is likely to arise from the use of the simple top-down strategy, since the information-flow component of the model helps to reduce and constrain the 'solution space' available to the designer.

Returning to the framework that is provided by the transformational model of the design process introduced in Chapter 8: the design transformations involved in this method can be viewed as forming a set of sequential steps, with feedback occurring automatically between them. The five basic steps, shown in Figure 10.5, are:

(1)   Construct an initial Data-Flow Diagram to provide a top-level description of the problem.

(2)   Elaborate this into a layered hierarchy of DFDs, supported by a data dictionary.

(3)   Use Transaction Analysis to divide the DFD into tractable units.

(4)   Perform a Transform Analysis on the DFD created for each transaction, in order to produce a Structure Chart for that transaction.

(5)   Merge the resulting Structure Charts to create the basic implementation 'blueprints', and refine them to include any necessary error-handling, initialization, and other exceptions.

Steps 1 and 2 are essentially those that make up the process that we are terming 'Structured Systems Analysis', while the other three can be considered as forming the process of Structured Design. This section concentrates on describing the nature of the first four steps, since the actions of step 5 do not involve major design decisions, although they play an important role in the form of the final design. (To do proper justice to the actions of step 5 also requires a more detailed description than can be provided in an overview such as this.)

10.3.1   Steps 1 and 2: Structured Systems Analysis

Most of the basic operations involved in these steps were outlined in Section 6.2, when discussing the use and the development of the Data-Flow Diagram. However, as Structured Systems Analysis is quite a large topic, which merits textbooks in its own right, it is appropriate to add a few more comments at this stage.

As might be gathered from their names, Structured Systems Analysis is essentially problem-driven in nature, while Structured Design is concerned with the form of the solution. For that reason, each process makes use of those diagrammatical forms that best support its particular purpose and provide for the necessary levels of abstraction.

The objective of the Structured Systems Analysis steps is to produce a functional specification that describes what the system is to do. Ideally this should constrain the form of the eventual implementation (solution) as little as possible. However, in practice it is often difficult to avoid making choices that will effectively constrain some architectural choices in the general form of the final solution, although the analyst is encouraged to

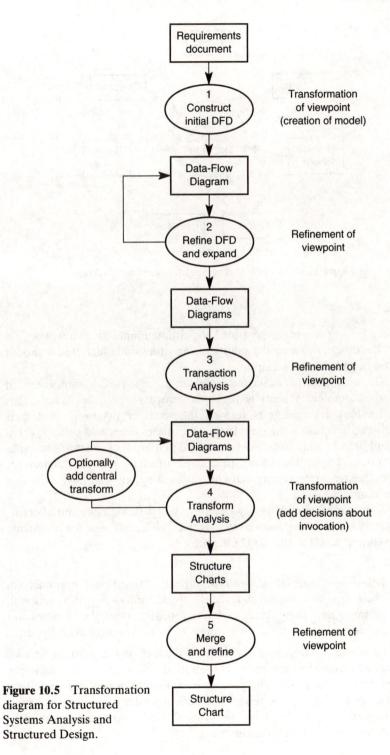

Figure 10.5 Transformation diagram for Structured Systems Analysis and Structured Design.

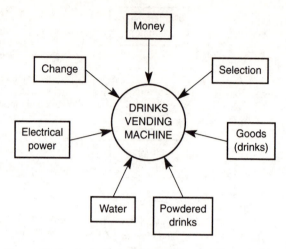

Figure 10.6 A context diagram for a vending machine.

avoid the former wherever possible. So, although analysis is not strictly a part of the design process, the reality of the situation is such that it should really be included in this chapter.

The most abstract description we can provide for a system is one in which the complete system is itself the process being described. This 'single-bubble' description is termed the 'context diagram', and it is basically the 'level zero' diagram that encapsulates the whole system with a single bubble; the only data flows described in it are those that are external to the system. Figure 10.6 shows an example of such a context diagram for a readily recognizable system. Of course, each system can have only one context diagram.

A context diagram having been produced (a valuable initial step), there are two commonly used strategies that can be adopted for producing the remaining levels of the DFD schema:

- *Top-down functional decomposition* is the 'traditional' approach, in which first the context diagram is divided into a set of 'functional' subtasks and then this process is repeated until the bubbles are considered to be sufficiently simple to be represented by P-Specs.

- *Event-partitioning* is a technique in which the thread of actions associated with each event is identified and used to form a simple bubble in the DFD. The process from this point may then be either compositional, in the sense of grouping related functions to form a higher level of DFD, or decompositional, using top-down techniques to refine the description.

In producing the Data-Flow Diagrams that form a major output from this step, the analyst (to employ the term usually adopted) is encouraged to use them for two purposes (De Marco, 1978; Page-Jones, 1988):

- drawing *physical* DFDs to describe the initial system model in terms of relatively concrete items (explicit names for users, form numbers, and so on);
- constructing *logical* DFDs, which use more abstract terms to describe the operations and data flow.

Examples of these roles were given in Section 6.2. The advantage of this subdivision is that the physical DFD is often easier to produce in the first place, and it can more easily be verified with the users (who can directly identify their problem in terms of its descriptive forms). However, the logical DFD is more valuable in terms of the next steps in the design process, and may also provide more insight into the design problem itself.

Of course, there are many aspects of a problem that cannot be captured easily by using the Data-Flow Diagram as the sole basis for the designer's model. Among other things, DFDs are concerned only with describing the flow of information, and not with its form or its persistence. For that reason, the DFD needs to be supplemented by other forms, with the choice of these depending on the problem itself. Besides the possible use of P-Specs, there will almost certainly be a need for some form of data dictionary. (In a large system, where the final DFDs identify very many processes, the data dictionary will be correspondingly large.) Other information about the problem may also need to be captured if the designer is to produce a complete model, such as

- frequency of information flow
- volume of data flow
- size of messages
- 'lifetime' of an item of information

In some cases, the flow of control may be a significant factor to be considered, in addition to any consideration of the data-flow element (Ward, 1986).

As with all apparently simple notations, actually producing a DFD requires a degree of practice. Both De Marco and Page-Jones offer suggestions to assist the inexperienced with this task (as do most textbooks that describe the different variations of this method). Some of the useful practices that are recommended are:

- Begin the task of identifying operations by considering the inputs and outputs of the system, since these are normally well defined in the user's requirements documents.

- Work inwards from these, if appropriate, otherwise outwards from the centre.

- Label carefully (following this advice is much harder than you might think).

- Don't try to handle exceptions and error conditions at this stage, since they will obscure the rest of the model.

- Don't flowchart (DFDs are used to model the *system*, whereas a flowchart models the operations of the *machine* that will eventually be used to implement the system).

Whatever the technique adopted (and however extensive the experience of the analyst), it is essential to be prepared to begin again, rather than to attempt to distort a model that is clearly wrong. (This provides one of the stronger arguments for performing this task with paper and pencil rather than some unfamiliar CASE tool, since the cost in personal time and effort of starting again is then much lower!)

10.3.2   Step 3: Transaction Analysis

The description of this step will be relatively brief, partly because this is not a major design transformation and partly because for less complex systems it may even not be required. The main purpose of the actions of this step is to separate the components of a large design into a network of cooperating subsystems, and this is done by identifying the transactions that are involved in the problem as a whole. The DFD components that correspond to each transaction are then grouped together and used as input to a transform analysis step, after which the resulting Structure Charts are recombined to provide the design model for the complete system. Figure 10.7 shows this process, together with those of steps 4 and 5, in abstract form.

The transaction analysis step can therefore be regarded as largely concerned with architectural design matters, its process part chiefly concerned with the identification of transactions. However, it is not quite so simple as that, as it is also necessary to consider some detailed issues about structure in anticipation of the final task of recombining the transformed transactions.

A transaction is usually considered to have five basic components:

- the *event* in the system's environment that causes the transaction to occur;

- the *stimulus* that is applied to the system to inform it about the event;

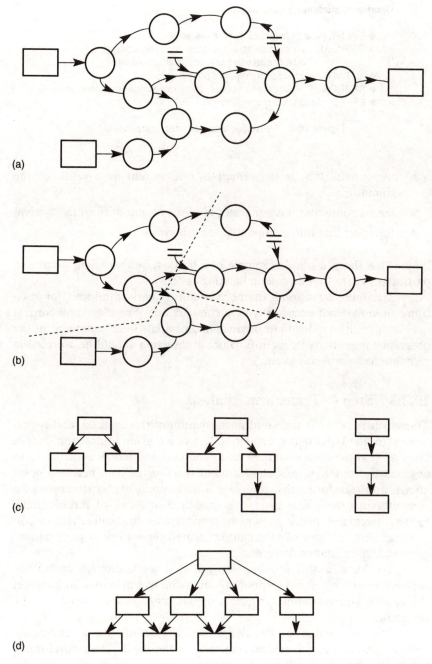

Figure 10.7 Transaction Analysis logic. (a) A complete system DFD from steps
1 and 2. (b) Step 3 Transaction Analysis divides into smaller DFDs. (c) Transform
Analysis creates Structure Charts in step 4. (d) Structure Charts recombined in
step 5.

Opening a student bank account

- EVENT: Student 'signs up' for a bank account
- STIMULUS: Information about student; university/college;
    date of opening account; grant source; etc.
- ACTIVITY: Add account details to bank's records
- RESPONSE: Free gifts to student; chequebook; monthly statements
- EFFECT: Student can spend money

Figure 10.8   A simple example of a transaction.

- the *activity* that is performed by the system as a result of the stimulus;
- the *response* that this generates in terms of output from the system;
- the *effect* that this has upon the environment.

Figure 10.8 shows a simple example of a transaction that might occur in a particular system (in this case, a banking system).

The later regrouping of the Structure Charts produced for each transaction may not necessarily be a complex one. For some problems, it may involve little more than organizing an initial CASE statement in the program's main body to identify which transaction should be selected in response to a particular event.

10.3.3   Step 4: Transform Analysis

Transform Analysis is the key transformation of this method, and is performed on the DFD that is created to describe a given transaction. It is in this step that the designer takes the nonhierarchical model constructed to describe the problem, modelled around the flow of data between operations, and transforms this to create a description of the structure of a computer program. This in turn is modelled in terms of the hierarchy formed from the order in which subprograms are called (invoked), together with the flow of information created through the use of parameters and shared data structures.

To see how this is done, we will first work through an outline description of the general form of this step, and will then seek to interpret the actions and operations in terms of our more general model of the design process.

The first action of the designer is to identify the operation or 'bubble' that acts as the **central transform** in the DFD. The central transform is the bubble that lies at the centre of input and output data flow – where these are considered to have their most abstract form (on the basis that they take their most concrete form when interacting with physical input/output devices). On occasion, however, it is not possible to identify a

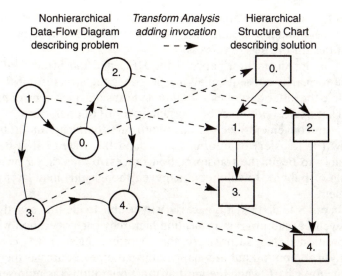

Nonhierarchical   *Transform Analysis*   Hierarchical
Data-Flow Diagram   *adding invocation*   Structure Chart
describing problem   – – ➤   describing solution

Figure 10.9   The operations of the Transform Analysis step.

clear candidate to act as the central transform, and in such a case the recommended practice is to create one – adding a further bubble in the position where the designer feels a central transform should occur. (While this may seem to be a slightly odd practice, a rationale for it will be given when we seek to interpret the transform structures.)

The basic form of the operations that are involved in the Transform Analysis step are depicted in Figure 10.9. A useful analogy is that used by Meilir Page-Jones (1988), in which he suggests that we regard the DFD as being a 'set of balloons, linked by strings'. To create the hierarchy, pick up the central transform balloon, letting the others dangle from it, and then turn the central transform into the 'main body' of the program. To stretch the analogy (and the balloons) rather hard: square off the balloons, so that the 'operations' become first-cut subprograms, and turn the data-flow arcs into invocation arcs (together with data flow), in order to form the initial draft of the Structure Chart.

A feature of this process that sometimes gives conceptual difficulty is that the flow arrows on the arcs seem to change direction when this transformation is made. This is because the arc in a DFD depicts data flow, while that in a Structure Chart depicts control flow (via subprogram invocation). The latter are added in this design step, and the former are subsumed into the data flow that is conducted via the parameters of the subprograms.

While this is by no means all that is involved in the Transform Analysis step, since a lot of work remains to be done to produce a proper Structure Chart that describes the form of the eventual system, it is sufficient for our immediate purposes, since it explains the essential nature of the transformation it contains. We now need to consider the implications of this for the design process.

A major distinction between the DFD and the Structure Chart is that the former is nonsequential and describes the structure of the *problem*, while the latter describes a *solution* in terms of a hierarchy of program units. That apart, both describe a system in terms of operations (which, of course, can conveniently be packaged into subprograms), and in terms of the flow (or transfer) of information around the system. It is therefore reasonable to begin the transformation process by making a one-to-one mapping of bubbles to subprograms, even though this may later require refinement.

In order to do this, it is necessary to be able to identify exactly where in the eventual subprogram invocation hierarchy each operation will need to be positioned. Not surprisingly, the operations most closely concerned with physical input/output are mapped onto the procedures at the base of the Structure Chart, while the most abstract operations (as represented by the central transform and the bubbles immediately around it) are mapped onto the top level of the chart.

This explains why it is sometimes necessary to create a central transform in order to be able to perform the transformation process. A system in which this extra step proves to be necessary corresponds to a situation where the chief role of the main body of the final program is to organize the sequencing of the calls to the subprograms. Since such a program main body performs no specific problem-oriented operations, it is unlikely to be identified as a bubble in creating the DFD. This is why it needs to be added to the DFD in the form of an 'empty bubble', in order to 'complete' the DFD so that the Transform Analysis operations can be performed in a consistent manner.

Once the first-cut Structure Chart has been produced in this way, quite a lot of work remains to be done in revising its form into one that is appropriate for implementation with a hierarchy of subprograms. Almost certainly, there will be additional work needed to sort out the detailed forms of any input and output; the functions of the DFD operations may need to be split between subprograms, or combined in some cases; and the needs of initialization and exception-handling need to be met through the creation of additional modules. On top of all that, there is a need to consider the quality of the structures created, and to maintain these by considering such factors as coupling, cohesion and information-hiding.

Transform Analysis is therefore a complex step, and in this subsection only a very general outline of the principal actions that it involves has been given. However, this description should be sufficient to provide an understanding of the nature and form of this transformation, leaving the details of the various refinements to be described in a more specialized text.

10.3.4   Step 5: Completing the design process

Where the Transaction Analysis step has identified a number of separate transactions, step 5 will involve bringing together the Structure Charts produced for the different transactions and resolving any overlaps or mismatches between these. As already mentioned, for systems in which these are essentially distinct options (as, for example, in a bank autoteller system, where the user may opt to deposit money, receive money or receive information), the linking may involve little more than adding a new top-level module that selects among the transactions. Equally, there may be some need to rationalize the lower-level modules, since there is the risk of some duplication occurring in their operations.

10.4   The role of heuristics in SSA/SD

Because the process of design for SSA/SD is much less tightly structured than that of JSP, its use is less likely to lead to such well-defined problems as the example of the structure clash in Chapter 9. The heuristics involved in its use are therefore less likely to be concerned with resolving problems that arise in the form of the solution than with assisting the designer to perform some of the actions involved in the major design transformations.

We have already encountered one significant example of a heuristic of this type, which is that of devising an 'empty' central transform when there is no obvious suitable candidate. This is a prime example of the use of a design heuristic to assist with the design transformations, as it provides guidance on the restructuring of a design model (which in itself may be quite correct) to allow a particular transformation to be applied to it.

Indeed, the very act of identifying the central transform during Transform Analysis is itself a form of heuristic. There are no prescriptive guidelines for performing this task, and the results of selecting different candidates will be quite different in their structure, as is demonstrated in the simple example in Figure 10.10, where the effects of selecting different candidates to be the central transform can be seen.

The technique of levelling, as used for developing a DFD, is probably a further candidate for classification as a heuristic, since the available guidelines are rules of thumb rather than systematic rules. However, since it is a normal operation during Structured Systems Analysis, the heuristic element is really concerned with the rules used for performing the operation, rather than with the act of performing it.

A second heuristic of this type is known as 'factoring'. This is a technique used for separating out functions within a module, where the operations of one module are contained in the structure of another. There are a number of reasons why we might want to do this, some of which are:

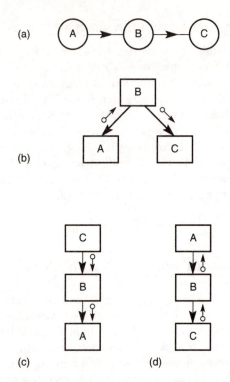

Figure 10.10 Selecting the central transform. (a) The Data-Flow Diagram. (b) Choose bubble B. (c) Choose bubble C. (d) Choose bubble A.

- to reduce module size (and hence complexity);
- to help with clarification of functions (and hence to assist with future changes);
- to help identify and reduce duplication of operations;
- to help with reuse of code.

Associated with the idea of factoring are the concepts of coupling and cohesion, which were introduced in Chapter 4 (page 70). Clearly, any factoring that we perform will need to take these into account. So these too might be considered as design heuristics, in that they can be used to help resolve particular issues and to assist with design choices.

Evidently the heuristics in SSA/SD are very likely to appear during 'normal' use of the method, and so are largely concerned with assisting in the performance of the regular design transformations. In the case of JSP, however, techniques such as program inversion are required only if the transformations generate a certain type of solution, and so heuristics are used only during a later stage of the design process.

10.5   Extended forms of SSA/SD

This section should perhaps include the terms 'variations' and 'developments' in its title, since SSA/SD has spawned a wide variety of derivatives. These can be classified as:

- *Variations*: the overall form of the process does not differ significantly, but slightly different notations or process models are used. There are a number of these, with perhaps the best known being that popularized by Gane and Sarsen (1979).

- *Extensions*: new features have been added to the process model, and new viewpoints have been included in the representation part. Most of these have been directed at assisting with design in the real-time domain (remember that this method was essentially developed to meet data-processing needs), and so these have tended to enhance the use of behavioural viewpoints in the design process. Particular examples are those due to Ward and Mellor (1985), Hatley and Pirbhai (1988) and Gomaa (1986; 1989).

- *Developments*: essentially refinements that have been added to the basic model over time without affecting the fundamental structure of the transformations. Much of the effort has been directed at improving the techniques used for data modelling (such as the addition of entity–relationship models (Page-Jones, 1988)).

The development of the basic method can probably be considered as having reached its most refined state of development in the description provided in Yourdon (1989). The extensions are in many ways methods that have quite different design processes and models, in terms of both the analysis and the design parts. While, from a methodological point of view, these merit separate attention, time and space have not permitted a separate survey of their features in this book.

10.6   SSA/SD: an outline example

A fully worked out example of the use of an analysis and design method such as SSA/SD is outwith the scope of this book. However, the fairly simple worked example that is provided here should be sufficient to give a strategic understanding of the mechanisms involved.

The problem

The problem chosen for this example is based on the development of a software utility that can be used to provide outline design documentation for an existing program, with the aim of using the documentation to help

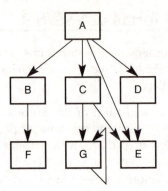

Figure 10.11   A Structure Diagram describing a Pascal program. (Procedure G is recursive.)

produce a Structure Chart that describes the program. In effect this can be considered as a form of 'reverse engineering' process that can be used to aid the maintenance of a program, by ensuring that the working documentation faithfully reflects the actual structure of the program.

To make the task somewhat simpler, the program being analysed is to be written in 'standard' Pascal, so ensuring that all the subprograms (procedures) are contained in a single source file. Even if we were to modify our goals to include programming languages that permitted separate or independent compilation, we should probably still adopt a strategy of 'separation of concerns' in the development of our solution, and begin the task of exploration by using the simplest case of the single source file.

Since the main requirement is to design a program that will be able to recognize any declarations of procedures and any calls to procedures in the input Pascal source file, the techniques involved are likely to be closely allied to those used in compiling. So, in an unconstrained situation, it would probably be most sensible to adopt a 'template' approach to the design of the system, involving the use of such software tools as the lex and yacc tools provided with the UNIX operating system. However, to provide the desired example, we will use the SSA/SD strategies instead.

To perform its task, the program will need to read through the source code of a Pascal program and identify the extent and forms of the relationships among its procedures. So for each procedure that is declared in the input source program, this 'reversing' program will need to print out a list of the procedures that it calls, either directly, or by making use of other procedures. This information can then be used to construct the eventual Structure Chart. (We will not attempt to develop the graphical routines that would be needed for constructing this directly from our program.)

In its simplest form, the output from our 'reversing' program can simply show the calling hierarchy for the input Pascal source text, but of course there is also scope to include information about the formal

					level	types
Level 1	A	>	B(list of formal parameters)		2	p
		>	C(	– ditto –)	2	f
		>	D(	– ditto –)	2	p
		>>	E(	– ditto –)	3	f
Level 2	B	>	F(	– ditto –)	3	p
	C	>	G(	– ditto –)	3	p
		>	E(	– ditto –)	3	f
	D	>	E(	– ditto –)	3	f
Level 3	G	>	G(	– ditto –)	3	p

>   procedure call at the next level
>>   call to a procedure at a lower level
p   procedure call
f   function call

Figure 10.12 Outline of the output form describing the program shown in Figure 10.11.

parameters used for the procedures. Figure 10.11 shows a Structure Chart that describes the form of a fairly simple Pascal program, while Figure 10.12 shows the type of output listing that our 'reversing' program might produce from its analysis of the code for the corresponding program, which can then be used to draw that Structure Chart.

While this requirements specification is not a very rigorous or complete one, it is probably not atypical of those often encountered, since few end-users are likely to have the skills necessary to construct detailed requirements documents. (Indeed, where relatively new products are involved, attempting to identify the complete requirements in advance may not even be desirable.) One of the benefits of an initial pre-design stage such as that provided by Structured Systems Analysis is the opportunity to clarify and resolve any ambiguities and identify any significant omissions.

The Structured Systems Analysis step

We begin by producing the context diagram, which is shown in Figure 10.13. For this particular problem, which, like a compiler, has a fairly simple 'batch' format, the context diagram is relatively simple, since there will be little or no interaction between the program and the user.

To develop the DFD, it is necessary to choose between top-down decomposition and event-partitioning. (Events are not necessarily associated with external actions: an 'event' in this context might well involve the recognition of a particular reserved word in the input.) In this case we will adopt the more basic top-down approach, in the absence of

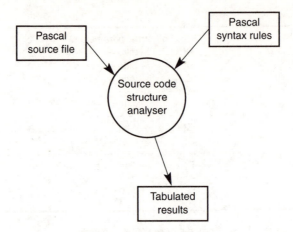

Figure 10.13 Context diagram for the 'reversing' program.

any features that indicate that either technique is likely to be the more appropriate.

Figure 10.14 shows a first attempt to produce a DFD describing this system. As often occurs in such a situation, this raises questions about the

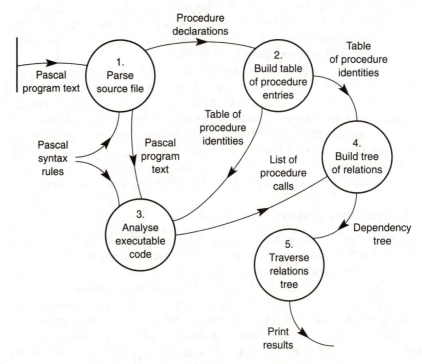

Figure 10.14 A first DFD for the 'reversing' program.

problem that lead us to refine or recreate the DFD. In this case, an obvious question that might arise is whether the solution will permit reading through the Pascal source file more than once. (Pascal was designed to permit single-pass compilation.) But we should avoid being diverted into considering eventual implementation in this way, and continue to concentrate on the more abstract task of analysis at this stage. (This point has been raised here to demonstrate how easily the task of analysis can overlap with that of design unless we take care to maintain an appropriate level of abstraction by a conscious effort. It also demonstrates how the design process might use note-making: a note of the above point should be made for consideration at a later stage.)

As it happens, further expansion of the DFD shown in Figure 10.14 leads rapidly to the conclusion that we have not chosen a particularly good set of basic operations. This is partly because operations such as 'parse' and 'build' are too vague, so complicating the task of expanding the bubbles,

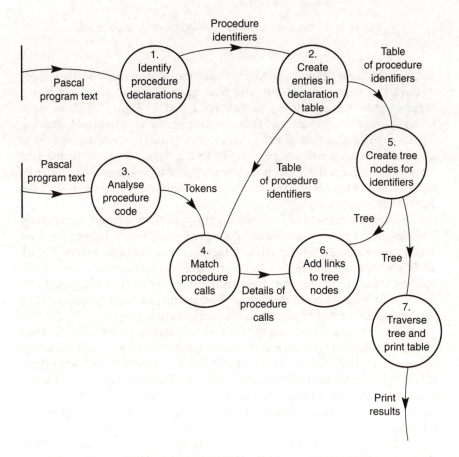

Figure 10.15 A second DFD for the 'reversing' program.

```
ProcedureDeclaration = ProcedureIdentifier
                ProcedureType        (* function or procedure *)
                Parameterlist        (* used for annotation *)

        (* do we really need ProcedureType? *)

TreeNode = ProcedureIdentifier
        ProcedureType
        list of parent nodes
        list of child nodes
        ParameterList        (* formal parameters only *)
        level                (* start high, migrate down *)


ProcedureCall = ProcedureIdentifier
            [caller]
            ProcedureIdentifier
            [called]

        (* what about recursive procedures? *)
```

Figure 10.16   A data dictionary for the 'reversing' program.

and also because attempting to constrain the solution to one that reads through the Pascal source file only once gives a convoluted form to the expansions of the operations in bubbles 1 and 3. Figure 10.15 shows a second attempt to construct a DFD, drawing on the experience of attempting to expand the first form. (Again, the point in showing this is to emphasize that we will not necessarily find a 'good' solution on the first attempt, and that a designer should be prepared to revise or even discard a model if it fails to meet all the requirements, and to develop anew with the experience so gained.)

The data elements involved in this problem are not particularly complex, and so the development of a more comprehensive description via such forms as the Entity–Structure Diagram is not really necessary. Figure 10.16 shows a simple first-level data dictionary, together with some notes that show where the designer has identified questions that will need to be resolved at some point in the future. The making of notes is, of course, a well-recognized practice already discussed in earlier chapters.

The process of levelling the DFD by expanding the bubbles can then be pursued until the designer determines that a suitable level of abstraction has been reached. Figures 10.17 and 10.18 show examples of such refinements for three of the bubbles in the top-level DFD (in the case of bubble 4, its description has been refined rather than levelled). For the moment there is no obvious expansion of bubble 2 and so this is left for future consideration.

The eventual DFD is shown in Figure 10.19, while Figure 10.20 shows a further refinement of the data dictionary; but there are still some

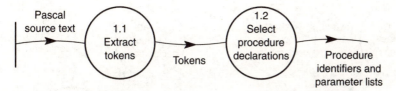

Figure 10.17 A first expansion of a DFD bubble.

issues needing to be resolved. For this problem, the eventual DFD is not particularly large, and so we can proceed to use it in full for the process of Structured Design. For a larger system, it might be necessary to use only the more abstract levels for the initial steps of the design process.

The analysis stage is also likely to form a significant source of designer's notes, where particular problems have been recognized but cannot be solved at this level of abstraction. One example of such note-making for this problem is likely to be prompted by the need to recognize the presence of recursive procedure calls, since too simple an approach to tracing procedure calls would be likely to throw the 'reversing' program into an infinite loop when it encountered a recursive procedure.

The Transaction Analysis step

For this particular problem, there is essentially only a single transaction, and so there is no need to separate out the DFD into separate transactions.

The Transform Analysis step

The key action that must be undertaken successfully to produce a well-balanced design is that of finding the central transform. In this problem

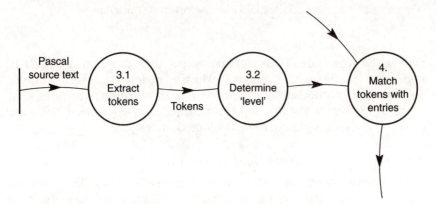

Figure 10.18 Further expansion of the top-level DFD for the 'reversing' program. It involves some global knowledge about 'level'.

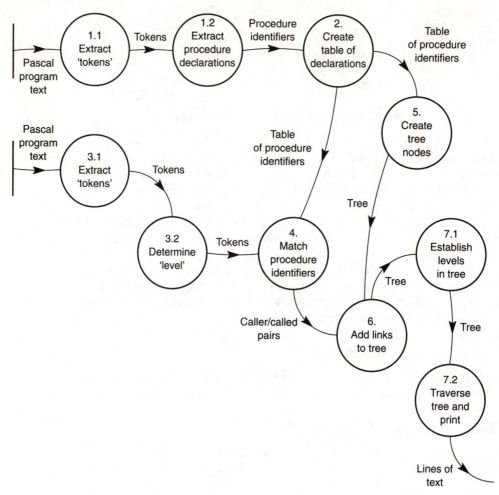

Figure 10.19 A more detailed DFD for the 'reversing' program.

neither the input data flows nor the output data flows are particularly significant features of the problem, which is mainly concerned with the creation and manipulation of the central information structures that describe the form of the Pascal program being analysed. Indeed, there are clearly two stages to the solution as adopted, namely:

● recognizing the procedure declarations;

● recognizing the procedure invocations (calls) and linking these to create the data structure needed in order to produce the final output.

```
ProcedureDeclaration = ProcedureIdentifier
                       ProcedureType          (* function or procedure *)
                       ParameterList          (* formal parameters *)

ParameterList = NumberOfParameters           (* count of parameters *)
                {FormalParameter}

FormalParameter = ParameterIdentifier
                  ParameterForm              (* VAR or VAL *)
                  ParameterType

       (* do we really need procedure type ? *)
       (* procedure type is needed if we want to annotate with data-flow
          information, as a function procedure is another parameter for
          this purpose *)

TreeNode = ProcedureDeclaration
           linked list of parent nodes
           linked list of child nodes
           level in tree                     (* established by traversal *)

ProcedureCall = ProcedureIdentifier
                ProcedureIdentifier          (* caller *)
                                             (* called *)

       (* what about recursive procedures? *)
       (* can be recognized by identical fields in ProcedureCall record *)
```

Figure 10.20 A revised data dictionary. While this has not been expanded fully, some of the questions raised have already been answered. Notes of both questions and answers should be kept on record in the data dictionary.

It turns out that, if we assess the qualities of any of the existing bubbles in the DFD (Figure 10.19) as candidates for the central transform, none of them are particularly suitable, since no bubble occupies a place between the two main tasks of the program as a whole. So this is where we create a further 'boss' bubble, positioned between bubbles 2 and 5. The new DFD that can then be produced from this is shown in Figure 10.21, and the new bubble will be used as the central transform.

Figure 10.22 shows the result of performing the first step in the transformation process, lifting the new bubble to the top of the diagram and letting the others trail below. The result of some squaring off and resolving of flows is then shown in Figure 10.23: the first rough Structure Chart describing the solution. This also reveals that the question of parsing the input has not yet been addressed and so will form a subproblem to be resolved separately (so perhaps we can make use of some degree of stylized design, anyway).

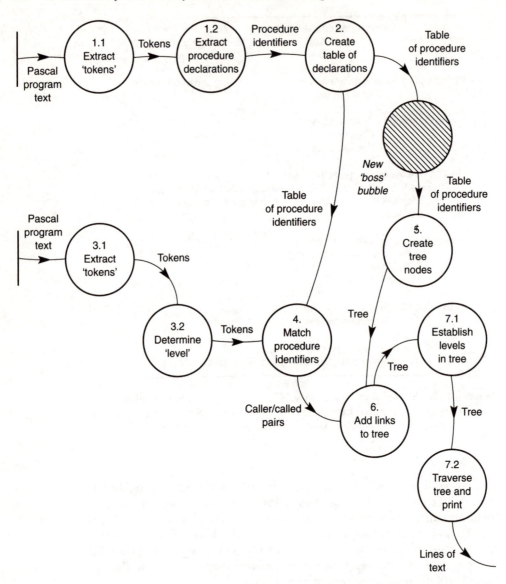

Figure 10.21 Adding the new 'boss' bubble to the DFD.

Finally, Figure 10.24 shows a rather more refined development of the Structure Chart, although obviously this is still by no means complete: lacking details of the 'parsing task', we still need to address such issues as:

• providing read and write modules;

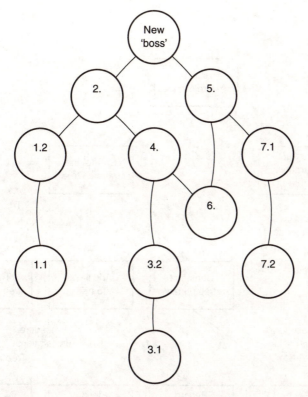

Figure 10.22   First step in reorganizing the components of the DFD.

- factoring out some of the functions that are really too large and complex to be contained in a single procedure;
- adding error-handling functions;
- adding the details for initialization and termination.

However, within those limitations the choice of the central transform has been fairly successful, in that the result appears to be a quite well-balanced tree of procedure calls.

As with all examples, this one is, of course, very much simplified. As a practical point, it should also be observed that producing even this first rough design required a number of attempts at performing the Transform Analysis step before the decision was made to adopt an empty central transform. The practical limitations of space prevent the inclusion of such iterations in this chapter, but their presence should not be forgotten.

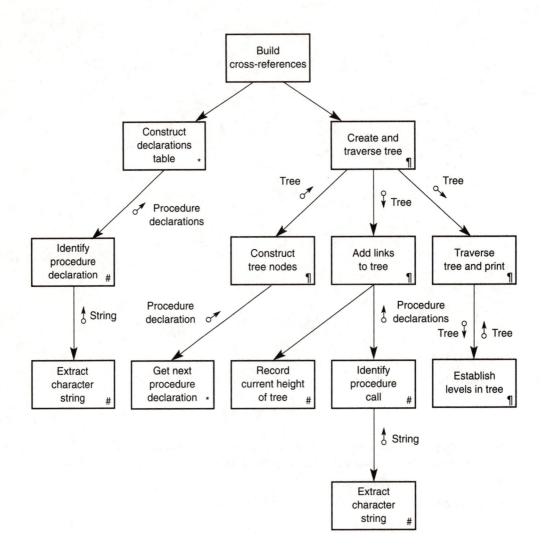

Figure 10.23   First rough Structure Chart.

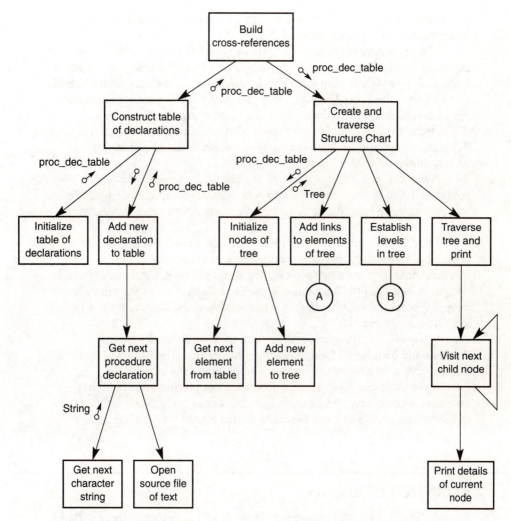

Figure 10.24   A more refined Structure Chart. (Items A and B require further expansion.)

SUMMARY

The very widespread use of the various forms of this method, together with its historical role in the development of software design thinking, make this an important method to introduce at this point. Indeed, in much the same way that ALGOL 60 has influenced the form of many subsequent programming languages, so SSA/SD has influenced the thinking behind many subsequent developments in design methods. It also provides an important contrast with JSP, both in its much wider scope and its (consequently) less prescriptive form.

The practices of Structured Systems Analysis have provided a very powerful set of techniques that can be used to assist with the initial stages of systems design. While analysis is not design, it is an essential precursor, and provides the initial problem modelling step that the designer is required to perform at some point. Indeed, there is a case for arguing that the distinction of title should not encourage a separation of role, in that it is the designer who should perform the analysis task as a part of gaining an understanding of the problem.

One way in which the value of Structured Systems Analysis is recognized is in its incorporation into other (later) methods of design. We will encounter an example of this when we study object-oriented design techniques later, in Chapter 12.

The Structured Design component would seem to be less widely adopted in its entirety, perhaps reflecting a general feature of design methods, that they are more prescriptive about the earlier activities of the design process than the later ones. Structured Design is certainly not a simple process if it is performed in a rigorous manner, although it can be very effective in practice.

Overall, the strong imperative content of Structured Systems Analysis and Structured Design practices has certainly assisted with their wide adoption by designers who have been brought up in the same imperative tradition. However, the limitations of placing undue emphasis on one viewpoint have also been recognized, as has been shown by the later developments and extensions that have been adopted into the method.

FURTHER READING

Connor D. (1985). *Information System Specification and Design Road Map*. Englewood Cliffs, New Jersey: Prentice-Hall International

Provides a quite comprehensive example of the use of this method and also shows how the same problem can be tackled using a number of other design strategies.

Page-Jones M. (1988). *The Practical Guide to Structured Systems Design*. 2nd edn. Englewood Cliffs, New Jersey: Prentice-Hall International

As the title implies, this is mainly concerned with the Structured Design process, although it also contains two useful chapters on Structured Analysis.

Yourdon E. (1989). *Modern Structured Analysis*. Englewood Cliffs, New Jersey: Yourdon Press

Provides the guru's own thoughts on developments in the method as a whole.

The real-time forms of the method are covered by rather fewer textbooks. Probably the most outstanding of these is:

Hatley D.J. and Pirbhai I. (1988). *Strategies for Real-Time System Specification*. Dorset House

Sets out one of the major forms of real-time extension in a clear and readable manner.

EXERCISES

10.1 Draw the context diagram for each of the following systems:

  (a) a bank autoteller machine;
  (b) a word-processing program;
  (c) a payroll package that is required to produce a set of printed pay-cheques each month, and to provide pay statements showing amount paid and deductions (national insurance, pension, income tax, regular subscriptions or donations).

10.2 For the Data-Flow Diagram shown in Figure 10.25 (on page 238):

  (a) identify your choice of the bubble that should be used as the central transform;
  (b) explain your reasons for rejecting the claims of each of the bubbles around it;
  (c) produce a first-cut Structure Chart from it.

10.3 Consider the needs of any error-handling procedures in the example system used in Exercise 10.2. Describe what forms of error-handling need to be provided, and consider the effects of including these as:

  (a) part of the Structured Systems Analysis model;
  (b) extensions to the first-cut Structure Chart.

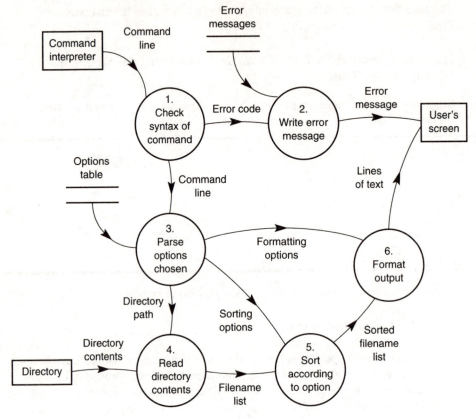

Figure 10.25   Data-Flow Diagram for Exercise 10.2.

11 Jackson System Development (JSD)

11.1 The JSD model

11.2 JSD representation forms

11.3 The JSD process

11.4 JSD heuristics

The JSD method emerged in the 1980s as a large-scale 'compositional' design strategy, based on the use of 'long-running' virtual processes to model the required system. Its detailed form evolved somewhat during the 1980s, although the changes were more in the nature of refinements and incorporation of accumulated experience, than major revisions of philosophy.

In this chapter we examine the concepts, forms and procedures of JSD, which shares much of the philosophy of JSP, although on a much larger scale of application. While JSD was intended for use with 'data-processing' problems, its use of parallelism and attention to time-ordering and event modelling has led to interest from the real-time design community, and there may well be some potential for further refinement and developments in the future.

11.1 The JSD model

Unlike the methods described in the preceding two chapters, which were devised in the early 1970s, JSD can be considered as a 'second-generation' software design method, since its development took place during the late 1970s and early 1980s. As a method, it encompasses both analysis and design activities, directed towards constructing a model of a system in terms of a set of 'long-running' interacting concurrent processes for its description, which is then transformed into a 'physical realization' of the model (namely, the detailed design). Although originally intended for use with the design of data-processing systems, JSD has the potential to be used in the design of a variety of problem domains, and the emphasis placed upon time-ordering of system activities makes it potentially well suited for use with large real-time systems as well.

JSD is generally regarded as having its roots in the thinking that stems from Hoare's ideas on communicating sequential processes (Hoare, 1978). In contrast to the SSA/SD design method described in the preceding chapter, JSD places emphasis on modelling the *actions* of the system in terms of their effects on the input and output data streams, rather than on using the direct functional tasks as the basis for the design model. As such, it is compositional rather than top-down in its form, and in some aspects it also comes close to the object-based paradigm that is described in the next chapter. Indeed, Henderson-Sellers and Edwards (1990) have argued that JSD occupies a midway point between these strategies.

JSD has undergone a certain amount of evolution since the original description in Jackson (1983). The form of the design process as described in Cameron (1986; 1988) contains some revisions to the design steps, while the description in Sutcliffe (1988) shows a rather different view of the structure of the method. This chapter examines both the original form of the method and the revisions it has undergone, together with some of the reasons for these.

JSD shares a number of major structural features with JSP, although its much larger problem domain means that it is correspondingly less prescriptive in nature. One of these common threads is the importance ascribed to incorporating time-ordering in the modelling process. JSD also shares with JSP the philosophy of using a model of the real world as the basis for system structure, meaning that changes in the external world can be mirrored as changes in the structure of the model, and eventually emerge as changes in the structure of the program(s).

The best framework for describing the broad process of JSD design is that provided by Sutcliffe (1988) and also used in Cameron (1988), where it is described in terms of the following three stages:

- a *modelling stage*, in which the problem is analysed and modelled in terms of the constituent entities and the actions that they perform,

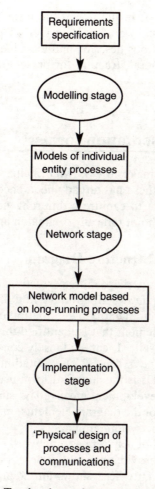

Figure 11.1 Top-level transformational model of JSD.

and where these entities are represented by 'long-running' sequential processes in the model itself;

- a *network stage*, in which the overall structure of the system is developed from that of the model by adding the details of interactions between entities, and between the entities and the external world;

- an *implementation stage*, in which the abstract design is mapped onto a 'physical' design.

Figure 11.1 shows these stages using the general transformational model we have adopted. (Note too that the terminology of JSD is sometimes somewhat idiosyncratic, as in the use of the term 'implementation' for a process that more normally would be described as 'physical design'.)

The following sections describe and examine the major features of JSD, using the same general structure for presentation as was adopted in the previous chapters.

11.2   JSD representation forms

The JSD design process makes use of two principal forms of diagrammatical description. One of these has already been encountered earlier in this book, but it is used here to capture a different viewpoint; the second is essentially new (although not radically original in any sense).

11.2.1   The Entity–Structure Diagram

This is an adaptation (or, perhaps more correctly, an interpretation) of the Jackson Structure Diagram described in Section 6.6. In JSD it is used to describe the 'evolution' of an entity over a period of time. In this context, an entity is an 'active' element that is identified through the operations of the modelling process itself. (It can be loosely considered to be a form of 'processing agent' in the system.) The notation used for an Entity–Structure Diagram (ESD) is the standard form used for a Structure Diagram, and the main development involved is simply one of making a different interpretation of the diagram elements, in order to adopt a rather different viewpoint of the system model.

In the JSD model of a system as a network of long-running sequential processes, the ESD provides a means of describing the behaviour of the sequential processes. Figure 11.2 shows an example of such an Entity–Structure Diagram, as developed for one of the entities in an Air Traffic Control (ATC) system (namely, an aircraft). For this problem, an aircraft has been identified as one of the entities whose behaviour should be modelled, and so this diagram is constructed as part of the modelling task. (The procedure for developing this diagram is described in the next section.)

Figure 11.3 shows the generic form of Structure Diagrams of this type; the overall basic sequence is concerned with:

- creation of the entity in the model;
- actions performed by the entity while in existence;
- deletion of the entity from the model.

An examination of Figure 11.2 shows that this conforms to this framework at the first level of abstraction. (Note that a JSD model is therefore

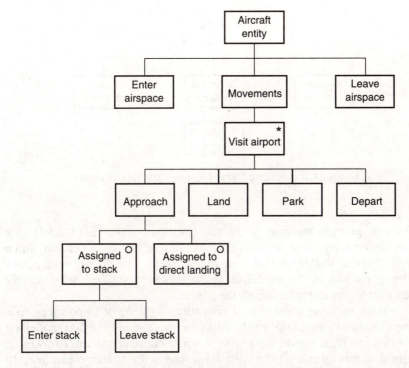

Figure 11.2 Example of an Entity–Structure Diagram (ESD) for an aircraft in an
Air Traffic Control system.

essentially of a dynamic nature, being concerned with specifying time-ordered behaviour.)

In this example, an aircraft becomes an entity of interest to the ATC system only when it crosses a boundary to enter the controlled airspace and it ceases to be of interest when it leaves that airspace. Between those events it might perform a number of actions, which can include:

- doing nothing (the aircraft just flies through);
- landing and taking off;
- being 'stacked' before landing.

This model allows for multiple occurrences of an aircraft being stacked, landing and taking off – although most of us would probably prefer that these events should be exceptional! Once again, time-ordering is import-ant: an aircraft must land before it can take off, and if it enters the landing stack, it must leave the stack before it can be assigned to the runway for landing.

For other systems, a suitable entity might be a person, as in Figure 11.4, describing a student who is on a course of some kind. Again, the

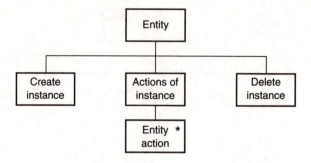

Figure 11.3   Generic form of Entity–Structure Diagram.

person in question becomes of interest (in terms of the JSD model) only when undertaking those actions that make him or her into a student, and a specific type of student at that (one registered for this course); and ceases to be of interest to the model on ceasing to be a student, whether this occurs through passing or failing the course.

Each of these examples of an entity might be of importance to a system designer using JSD. In the first case, we can assume that modelling aircraft behaviour would be required when constructing an Air Traffic Control system intended to provide assistance to the human controllers. In the second, in order to create a system that will be used to maintain student records, the designer will need this model of student activity in order to help identify all the situations that the system will be required to handle. (We will examine the criteria used for the selection of suitable entities in Section 11.3, where we study the JSD procedures.)

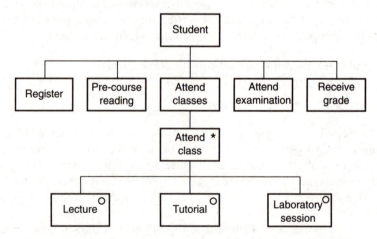

Figure 11.4   Entity–Structure Diagram for a student on a course.

Figure 11.5 The System Specification Diagram (SSD) for a pipeline (data stream).

11.2.2 The System Specification Diagram (SSD)

The System Specification Diagram is basically a network diagram that identifies the interactions between the entities that make up the model of the system. These interactions take place by two basic mechanisms for interprocess communication, which are:

- A *data-flow stream*, in which messages are passed asynchronously between the entities concerned, using some form of pipeline mechanism, as shown in Figure 11.5. A data-flow stream acts as an FIFO queue, and is assumed to have infinite buffer capacity, so that the producer process is never blocked on a write operation to the buffer of the stream. In contrast, the consumer process *is* blocked if it tries to read from a buffer when no message is available, as it has no means of checking whether data is available before issuing a read request.

- A *state vector* that describes the 'local state' of a process at a given time. By inspecting this state vector, one entity can obtain required information from a second entity, where this is contained in its current state. The state vector will typically consist of the local variables of a process, including its program counter which is used to indicate the current state of execution. (This concept applies to the long-running 'virtual' processes used in the designer's model as well as to the 'physical' processes used in the eventual implementation.) Figure 11.6 shows an example of state vector inspection. Since the 'inspected' process may also be executing during the inspection process, there is a degree of indeterminacy present in this mechanism.

The notation used for SSDs has further elements to denote such features as multiplicity of data transfer operations and multiplicity of processes.

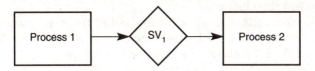

Figure 11.6 The SSD for a state vector inspection. Process 2 inspects the state vector of Process 1.

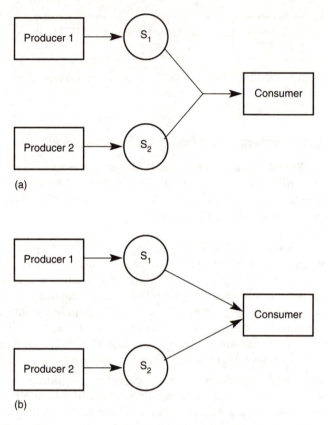

Figure 11.7 Processes with multiple input streams. (a) Using a rough-merged form. (b) Using separate 'read' operations.

In particular, where a process reads from more than one stream, we can distinguish between the cases in which data is read from either stream as available using the 'rough-merged' scheme (Figure 11.7(a)), and those in which the inputs remain distinct (Figure 11.7(b)). In the first case, the consumer is required to organize the handling of multiple inputs through one read operation, while in the latter it must organize the sequencing of consumption from the two sources. However, beyond observing the presence of these structures, we will not explore the SSD notation in any further depth in this chapter.

(To look a little way ahead at this point: there are some obvious similarities between these mechanisms and those used in MASCOT for the Channel and Pool structures, as described in Chapter 13. The parallel should not be drawn too closely though, as the SSD provides a much more abstract level of description than the ACP diagram, which is concerned with physical design objects and their interactions.)

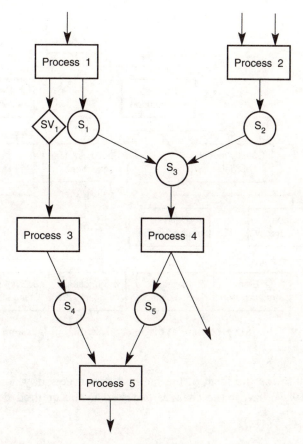

Figure 11.8 A simple example of a segment from an SSD.

Figure 11.8 shows an SSD describing a very simple network in a system. The circle is used to label a data-flow arc, and an entity is represented by using an oblong box. Those who are more accustomed to the conventional Data-Flow Diagram notations might find this confusing. The diamond shape used to describe the state vector is associated with a particular entity by means of the labelling attached to it.

11.3   The JSD process

The procedures involved in the 'process part' of JSD have undergone a certain amount of revision and repackaging since the method was first introduced. Figure 11.9 uses an Entity–Structure Diagram to describe the JSD process as it was originally presented in Jackson (1983), while

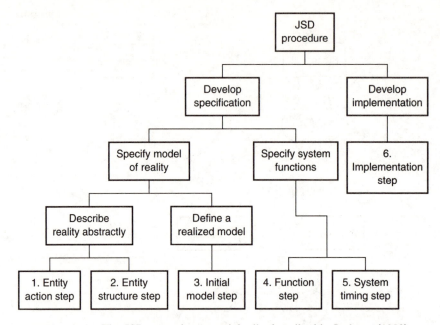

Figure 11.9   The JSD procedure as originally described in Jackson (1983).

Figure 11.10 shows the form of the method as subsequently described in Cameron (1986). Two basic changes occurred in the method during this interval:

- The first two steps of the method as it is described in Figure 11.9 have been merged in Figure 11.10. The change involved can be considered as being largely cosmetic, as the two steps are so closely related.

- The function step of Figure 11.9 has evolved into two separate steps in Figure 11.10 (the interactive function step and the information function step). We will examine the roles of these in a little more detail later. This modification is a more significant development than the previous one, since it gives additional structure to the design process for a task that is generally seen as posing difficult problems for the designer.

In Section 11.1 the JSD design process was also described in terms of the three-stage outline used more recently by both Sutcliffe (1988) and Cameron (1988a). These stages differ slightly from the abstractions used in the other two forms, and the corresponding mapping of the design activities is shown in Figure 11.11. By comparing this with the descriptions of the earlier forms, it can be seen that the modelling stage can be identified as

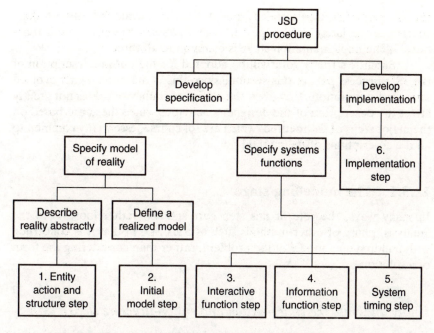

Figure 11.10 The JSD procedure as revised by Cameron (1986).

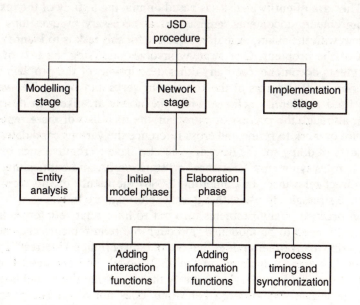

Figure 11.11 The three-stage model of JSD as used in Sutcliffe (1988) and
Cameron (1988a).

the first part of Jackson's 'specify model of reality', while the network stage comprises the latter part, together with Jackson's 'specify system functions'. (The implementation stage is common to all three.)

Sutcliffe's framework will be adopted for the outline description of the JSD process part in this section, since this is the most highly evolved structural description. However, the choice of framework does not greatly affect the description of the designer's activities, since these are based on the major steps of the method, which are, of course, essentially common to all the descriptions of the method.

11.3.1   The modelling stage

In many ways, the role of this step corresponds (rather loosely) to the 'analysis' phase of other methods such as SSA/SD, in that it is concerned with building up a model of the problem, rather than considering the form of a solution.

Entity analysis (the entity–action and entity–structure steps)

Jackson and others have recommended that a designer should begin this task by analysing the requirements documents in order to identify the entities in the system, the actions that they perform, the attributes of the actions, and the time-ordering of the actions.

This task of entity analysis is based on making a study of the text of the requirements documents, augmented as necessary by questions and interviews with the client. A major objective for this task is to identify the entities of the problem. One strategy involves analysing the text of the requirements documents (and any other descriptions of the problem that can be obtained) in terms of the constituent verbs and nouns. The verbs can be used to identify actions, while the nouns are likely to describe entities, although the process of extracting the final lists of these requires quite a lot of work to refine and cross-reference the various candidates. In the process of doing so, the designer will also have to remove such extraneous items as synonyms, 'existence' or 'state' verbs, and entities that are not of direct relevance. In Cameron (1988b) the nature of this step and alternative strategies to use within it are explored more fully.

In practice, many problems turn out to have relatively few entities that actually need to be modelled, although the requirements documents may describe many other entities that are of only peripheral interest. These other entities are not included in the JSD model, and are described as 'outside the model boundary'. An entity that is outside the model boundary is one whose time-ordered behaviour does not affect the problem directly, but which may act to constrain the entities used in the design model.

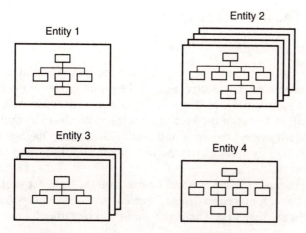

Figure 11.12 The JSD model at the end of the modelling stage. The notation is intended to indicate many instances of entities 2 and 3.

As an excellent example of this distinction between entities and items outside the model boundary, Jackson (1983) develops an example of a simple banking system. A major entity that is identified for the model is the 'customer', which performs such actions as opening and closing accounts, and paying in and withdrawing funds. The bank manager, on the other hand, is dismissed as being 'outside the model boundary', because modelling the time-ordered behaviour of the bank manager does not help with developing a model of how the banking system operates, which is the problem.

Once the entities and actions have been identified and correlated, the designer needs to add time-ordering to the list of actions for an entity. Figure 11.2 showed an example of the type of diagram that results from doing this, namely a Structure Diagram that describes an entity (in that case, an aircraft). As a further part of this task of analysis, the analyst will also seek to identify those attributes of the aircraft's actions that are of interest to the modelling. These may include information about:

- flight number
- call-sign
- position

and any other features that may be of assistance in distinguishing any one aircraft from the others in the airspace at a given time.

Figure 11.12 shows in a symbolic manner the state of the JSD model at the end of the modelling stage. At this point in the design process the model consists of a set of (disjoint) process models for the major entities of the problem.

11.3.2   The network stage

The initial model phase

This phase involves the designer in linking the entities defined in the first step, and beginning the construction of the initial model of the system as a whole. Not surprisingly, as this initial model is concerned with modelling the interactions between the various entities, it produces a combination of System Specification Diagrams and Entity–Structure Diagrams, with the added functionality arising from the fact that the operations of this step are contained in the SSDs.

The task of creating a model begins with the designer seeking to find the input that is required to 'trigger' each action of an entity that has been identified in the first step. Each such input will be either:

- an input corresponding to an event that arises externally to the system – for example, the radar detects a new aircraft in the control zone;
- an input generated internally by the system – for example, when interest is added to the bank account every six months.

This step is concerned with identifying instances of the first group of inputs, while the modelling task involving the second group forms the subject of the next phase (through the interactive function step).

The procedure for identifying the inputs is first to identify the external actions of the model, and then to determine how the corresponding event for each one of them will be detected in the real (external) world. For example, for the Air Traffic Control system, we can see that a new aircraft entity will usually be instantiated when the radar detects a new signal in the control area, and so this external event can be linked with a particular action of the entity (in this case, the 'action' of being created).

A part of this task of adding inputs (and outputs) to the model processes involves the designer in choosing the forms that these will take (data stream or state vector). Initial decisions may also be required where multiple data-stream inputs are required (for example, deciding whether or not to adopt a rough merge).

Tasks such as error-handling may also be included at this stage, although, as with all design methods, this needs to be kept at a suitable level of abstraction. However, such system needs as the detection of spurious events and their removal would certainly need to be identified in this phase.

On completion of this phase the designer should possess a fairly complete diagrammatical representation of the basic design model, together with textual descriptions of the properties that are to be associated with the actions performed by the entities.

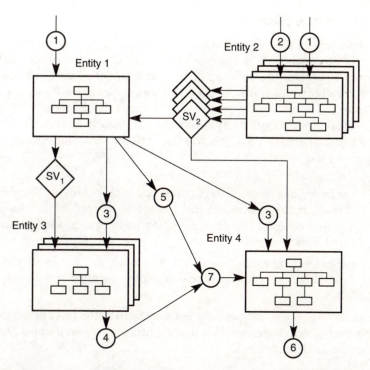

Figure 11.13 The JSD model at the end of the initial model phase of the network stage.

It is during this second stage that the designer begins to transform the model of the problem into a model of the solution. However, it is important to appreciate that the model developed during this stage is still relatively abstract. It may well be expressed as being formed from a very large (impractically large) number of sequential processes running concurrently. Figure 11.13 shows the state of the JSD design model at the end of this initial model phase, using the same form as before. Resolving this model into a practical detailed design is a task that is deferred until as late as possible, and so the elaboration phase continues to build on the same abstract model.

The first two steps of the elaboration phase (essentially corresponding to the rather complex function step of the original descriptions of the JSD process) provide a less well-defined set of actions for the designer than those of the initial model phase, since they are concerned with making a major design transformation, and one that is driven very strongly by the problem domain and the problem itself. While JSD is relatively prescriptive in the early analysis steps, this part of the network stage requires much more in the way of creative thinking.

The elaboration phase

The main role of this phase was identified in the description of the role of the previous phase. It is through the activities of this phase that the designer completes the creation of the basic model of the problem, and begins creating a model that is concerned with the solution, by adding extra processes to the network to perform the system-related tasks.

This major transformation was not particularly well defined in the earliest descriptions of JSD, but was later refined into two separate transformation tasks, which are:

- the *interactive function* step, concerned with identifying those events that affect the system and that cannot be derived from considering external actions, and then designing additional processes that will provide these events;
- the *information function* step, which adds the processes and data flows that are required for generating the eventual system outputs.

This phase is now also seen as incorporating most of the tasks of the former *system timing* step, which involves making decisions about the synchronization of the model processes.

Elaboration phase 1: the interactive function step

An example of such a function has already been mentioned, namely that of adding interest to a bank account at predetermined intervals. While 'normal' transactions can be identified through examination of a customer's actions (paying-in using a deposit slip, or withdrawing funds using an auto-teller), this one arises as a function of the system, and so is not among the actions identified for a major entity of the design. So in this part of the modelling phase, the designer needs to identify such actions of the system, and to determine how they are to be incorporated into the design model.

The recommended procedure for this task is to examine the original requirements specification again, this time with the aim of identifying some of the issues that were not dealt with in the initial model. In particular, at this point the designer is required to consider in turn each action that needs to be internally generated, and *when* this action should be generated. The output from this analysis might be expressed in terms of other actions ('when the day of the week is a Friday') or of some form of external input. The designer may also need further information from the model to determine the details of the actions to be performed, together with the values of their associated attributes.

The refinements to the design model that result from the decisions made in this step will involve:

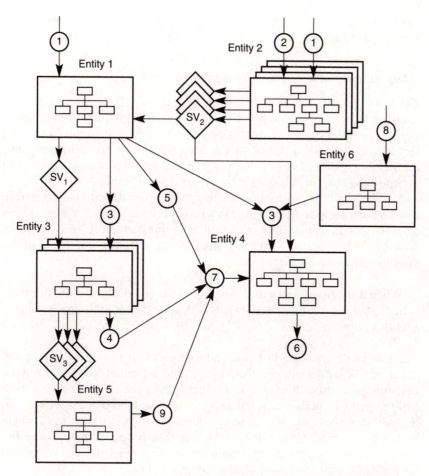

Figure 11.14   The JSD model at the end of the interactive function step
(elaboration phase of the network stage).

- adding ESDs that describe the behaviour of the new processes
  required for these functions;
- revising the SSD (or SSDs) which describes the system, to show the
  extra processes and the interactions that they will have with the rest
  of the model.

Figure 11.14 shows the state of the symbolic JSD model at the end of this
step of the elaboration phase, including the new processes that have been
added during this step. (In the example represented by Figure 11.14, it has
been assumed for simplicity that the SSD is simply extended to incorporate
the changes arising from this step. However, this is likely to be rather

unrealistic for any real system, since adding new processes may well also require modifications to be made to the existing form of the SSD.)

Elaboration phase 2: the information function step

Up to this point, the JSD modelling process has been concerned with handling system inputs, and it is only at this stage that the JSD designer begins to consider how the system outputs are to be generated. In particular, the design task involved in this step is centred on identifying how information will need to be extracted from the model processes, in order to generate the outputs required in the original specification.

Many of the rules for determining the outputs that are required from a system are likely to be provided in a relatively 'rule-based' manner in the original specification. They may well be expressed using such forms as 'when x,y and z occur, then the system should output p and q', as in the example requirement that:

> 'When it is Friday, and within six days of the end of the month, print a bank statement for the account, and calculate the monthly charges due at this point.'

The task of determining how such a requirement is to be met in terms of the model is somewhat less prescriptive than we might like it to be. One recommended procedure is first to identify how the information can best be obtained (through a data stream or from a state vector inspection); to assume that the task of extracting this can be performed by a single process; and then to use JSP to design that process. In practice, the complexity of the processing required may well need the use of several processes, in order to resolve JSP structure clashes.

Once again, the effect of this step is to further refine and extend the process network, and hence the SSD(s) describing it, and to create yet more ESDs to describe the actions of the additional processes. Figure 11.15 shows the effects of this step in terms of its effect upon the symbolic JSD model. However, at this point the task of network development is relatively complete, and so the designer can begin to consider the behavioural aspects of the system in greater detail.

Elaboration phase 3: the system timing step

Up to this point, the JSD design model describing the designer's solution has effectively been based on the assumption that it consists of a network of essentially equal processes. However, this will often be an unrealistic assumption, and one of the major tasks of the present step is to determine the relative priorities that will exist among processes. For example, in an Air Traffic Control system, we may be regarding the processing of the

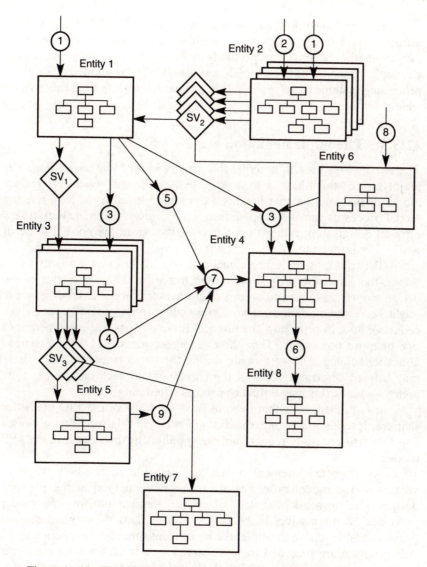

Figure 11.15   The JSD model at the end of the information function step
(elaboration phase of the network stage).

signals from the primary and secondary radars as of higher priority than
(say) the updating of a display screen.

This in turn leads to consideration of the scheduling of processes
(remember, though, that we are still talking about a model, not about actual
physical processes). The consideration of how processes are scheduled, and
by what criteria, helps with determining the basic hierarchy for these
processes, and this hierarchy forms the principal output from this step.

It is perhaps this stage, in particular, that makes JSD appear very attractive as a design method for real-time systems, although on closer inspection the benefits are probably not as great as might be hoped. Certainly, though, although JSD was essentially developed with data-processing systems largely in mind, it is capable of being used much more widely.

11.3.3   The implementation stage

The terminology used to describe this activity is apt to be misleading. The major task of this phase is to determine how the still relatively abstract model of the solution that has been developed in terms of long-running model processes can be mapped onto a physical system. It is therefore a physical design step, rather than 'implementation' in the normal sense of writing program code.

This phase is therefore concerned with determining, among other things, the forms that may best be used to realize the components of the design model, such as state vectors and processes (in the latter case, some might be realized as physical processes, while others could become procedures); and, in turn, how the physical processes are to be mapped onto one or more processors. This phase is also constrained by the decisions about scheduling that were made during the network phase, since these may help to determine some of the choices about such features as hierarchy, and how this may influence process scheduling.

It is in this phase that most use can be made of the JSD heuristics that are described in the next section. (There are relatively few of these, and they are generally recognizable as parallels to those used in the JSP model.)

An important element of this step is to determine how the state vectors of the model processes are to be implemented in the physical design. The form adopted will, of course, depend on how the model processes are themselves to be realized, as well as the implementation forms available. As an example, the concurrent threads of execution in an Ada program are provided by tasks, and where these are contained in a single compilation unit (or package), they can have shared access to data, types and constants, and so can be used to model the state vector mechanism quite closely. However, if the model processes are mapped onto (say) MASCOT Activities (as described in Chapter 13), then each will occupy its own virtual address space, and there is no mechanism that permits direct access to the address space of another process. So in such a physical implementation form, a quite separate mechanism needs to be provided for the state vector form of communication. (These issues will be examined again in Chapter 13.)

Figure 11.16 shows the Transformation Diagram for the complete JSD design process (as always, this omits any of the revisions or iterations

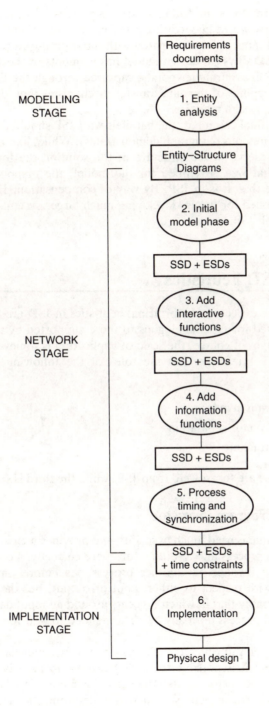

Figure 11.16 The complete JSD transformation model.

that will normally occur during the design process). One feature of this that is particularly worth highlighting is the more comprehensive nature of the final design model when compared with those produced from JSP or SSA/SD. The JSD physical design model has elements of the structural, functional and behavoural viewpoints, captured through the ESDs, SSDs and physical mappings of the data transfer mechanisms that together make up the physical design model.

As a final comment, the parallels with JSP should not be drawn too far (as the previous paragraph demonstrates). While, like JSP, this method seeks to preserve in the structure of the solution the form of the basic structure that was developed for the model, the mapping is much less prescriptive than it is in JSP. By way of compensation, JSD is a method that is intended for use in developing much larger systems than would be possible with JSP.

11.4   JSD heuristics

As might be expected, the principal heuristics in JSD are largely (but not entirely) used for tasks analogous to those supported by the heuristics of JSP, although, of course, the scale of application is somewhat larger. This section very briefly reviews the roles of the following three forms of heuristic:

- program inversion
- state vector separation
- backtracking

Two of these are 'borrowed' from JSP, while the third is specific to JSD.

11.4.1   Program inversion

This technique is used much as in JSP, and provides a means of transforming a model process into a routine (or, more correctly, a coroutine), which can then be invoked by another process. As before, inversion can be organized with respect to either input or output, but the most common form is probably that in which it occurs around an input data stream, with the inverted process normally being suspended to wait for input from that stream.

One point in which the JSD model differs somewhat from that used in JSP is that it is possible for a JSD process to have both data-stream inputs and state vector inputs. The use of inversion is really only appropriate for data-stream inputs, which are deterministic and well-formed, whereas state vector inputs are essentially nondeterministic (the value obtained will depend upon exactly when the state vector was last updated) and so do not fit well into the inversion mechanism.

Program inversion is essentially a technique used during the implementation stage, when the designer begins to consider the detailed organization of a solution. Prior to that, the design activities are based on a more abstract model and are less concerned with the actual details of physical program organization.

11.4.2 State vector separation

This heuristic is specific to the multiple-process nature of the JSD model, and has no real analogy in JSP. It is used to improve efficiency where a JSD model has many processes of a given type. For example, in the ATC problem there might be many instances of the 'aircraft' process; and in a banking system there might be many instances of the 'customer' process. All the instances of a particular process can use the same code to describe its structure, but each will require to store different values for the local variables that define its state.

The situation is analogous to that which often obtains in multi-processing operating systems, where one solution adopted to improve memory utilization is 're-entrancy'. This involves the system in maintaining copies of the data areas used by each process, but storing only one copy of the code. (The data area for a process includes its program counter, used to determine which parts of the code are to be executed when it resumes.)

The method used to handle multiple instances of a process in JSD is to adopt a more abstract version of the above, and the design task involved is concerned with organizing the details of the re-entrant structures. The term used for this is 'state vector separation'. Since this is a task that is very much concerned with the physical mapping of the solution, it is normally performed during the final implementation stage.

11.4.3 Backtracking

Once again, the basic concepts involved in this heuristic have been derived from the experience of JSP. However, unlike the previous two heuristics, this one is normally used during the initial analysis tasks, rather than in the later stages of the design activity.

Backtracking helps handle the unexpected events that might occur in an entity's life history, such as its premature end. Once again, the purpose of this heuristic is to restructure any untidy nested tests and selections, and to handle those iterations whose completion may be uncertain. The details are largely similar to those of the technique used in JSP and we will not go into any further detail here.

Overall, the principal JSD heuristics are as prescriptive as might be expected for such a method, and compare not unfavourably with those used in the much less ambitious JSP. Perhaps the main point to make, though, is the relative lack of any heuristics that can be used with the (more rigorous) early stages of modelling – which is where it would be useful to be provided with some means of utilizing the experience of others.

SUMMARY

The JSD method provides a very different set of abstractions for use by the designer from those described in the preceding chapter. And, as will be evident from the material of this chapter, JSD is a relatively extensive design method that does not readily lend itself to being used in any form of subset. Indeed, there are good arguments why we should not use JSD on small systems, since the activities involved in following the full JSD procedures are apt to be lengthy, and hence out of proportion to the benefits that are likely to be obtained from its use (Floyd, 1986). That is not an argument for not using JSD at all, simply one for using it only where appropriate. (To complain that a tractor does not have the acceleration of a sports car is to miss the point of its purpose and effectiveness in much the same manner.)

The larger scale of application of JSD means that it is less prescriptive than JSP, while sharing much of the basic philosophy about design. However, it is the later stages of JSD that are less prescriptive (particularly the information function step and the system timing step), while the initial analysis and model-building are much more highly structured.

The role of the implementation stage is also important, for it is in this transformation to a physical design that it is possible to undo many of the benefits of a good structure. Again, the JSD guidelines for this task are rather less extensive than might be hoped, but as we have continually observed throughout this book, this is in the nature of the design problem itself, and there are definite bounds upon the degree of rigorous guidance that we can expect.

Overall, though, the argument that JSD as a compositional method is more systematic than the decompositional approach illustrated in Chapter 10 seems to be justified. The early analysis steps are relatively rigorous, and the 'creative' activities are deferred until a fairly sound model has been constructed. However, as we have also observed in the earlier parts of this book, any attempts to draw comparisons between design methods are apt to be two-edged, and we should particularly beware of drawing comparisons about the design strategy when it is considered apart from a particular problem or problem domain.

There is now a quite solid base of experience with the use of JSD in the development process. In particular, there is some support available in terms of introductory textbooks, and particularly in terms of good case-study material – Cameron (1988a) and Sutcliffe (1988) contain quite extensive case-study material. As a method, it may still be capable of further development, and it has certainly exercised a wide influence on design thinking.

FURTHER READING

The range of textbooks currently available is still relatively limited, although the existing ones complement each other quite well in terms of approach and style.

Cameron J. (1988). *JSP and JSD: The Jackson Approach to Software Development*. 2nd edn. Washington DC and Los Alamitos, California: IEEE Computer Society Press

The author has been one of the codevelopers of JSD, and has published quite widely on its application. Somewhat more than half of the book is dedicated to JSD, and while, like all IEEE tutorials, it is largely composed of reprinted papers, it has a much stronger tutorial element than is usual. A major source-book, but not so well suited to providing an initial introduction.

Sutcliffe A. (1988). *Jackson System Development*. London: Prentice-Hall

A compact book, written with a clear style, and providing two useful case studies in its appendices. It is not extensive enough to act as a complete practitioner's guide, but would provide a good introduction to the techniques of the method.

Ingevaldsson L. (1990). *Software Engineering Fundamentals: The Jackson Approach*. Bromley, Kent: Chartwell-Bratt

A short text that is constructed around a running example. It has a rather strong DP flavour, and the author makes excellent use of annotated diagrams to help make his points.

EXERCISES

11.1 Construct an Entity–Structure Diagram (ESD) that describes:

(a)   the 'customer' of a public lending library;
(b)   the operational cycle of an automatic washing machine;
(c)   the 'customer' of a car-hire firm.

11.2 Where a process has two data streams, there is a choice between receiving data from these separately and combining the data flow using rough merge. Discuss the benefits and disadvantages of each scheme, and for each one suggest an instance in which it would be appropriate to use such a form.

11.3 For the lending library of Exercise 11.1(a) above, consider what operations of a library records and issues system will need to be modelled by using:

(a)   interaction function processes;
(b)   information function processes.

12 Object-Oriented and Object-Based Design

12.1 Introducing the notion of the 'object'

12.2 Design practices for the object-oriented paradigm

12.3 Object-Based Design (HOOD)

12.4 Object-Oriented Design

12.5 HOOD: an outline example

This chapter examines a set of design abstractions and practices that differ quite markedly from those described in the previous chapters. At a very simple level, this can be regarded as a change in strategy from modelling action-oriented abstractions (functions, operations, processes, entities) to modelling abstractions based more directly on the concept of the abstract data type (ADT). Creating the design model is then no longer based on design elements performing actions but instead is based on design elements that have things done to them.

The first part of this chapter examines the nature of objects and considers their potential as design abstractions. It then goes on to review some current practices in the design of systems around these abstractions.

12.1   Introducing the notion of the 'object'

12.1.1   The scope of the problem

This chapter is concerned with what must be the most incompletely developed of the design strategies that are described in this book. To some degree this lack of a set of clear design practices has been compounded by the extent to which the term 'object-oriented' has acquired multiple interpretations, and, indeed, two distinct interpretations of this term will be examined in this chapter. (To help distinguish between the general and the specific, the term 'object-oriented', in lower case, will be used when referring to the general paradigm; upper-case leading letters will be used for the specific methods that are based on this strategy.)

The development of 'object-oriented' systems (regardless for the moment of the exact interpretation of the term) received much attention in the 1980s and early 1990s. Unfortunately, this has not led to any consensus about the meaning of the relevant concepts, nor to any very prescriptive design methods based on them. Indeed, the words used by Tim Rentsch (1982) now seem to have been truly prophetic:

'My guess is that object-oriented programming will be in the 1980s what structured programming was in the 1970s. Everyone will be in favour of it. Every manufacturer will promote his products as supporting it. Every manager will pay lip service to it. Every programmer will practice it (differently). And no one will know just what it is.'

The shift of viewpoint that the object-oriented paradigm involves is one that reflects the development of the imperative programming languages used to implement so many systems. Early programming languages such as FORTRAN and COBOL provided powerful structures for expressing actions, but had only relatively primitive forms for modelling the relationships that could exist between the data elements of a program. In the evolution that has led to the more recent imperative programming languages, such as Ada, Modula-2, C++ and Eiffel, and through the influences of Pascal and Smalltalk especially, there has been a gradually changing emphasis, with increasing support within a language for implementing and using abstract data types.

When designing an abstract data type, one normally seeks to establish the properties of the type elements, and to identify the operations that are performed upon them. In doing so, it is good practice to avoid making any implementation-specific assumptions and decisions. Given that information-hiding practices are now better supported by modern programming languages, it is not surprising that there has been a corresponding interest in developing and constructing systems based on the concept of the ADT, and much of this can be grouped under the heading 'object-oriented'.

Unfortunately, the relative success of the development of ways of implementing object-oriented structures (frequently termed 'object-oriented programming structures' or OOPS) has not been matched by the same degree of success in designing around these concepts. The various techniques and procedures that may be collected under the heading of 'object-oriented design' (or OOD) have yet to provide any really satisfactory systematic practices for developing a design model centred on any form of 'objects'.

While this chapter cannot hope to provide a detailed 'road-map' through this shifting terrain, it will seek to:

- identify some ideas about the nature of an 'object';
- describe some design practices that are based on modelling of objects and their interactions;
- provide some general pointers to other work in this field.

The rest of this introductory section is therefore largely concerned with the first of these points.

12.1.2   A brief history

The full history of the 'object concept' is quite long and complex; perhaps the best review of the whole object-oriented paradigm is given in Booch (1991), which includes a survey of historical issues. For our purposes, a much briefer outline covering a number of salient points should suffice.

The digital computer is basically an *action-oriented* device: its primitive operations (instructions) are concerned with actions (arithmetical operations, logical operations, copying of data, and so on). So it is not surprising that the early programming tools were themselves action-oriented in nature. Assembler code and early high-level languages such as FORTRAN have forms that are almost entirely concerned with describing the structure of actions, and provide little in the way of facilities for modelling *data structures*. Figure 12.1 shows the way in which the balance between these has evolved with programming language development.

So it is hardly surprising that the longer-established software design methods have generally provided an action-oriented emphasis in their approach to the construction of a model for a solution, with functional decomposition providing a rather extreme example of such a design strategy. Only in the more recent forms, such as that of JSD, do we see a more even balance occurring between the elements of the model that are concerned with the actions and those concerned with the data. Even then, the design steps themselves are still directed towards developing the model by considering action-oriented features of a problem.

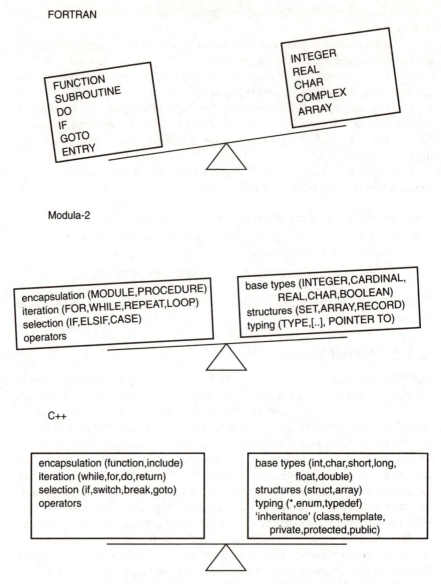

Figure 12.1 The relative distribution of programming language features between actions and data-modelling.

However, quite early on in the development of programming tools, the idea of modelling the structure of a problem around the concept of 'passive' objects of some form began to be explored. Simula in particular is generally considered a significant forerunner of the development of the object-oriented paradigm, not least for its introduction of the 'class', a concept which will be considered later in this section. (Such an approach to modelling a problem could perhaps be considered as 'noun-oriented' rather than 'verb-oriented'.) The Smalltalk system extended this model still further and introduced these concepts to a much wider audience.

In a relatively early and highly influential paper, David Parnas (1972) had already identified the benefits that could be gained through designing on the principle of information-hiding, which, as will be seen in the next subsection, is one of the characteristics of an object-oriented system. However, Parnas recognized that, while the principle was valuable, it was difficult to find any procedural form of design action that could be used for generating designs in such a way as to ensure they would possess the necessary properties. Unfortunately, as we will see, it appears that the efforts of the next two decades have failed to improve upon this position to any significant degree.

However, while the idea of information-hiding (encapsulation) might not have been easily incorporated into design practice, it has certainly been widely adopted in the design of new programming languages. Particular examples include the Modula-2 MODULE construct, and the Ada package.

12.1.3 The properties that distinguish an object

The concept of an 'object' is a relatively elusive one. It is certainly more easily identified in terms of solution-oriented concepts than of problem-oriented concepts, which perhaps reflects the relatively early stage of development of the techniques of what can best be termed 'object-oriented analysis' when compared with those of design. There are still relatively few research papers addressing this problem of analysis, and very few books – Coad and Yourdon (1991a) and Shlaer and Mellor (1988) being perhaps the best-known of these.

For our purposes, we can regard an object as some form of entity that performs computations and has some kind of local state that may be modified by the computations. On this basis, an object possesses a *state*, exhibits *behaviour*, and has some form of distinct *identity*, as illustrated in Figure 12.2. (In many ways, this is very close to the concept of an abstract data type, although perhaps we would not usually consider that an ADT 'performs computations'.)

While this is hardly a rigorous definition, it is sufficient for us to be able to identify the prime characteristic of an object, which is this unification of algorithmic components and data abstraction. This combination of two different aspects that need to be described through the use of all four of the major viewpoints (function, behaviour, structure, data modelling) in turn creates two of the main characteristics of a design that has been developed using object-oriented principles: that it will possess

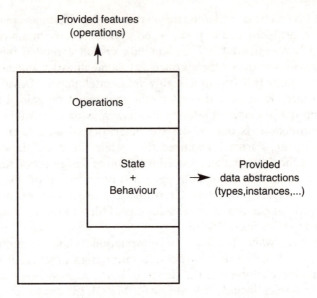

Figure 12.2   The basic properties of an object.

- relatively little global data; and
- a structure that is a network, rather than a tree.

This can be compared to the form of design produced by a procedure such as Structured Design, as described in Chapter 10. The description of the resulting solution can be represented as a Structure Chart, which is of course treelike in form; as the method provides no direct guidelines for creating local data structures, any data structures in the solution are likely to be global in scope.

An object-oriented model adds a framework to this basic concept of an object, in order to make what Booch terms the 'object model'. Booch considers that this model has four major elements:

- abstraction
- encapsulation
- modularity
- hierarchy

and these are briefly reviewed below. (We should note here that some authors merge modularity with encapsulation.)

Abstraction

Abstraction has already been identified as playing a major role in the design process in general. It is concerned with describing the external view of an object (that is, the 'essential features'). It provides a concise description of that object, which can then be used to reason about its behaviour, and about its relationships with other objects, without a need to possess any knowledge about its internal details.

It is an essential property for any form of design object that its characteristics should be capable of being identified in an abstract manner. For the 'object-oriented' forms of design process, abstraction performs an important role in modelling the objects in a system, and indeed object-oriented design is largely about how to select the 'correct' set of abstractions for use in modelling a problem.

Encapsulation

This is basically another term by which to describe the concept of information-hiding, whereby we seek to conceal those features of an object that are not essential to its abstraction. By concealing the implementation details of an object, it is then much easier to make changes to them without creating side-effects for the system as a whole. Obviously, the concepts of abstraction and encapsulation are largely complementary, and some authors would not separate them in this list of properties.

Modularity

Again, this concept is one that we have already encountered in a number of different forms. Basically it is concerned with partitioning the model of a system into individual components (often termed 'separation of concerns'), and an important criterion in evaluating any choice of components is the complexity of the interfaces between the resulting modules.

For many action-oriented design strategies, the basic level of modularity is the subprogram, and the interconnection mechanism is a combination of the subprogram-calling mechanism (invocation) and the parametrization of the subprogram interface. For the object-oriented strategies, this concept takes on a somewhat wider connotation, and the form of the corresponding interface may be more complex in nature.

The 'correct' choice of modules is in many ways as critical for the success of any design process as the choice of abstractions. However, it is also a more implementation-based decision, and one that may need to take into account the features of the programming language that is to be used to realize the design, as well as the configuration of the hardware components of the final system.

Hierarchy

Hierarchy is mainly concerned with establishing some form of ranking for the abstractions that make up the system model. In the case of Structured

Design, the abstractions will usually be realized as subprograms, and so the appropriate form of hierarchy to consider is that of subprogram invocation. For the object-oriented paradigm we need to consider two further hierarchies, which are based on:

- class structure
- interdependency of objects (the 'uses' relationship)

Class hierarchy   The hierarchy based on class structure leads us to consider the concept of **inheritance**, by which the properties of an object can be derived from the properties of other objects. The question of the relative importance of inheritance for object-oriented design comes close to being a theological issue. Since there seem to be no design practices that are currently able to handle this feature, although it is well supported by programming language structures, we will focus our attention solely on identifying some of its major features, and will not attempt to classify its use.

The concept of a class can be considered a natural development of the concept of a *type* as used in a programming language. While the concept of type is normally applied to data objects (including the data elements of ADTs), the class notion is much more general, and a class can be considered an abstraction of an object, with an object forming an instance of a class. We can therefore expect that a class specification will describe behavioural features as well as data structures and that, further, these features may be made *visible* to other objects or kept *private* to the class.

In a programming language it is possible to construct new types from existing types, typically by compounding them in some way (records, sets, arrays), or by defining a subrange type. We can do much the same sort of thing with classes, but the associated inheritance mechanism used to create subclasses is much more complex than that needed for creating dependent types, since it needs to incorporate not just static data relationships but also behavioural qualities.

The members of a class will share common structures and common features of behaviour. For example, a bank may provide customers with many different forms of account, which may have different rules about how interest is paid, how charges will be applied, the minimum balance required, withdrawal notice, and so on. However, all these forms are clearly recognizable as members of the class of bank account, and share some common structures, such as:

- current balance
- identity of owner
- date of creation

as well as some common operations, such as:

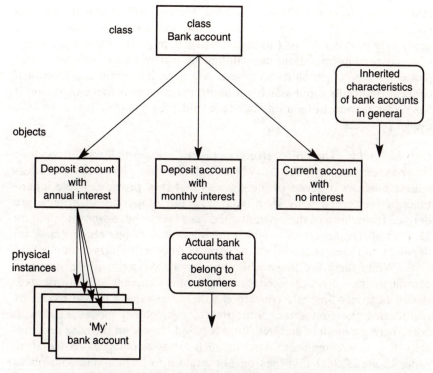

Figure 12.3 The concepts of class and inheritance.

- creation of a new account
- addition of interest
- withdrawal of part of the balance

For this example, therefore, the class of 'bank account' provides a description of these common properties and behaviour, while the detailed form of a particular type of account will depend on the rules applying to that subclass. (For example, some accounts may pay no interest, others may pay interest annually, quarterly or monthly, and so on.) The behaviour of the eventual physical objects (*my* bank account) will, of course, also depend on the values assigned to the data structures (the *amount* of my current balance). For design purposes however, the designer is only concerned with the abstractions involved in the class (bank account), and the subclasses (three-year account, current account, high-interest deposit account, and so on). Figure 12.3 illustrates these points concerning the class concept.

Inheritance is the mechanism by which objects acquire the general properties of their subclass, including those inherited from the parent class(es). (It is this relationship that forms the hierarchy associated with inheritance.) In our example, any bank account will inherit the general properties of bank accounts in general, but may have some features that apply only to that subclass (minimum balance, interest period, and so on), while some of its operations may contain algorithms that apply only to that particular type of account. So inheritance is an important constructional concept (hence its rapid assimilation into programming languages), but it has so far proved to be a difficult task to design this class hierarchy into design practices.

Uses hierarchy   The object structure hierarchy essentially corresponds to the uses relationship (Parnas, 1979) and it describes a hierarchy that exists among modules in terms of the services that they provide. While inheritance is concerned with identifying how the properties of objects are derived from those of their parents, the uses hierarchy, as shown in Figure 12.4, identifies the extent to which the operations of one object (module) depend upon the availability of the services of other objects (modules).

While there are those who consider the concept of inheritance as central to the object-oriented paradigm, many current 'object-oriented' design practices are only concerned with developing a design model by considering the first three properties of the 'object model', and with constructing a module hierarchy that is based largely on the uses relationship. It is now common to describe such forms as being *object-based*, in order to make clear that they do not attempt to include decisions about inheritance, and this terminology will be used in the rest of this chapter and wherever this distinction requires to be made.

The description provided in this section should not be considered as forming a definitive framework. Booch identifies other (minor) elements besides these four (namely typing, concurrency and persistence), and other authors place less emphasis on modularity (Coad and Yourdon, 1991b).

A valuable contribution to capturing the essentials of the 'abstract object model' is provided in Snyder (1993), which summarizes an attempt to draw up a list of 'core concepts' for such a model, which will avoid the confusions caused by variations in terminology. For this model, an object is considered to be

'an identifiable entity that plays a visible role in providing a service that a client (user or program) can request.'

A summary of the core concepts of the proposed model is given below: it seems to summarize the issues of the object-oriented paradigm very well.

- *Objects embody an abstraction* that is meaningful to their clients.
- *Objects provide services* characterizing the abstraction that is embodied in an object, where such a service may access or modify data within an object and may affect other objects.

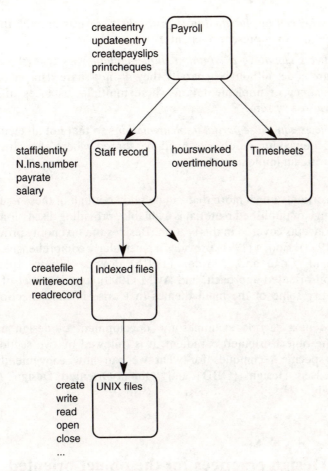

Figure 12.4 Examples of the uses hierarchy between objects.

- *Clients issue requests* for the services that are provided by objects.
- *Objects are encapsulated* so that clients cannot directly access or manipulate data associated with objects.
- *Requests identify operations* in terms of the service that an object is required to provide.
- *Requests can identify objects*, so that in issuing a request a client can identify the object that should service it.
- *New objects can be created* to support parallel operations and the time-varying behaviour of a system.
- *Operations can be generic* in that a service can have different implementations for different objects.

- *Objects can be classified in terms of their services* through the interface that they present to clients.

- *Objects can have a common implementation* so that objects may share code, although generally they do not share data, making for efficiency of implementation where multiple instances of objects exist in a system.

- *Objects can share partial implementations* so that not all elements of the behaviour of objects need be shared where the objects are sharing an implementation.

There is certainly much more that can be said about all of these issues, and a wide range of published material is available, providing discussions of the various concepts covered in this section. Besides the taxonomy provided in Snyder (1993), Booch (1991) provides a particularly comprehensive review of the field; Coad and Yourdon (1991b) provide a more specifically application-oriented approach; and ACM (1990) contains a set of papers that identify some of the main themes that arise in the object-oriented paradigm.

The next section examines the development of design methods around the object-oriented paradigm; it is followed by two sections that examine specific techniques for what we can now conveniently term 'Object-Based Design' (OBD) and 'Object-Oriented Design' (OOD) respectively.

12.2 Design practices for the object-oriented paradigm

In the preceding section, it was remarked that in identifying the benefits that could be obtained through using the principle of information-hiding, Parnas (1972) also recognized that it was difficult to produce such structures by following any well-formed set of procedures. By the time that the object-oriented philosophy began to coalesce in the late 1970s, it was obvious that this difficulty with providing any form of design process that handled encapsulation still remained as a significant problem, and, indeed, that the problems were increased by the wider scope of the object-oriented model.

A further spur to finding a design process that encompassed object-oriented principles came from the development of Ada, which became an ANSI standard in 1983. While Ada is not strictly an Object-Oriented programming language, it can be considered to be Object-Based in its form, since the structures of Ada support the use of:

- abstraction, both in terms of data typing and through the generic mechanism, with the latter allowing for some abstraction in the description of the algorithmic part;
- encapsulation, since the scope of data instances can be controlled via the private/public mechanism;
- modularity, through the use of the package construct (and arguably by using the task and the procedure).

However, although Ada has its generic mechanism, which can be used to support a definition of an abstract data type that is not bound to any specific base types, this is really a form of 'template' rather than a means of providing inheritance. (A good summary of Ada is provided in Barnes (1989), while the Appendix to Booch (1991) provides an analysis of a number of programming languages, including Ada, and evaluates the features of each one in terms of its object-oriented characteristics.)

Abbott (1983) proposed a strategy for developing a design around 'object-oriented' concepts in such a way that it could be implemented using the main features of Ada. His approach was based on identification of the objects in a textual narrative describing a solution. This was developed and extended by Grady Booch in the first edition of his book *Software Engineering with Ada* (Booch, 1983). Booch also added a diagrammatical notation to assist in describing the final structure of a design. The main steps in this design strategy are:

- produce a written description of a 'rough' design solution;
- analyse this description in terms of the nouns and the verbs, using the former to help with identifying the design objects and the latter to help with identifying the operations (or 'methods') associated with the objects;
- refine the descriptions of the objects to help produce a more complete solution.

The next section will look further at this strategy, and so we will not pursue it at this point, other than to observe that, while this technique can undoubtedly be made to work successfully, it does not readily scale up for use with very large systems. Its use also requires the designer to possess some initial degree of intuitive understanding of how a solution might be formed, in order to help with producing the initial rough design. These points were recognized by Booch, and in the second edition of *Software Engineering with Ada* he moved away from dependence on this technique, and also developed further the notation used for describing the solution (often termed 'Boochograms'!).

This strategy for developing a design has some attractions as well as some obvious limitations; in trying to overcome the latter, the developers

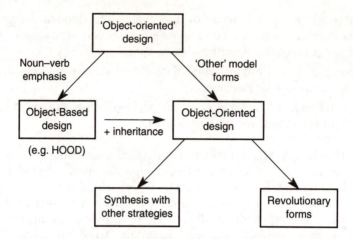

Figure 12.5 Evolution of object-oriented design strategies.

of object-oriented design methods have generally followed one of the two paths illustrated in Figure 12.5. These are:

- to find another strategy that can truly be termed Object-Oriented (and hence usually featuring the early inclusion of inheritance in the design model);
- to improve on the noun/verb strategy, while retaining the (relatively successful) Object-Based emphasis.

Most effort has probably gone into the first route, although so far it has met with relatively little success in terms of producing a convincing form of systematic design method. For example, while both Booch (1991) and Coad and Yourdon (1991b) offer various ideas based heavily on heuristics drawn from the experience of well-practised users, neither proposes any well-formed design strategy in a procedural sense. (In terms of the model that we have used so far, their methods provide only a representation part and some heuristics, and lack a real process part.) This lack of maturity in the object-oriented methods is also recognized in Pressman (1991), which provides some further simple examples of the concepts involved. Good comparative analyses of more recent developments in object-oriented design practices can be found in Fichman and Kemerer (1992) and Walker (1992), although it is perhaps a significant indication of the current state of practice that there is very little overlap between the sets of methods that they use for their comparisons!

The second route has been pursued further in the HOOD strategy (Hierarchical Object-Oriented Design). Despite its acronym, HOOD uses an Object-Based approach, and a description of this method forms the main topic of Section 12.3. HOOD makes use of two forms of hierarchy (one of which is essentially a functional breakdown, while the other is a uses hierarchy), together with a (further) form of notation intended to help pull these together. Since the next section discusses this method in much more detail, we will not describe it further here, other than to observe that there seems to be little experimental evidence so far to indicate that this approach is significantly better able to handle the design of large systems than the earlier practices based on this strategy.

One of the major problems that affects all object-oriented design strategies is the question of how to create an initial design model that is based on 'real-world' objects. An obvious step would seem to be to develop an analysis strategy that would allow a problem to be analysed in an object-oriented manner, which would then lead on directly to an object-oriented design. As mentioned in the previous section, techniques incorporating such strategies have been developed – see Coad and Yourdon (1991a), Pressman (1991) and Fichman and Kemerer (1992) – but it would be fair to say that they are even less mature than those used for the design task.

To some extent, the slower progress of development of analysis techniques is quite understandable. The object-oriented design techniques are very much 'detailed design' techniques that focus on exploiting the characteristics of the implementation media. In other words, once we have decided on the objects to be used (the tricky bit), we can concentrate on deciding how to model these by using a given set of programming features – which is a somewhat easier task, since many programming languages provide a relatively well-defined object-related framework. For the task of analysis, on the other hand, the focus of attention is on the original problem, and it is much harder to fit this into an object-related framework, since so much of the emphasis is placed on the difficult task of identifying suitable objects in the problem domain.

In some ways the activities involved in an object-oriented analysis procedure are not unlike those performed during the model-building stages of the JSD method. However, the Jackson entities generally possess simpler properties than those ascribed to objects, and they are more readily identified from analysis of a description of a user's needs, since such a description is likely to place greatest emphasis on the functionality of the intended system.

12.3   Object-Based Design (HOOD)

12.3.1   The choice of HOOD

Since one of the motivations for developing Object-Based Design strategies has been to provide a means of designing for Ada, it is appropriate to select one of the Ada-oriented methods as an example of such a strategy.

HOOD forms a good basis for this section, since it is fairly widely publicized, and, while targeted at Ada, there seems no reason why it should not be used with languages such as Modula-2 and C++. However, being an Object-Based method according to our earlier definition, it provides no real guidelines on developing effective ways of using the inheritance property provided through the class mechanism of C++.

The HOOD (Hierarchical Object-Oriented Design) method was developed for the European Space Agency by CISI–INGENIERE, CRI and MATRA, and it is now in its third version (ESA, 1989; Robinson, 1992). The process part is based heavily on the form used in Booch's earlier work (Booch, 1983), together with some input from MATRA's 'abstract machines' approach.

The same general format will be used in this section that was adopted for describing the design methods of the previous chapter. A description of the representation forms is followed by an outline description of the process part, and finally comes a review of the available heuristics.

12.3.2   HOOD representation forms

The difficulty of identifying and modelling both problem and solution 'objects' using diagrammatical forms means that, in common with many other approaches to object-oriented development and design, HOOD leans heavily on the use of written text to describe the abstract design models. It does, however, have a diagrammatical representation, although this essentially provides only a structural viewpoint on the design model, and so is used mainly to represent the outcome of design rather than to support the transformation steps. There are no specific forms used for capturing behavioural, functional or data-modelling aspects of the object model.

In order to explain the form of the diagrams, two further HOOD concepts must be described:

- HOOD recognizes the existence of both 'passive' and 'active' objects in a system. A **passive** object essentially provides a service, in that it provides a set of operations and associated abstract data types. The operations of a passive object can be activated only when control is passed to them directly, as occurs during the invocation (calling) of a procedure (subprogram). An **active** object can provide a parallel thread of execution that can respond to synchronous and asynchronous 'events' (or timeouts). Active objects may interact with both passive and active objects, but passive objects may make use only of other passive objects, and so cannot be used to activate active objects.

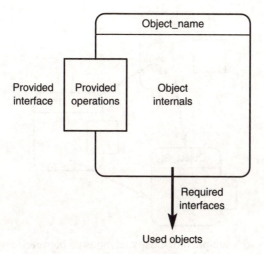

Figure 12.6 The HOOD graphical representation of a passive object.

- The hierarchy described in a HOOD diagram can also take two
  forms. The first is a **uses** hierarchy, of the form described by Parnas
  (1979). Such a hierarchy shows the dependence of one object on the
  services provided by other objects, as shown earlier in Figure 12.4.
  For this relationship, the above rules governing interaction between
  active and passive objects will apply, with the added constraint that
  passive objects may not use one another in a cyclic manner. The
  second form of hierarchy is based on **functional decomposition**,
  whereby an object may be internally decomposed into child objects.
  The child objects provide the functionality of the enveloping object.

We will examine these concepts further in looking at how the representation form can be utilized. The relationships with the Ada task, package and
procedure structures should be fairly obvious; in that respect the notation is
not unlike the Structure Graph notation discussed in Section 6.5, since it
supports many of the same Ada-oriented concepts.

The basic form of representation used to denote a passive object is
that shown in Figure 12.6. The outer bounds of the object are indicated by
a box with rounded corners. An object has an 'object identifier' at the top
of the box, and a 'boundary box' on its perimeter, which lists the 'provided
operations' that are visible for this object. The uses relationship is then
represented by a broad arrow drawn between object boxes, as can be seen
in Figure 12.7, which shows such relationships between a number of
passive objects.

An active object is described by essentially the same form, but an
additional zig-zag arrow is also drawn next to the 'provided operations' box

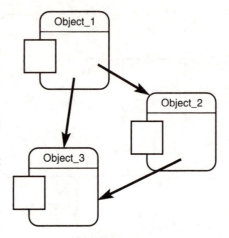

Figure 12.7   An example of the uses relationship between several passive objects.

to denote the use of an external trigger, to show that the associated 'provided operation' is invoked in response to an event, rather than by a fully synchronous procedure call. (This aspect of the notation seems rather clumsy, especially when it is compared to that of the Structure Graph.) Figure 12.8 shows an example of the representation of an active object.

The parent–child decomposition is shown by drawing the child objects inside the parent object, as shown in Figure 12.9. The provided operations of the parent object are also linked to those of the child objects,

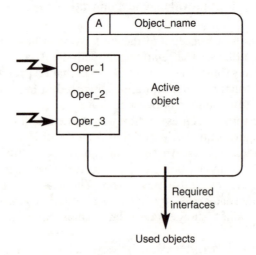

Figure 12.8   The HOOD graphical representation for an active object.

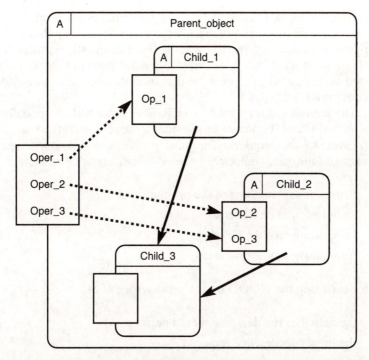

Figure 12.9 Parent–child decomposition in HOOD. (This is indicated by dashed
   lines, with solid lines being used to show the *uses* relationship.)

to indicate which child object will be responsible for implementing each
operation. In Figure 12.9, the objects Child_1 and Child_2 supply the
provided operations of the parent object. Data-flow arrows can also be
used to show the flow of data between child objects.

Where an active object is decomposed in this way, there is the added
possibility of decomposing it into a mix of active and passive child objects.
An example of this is also shown in Figure 12.9, where Child_3 is a passive
object.

There is not much else that can usefully be said about the HOOD
notation at this point, other than to remark that it can be extended to
include descriptions of exception-handling, and also that it includes a form
of class object that relates fairly closely to the Ada generics mechanism. A
HOOD class object, however, only provides a form of object 'template',
rather than capturing all of the properties of a true object-oriented class
mechanism, and inheritance in particular.

12.3.3   The HOOD process

The descriptions of the preceding subsection may already have made it
clear that the structural viewpoint provided by the HOOD diagrammatical

form is really only well suited to describing the final outcome of the design process. So the process itself remains largely based on manipulating textual descriptions of the design model – a form that is inherently unsuited for use with large systems. (This is actually a general problem for the object-oriented design paradigm, yet to be convincingly overcome by any of the object-oriented strategies.)

The overall strategy used in HOOD is described as 'globally top-down' in form, and it consists of a sequence of refinements to an object-based model of the problem. The basic process can be summarized as a sequence of four transformations, termed design 'steps'. These are:

(1)   definition and analysis of the problem

(2)   elaboration of an informal strategy

(3)   formalization of the strategy

(4)   formalization of the solution

and for each step the HOOD design process identifies:

- the activities the designer should perform
- the input 'documents' required
- the output 'documents' to be generated
- any validation procedures to be used

An outline description of the main transformations involved in the HOOD design process is shown in Figure 12.10. As elsewhere, this section will not attempt to describe all the details of this process, and of the documentation issues in particular for which the reader is referred to ESA (1989) or Robinson (1992). Since an example of the operations involved in steps 2–4 of the process is provided at the end of this chapter, we will mainly focus our attention on outlining steps 1 and 2 in this section.

The first activity of the design process in step 1 requires the designer to perform an initial analysis of the problem. This is really a major task, and ideally would itself be undertaken in an object-oriented fashion, so that the analysis of the problem in terms of its constituent objects could be used to provide guidance to the designer in the next task, which is to identify suitable candidates for solution (design) objects.

In the absence of suitable analysis techniques, Booch originally recommended the use of Structured Systems Analysis for this task, while the HOOD developers have suggested that SADT provides a good alternative form. Both of these analysis techniques are, of course, based on the use of functional decomposition rather than on a true object-oriented strategy, and so their use should perhaps be regarded as a step towards the ultimate objective of a fully object-oriented design process.

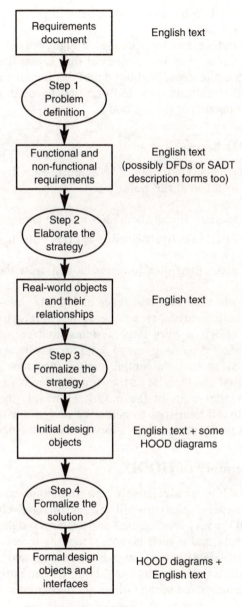

Figure 12.10   HOOD process diagram.

The unsatisfactory form of step 1 (in terms of building an object-oriented model from the beginning) leads to the difficulties of step 2. This step essentially requires the designer to 'rough out' an initial architectural solution to the problem, which can then be analysed to provide a more detailed object-based design model. (One way of performing this analysis is shown in the example below.)

Step 2 therefore has to act as a 'bridge' between the function-oriented model produced by the analysis of step 1, and the object-centred needs of the succeeding steps. Without doubt this remains an inelegant and poorly structured transformation, and one that needs to be improved in any future developments of the method.

12.3.4 HOOD heuristics

This section is of necessity rather brief. A cynic might indeed conclude that two views could be taken at this point:

- HOOD is too new for any heuristics to have emerged;
- the process part effectively consists entirely of heuristics!

Readers should make their own judgements and draw their own conclusions.

Whatever the view that one takes of HOOD, however, it is clear that the noun–verb analysis technique is not likely to prove wholly adequate when designing very large systems, and so needs to be supplemented. The most promising way of doing so may lie in seeking ways of improving step 1, so that the initial analysis provides a good object-oriented model that can then be further transformed by using the current techniques on smaller units of the model. However, the emergence of some well-established heuristics to guide the designer with handling particular structures would certainly be a welcome development.

12.3.5 A summary of HOOD

In many ways HOOD is a relatively new technique, and so any views expressed in a summary such as this will be based on relatively little exposure to its use. HOOD is very much aimed at designing systems that are to be implemented in Ada, and as such it is able to identify successfully some ways of using the major Ada structures (such as the package and the task).

Perhaps the main reservations about its 'integrity' as a design method can be summarized in the following observations:

- The design model should ideally capture the behavioural, functional, structural and data-modelling viewpoints in a balanced manner. However, the emphasis in textual analysis is on building a description that contains a mixture of the behavioural, functional and data-modelling aspects, and the process of extracting the structural viewpoint of the model from this is far from being well-structured.

- The diagrammatical representation is not really used in the design process, and does not aid the design transformations in any way, so that these only involve the (rather loosely structured) description provided through the use of natural language in order to capture the design model.

- It is not clear that the process itself will scale up well for all problems (although it is likely that it can be scaled up for those problems where it is at least possible to identify a clear parent–child hierarchy).

HOOD extends the basic object model in a number of ways: adding parent–child decomposition, including the concept of active objects in the design model, and providing a diagrammatical form that is able to encompass these (although not in a particularly elegant way). However, it confines itself solely to the three object characteristics of modularity, encapsulation and abstraction and makes no attempt to capture the concept of the class hierarchy. The next section briefly reviews some of the current ideas about how this further characteristic might be incorporated into the design process and goes on to examine a brief example of the use of HOOD.

12.4 Object-Oriented Design

12.4.1 A paradigm in search of a method?

Whatever one's view about the strengths and weaknesses of the top-down and text-based strategy that was described in the previous section on HOOD, it does at least provide a designer with *some* guidelines for organizing a design around the ideas of modularity, encapsulation and abstraction. Equally, though, it provides no real guidelines to help with incorporating classes of objects into a design by using the mechanism of inheritance.

There are two possible approaches to producing a truly object-oriented design method:

- adding extra features to the object-based strategy, so as to include support for true object-oriented structuring;
- producing a completely different strategy.

To date, no clearly successful solution to this problem has emerged from either of these approaches. Most writers would probably support the line that the first has now been discarded, mainly because inheritance is too deeply embedded in the object-oriented concepts to be added on in this way. So if we are to make use of inheritance in the design model, it will need to be included in the model at a relatively early stage of the design process.

Fichman and Kemerer (1992) have analysed a number of techniques for analysis and design that can be categorized as either 'conventional' or 'object-oriented' in their strategies, in order to determine how radically different these really are. Their conclusion is that the object-oriented approach *is* radically different from both the process-oriented and the data-oriented methods. However, even within the supporters of the object-oriented approach, there is a division between those who consider that object-oriented systems should be developed through synthesis, in which the object-oriented approach is linked to more 'traditional' structured design techniques, and those who advocate revolution, requiring that the analyst and designer should take a fundamentally different approach to the whole question of design. Considered from the viewpoint of the 'transformational model', it is difficult not to sympathize with the latter view, since the viewpoints and structures used in both process-oriented and data-oriented analysis and design are very different from those used in object-oriented analysis and design.

Perhaps one of the more successful attempts at synthesis is the Object-Oriented Analysis approach of Schlaer and Mellor (1988), and it may well be that the analysis task provides better scope for the synthesis approach than the design task. Certainly object-oriented design as currently practised is a very 'fuzzy' process when compared to the other methods that we have examined, being what Booch (1991) describes as a process of 'round-trip gestalt design'. Only time will tell whether this is a transient state of affairs that reflects the relative immaturity of the object-oriented discipline, or whether it is a symptom of deeper structural difficulties that are inherent in the object-oriented model itself.

This section, therefore, very briefly reviews some ideas about notation, and about process, but makes no attempt to analyse these approaches in the manner used elsewhere in this book.

What of the future? Well, efforts are likely to continue to find some way of organizing the production of object-oriented designs in a more methodical manner than at present. While radical breakthroughs currently seem unlikely, technological forecasting is notorious for its pitfalls, and its inability to foresee quantum steps in a technology. So the possibility of a more systematic approach to object-oriented design should not be ruled out for the future. Even if no major breakthroughs occur, the benefits provided by object-oriented structures suggest that the paradigm is here to stay, with or without a systematic method.

12.4.2   Notations for Object-Oriented Design

Booch has suggested that a set of different notations is required in order to separate the independent kinds of decision that are involved in designing object-oriented systems. He has therefore proposed that the following set of six graphical forms could all be of use during the development of an object-oriented design:

- class diagrams } to provide a *logical* view of the
- object diagrams } system

- module diagrams } to provide a *physical* view of the
- process diagrams } system

- state transition diagrams } to provide the *dynamic semantics* of
- timing diagrams } the design

For a full description of these forms, and of their use, the reader should consult Booch (1991). In this section, we will briefly examine the three least familiar of these, which are the first three forms from the above list.

Class diagrams

Class diagrams aim to capture ideas about the relationships between the object classes in a system, and hence this is the form that can be used to express the notions about inheritance that are lacking in the object-based approach. The basic components of this form are shown in Figure 12.11, and are:

- the *class* itself, shown as a 'blob' or 'cloud', with its boundary drawn with dashed lines;
- the *class relationships*, which are denoted by labelled arcs, with the form of the line and the choice of line terminators being used to indicate specific types of relationship (for example, uses, instantiates, inherits);
- the *class utility*, which is a shadowed 'blob' representing a single free subprogram (or a set of these), where such an entity is supported by the implementation forms available.

Since there are eight forms of class relationship that can be represented in this way, the representation form has to provide a lot of detail (and can require fairly extensive textual support). This is, however, a situation where such a degree of detail is appropriate, since such information is only likely to be available when the design process is in a fairly advanced state.

(As a general point, it should be remarked here that the use of 'shadowing' as a convention in such representations is not very convenient for those lacking a suitable computer-based and method-specific diagram editor!)

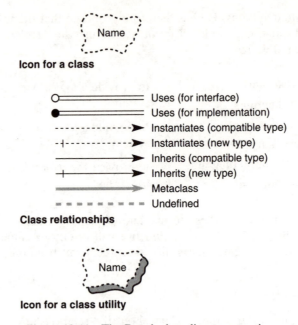

Icon for a class

Class relationships

Icon for a class utility

Figure 12.11   The Booch class diagram notation.

Object diagrams

These are primarily concerned with describing objects and their relationships. The symbol for an object is again a 'blob', but this time drawn with a solid line to show that this is an instance rather than a class. An example of such a diagram is shown in Figure 12.12.

The particular relationships that are captured by this form are concerned with the sending of messages between objects. A further notational extension (termed 'object visibility') can be used to indicate the way in which the exchange is managed (for example, by passing parameters, or by using shared data items). A further addition provides information about the synchronization form to be used between the objects (this information will be particularly important where objects can exist in parallel).

Module diagrams

Module diagrams are much closer in form to the style of diagram that is used with HOOD, which is, perhaps, not surprising, since both are concerned with modelling the physical structure of the system. However, there are also some similarities to the Structure Graph notation that was described in Section 6.5. The terminology is Ada-influenced (there are symbols for a task, as well as for generic subprograms and packages).

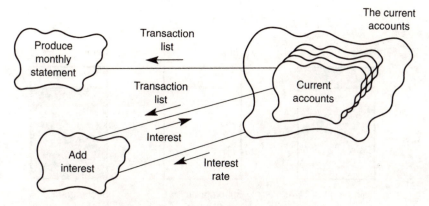

Figure 12.12 The Booch object diagram.

Figure 12.13 shows an example of such a diagram. Subprograms are denoted by upright boxes, and packages by upright boxes with sub-boxes on one surface (presumably to indicate that they provide external interfaces). Tasks are denoted by parallelograms, in close analogy with the form of the Structure Graph. Subsystems are not shown in the diagram, but are denoted by boxes with rounded corners.

Other notations

In contrast to the emphasis that Booch places on the use of diagrams in constructing and manipulating the object-oriented model of a system, Coad and Yourdon (1991b) use a much less comprehensive set of notations in their work. They use a form of diagrammatical representation that is termed 'class-and-object' notation, which can be used to describe both inheritance between classes and the instantiation of a class into objects. Beyond that they make little use of diagrammatical forms.

Wasserman *et al.* (1990) have reviewed the requirements of object-oriented description forms, and have proposed an 'Object-Oriented Structured Design' notation that is considered to be method-independent. Their approach pulls together many of the issues described in this chapter and the notation proposed is intended to be used for supporting both object-based and object-oriented forms. No particular design process has yet been proposed to complement the notation, and it has also been suggested that it can become overcrowded and hence difficult to read (Sutcliffe, 1991). This observation could perhaps be applied quite widely to object-oriented notations, since they are generally used to model detailed physical design issues.

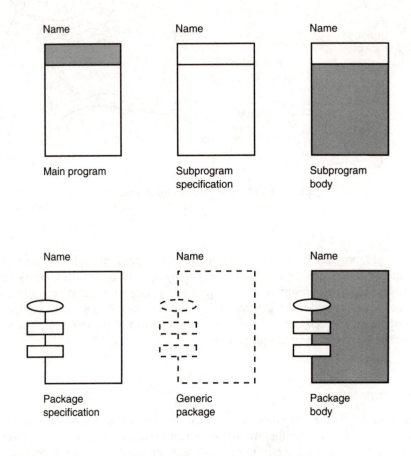

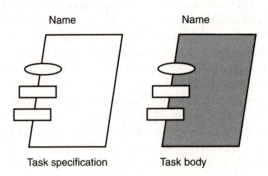

Figure 12.13 The Booch module diagram.

12.4.3 The Object-Oriented Design process

As yet, there is really no design process that can be described as fully incorporating the use of the principal object-oriented concepts. Booch has taken the view that the design of an object-oriented system cannot be readily classified as either compositional or decompositional, and that it is likely to involve the designer in using a mix of strategies with no specific ordering imposed upon them. Coad and Yourdon similarly discuss tasks and criteria, rather than overall structure, and can probably be assumed to have a generally similar view of the design process itself.

Sutcliffe (1991) has reviewed a number of design methods (including those described in the earlier chapters) and has sought to determine how far each goes towards meeting object-oriented criteria. Not surprisingly, no one method emerges with strong credentials, although many are able to provide strategies that incorporate some of the object-oriented viewpoints.

At this time, therefore, we can only conclude that there is no identifiable systematic design strategy that can be used to produce fully object-oriented designs. Although a number of strategies have been proposed, none has yet been really tested in any very convincing way beyond fairly small 'trial' problems, with the possible exception of that proposed by Booch (Fichman and Kemerer, 1992). Indeed, the argument that the object-oriented philosophy is such that prescriptive strategies cannot be used to create these structures may well prove to be true, although it would be difficult to prove this.

12.5 HOOD: an outline example

To demonstrate the transformations that are used in steps 2–4 of the HOOD design process, we will use our example of a program to analyse the structure of Pascal program source code that was introduced in Chapter 10. This is a further development of the object-based solution beyond that which was first introduced in Budgen (1989). A summary of the problem is given in Figure 12.14 as a reminder of what is required.

Step 2: Elaboration of an informal strategy

For HOOD, as well as for other object-based and object-oriented methods, this initial architectural design task has so far proved to be difficult to structure in any very systematic manner. Basically it is one in which the designer outlines an intended solution to the problem defined in the 'analysis' step. Ideally the former will have identified the objects contained in the real-world problem, and these can then be directly linked to objects in the solution (rather along the lines of the JSD entity-analysis and structuring process). However, existing analysis methods fall rather

(a) Statement of requirement

The program is to perform 'dependence tracing', using as its input the source code of a Pascal program. For each procedure declared in the input Pascal code, the program will need to print out a list of those procedures that it calls, from which we can then construct a Structure Chart that represents the organization of the Pascal program.

(b) An example of a Structure Chart

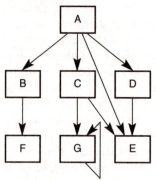

(c) Suggested output for this Structure Chart

Level 1	A	>	B(list of formal parameters)	2	p
		>	C(–ditto–)	2	f
		>	D(–ditto–)	2	p
		>>	E(–ditto–)	3	f
Level 2	B	>	F(list of formal parameters)	3	p
	C	>	F(list of formal parameters)	3	p
		>	E(–ditto–)	3	f
	D	>	E(list of formal parameters)	3	f
Level 3	G	>	G(list of formal parameters)	3	p

The symbols used are:
- \>   procedure call at next level
- \>>   call to a procedure at a lower level
- p   procedure call
- f   function call

Figure 12.14   Requirements for a Structure Chart (call graph) analysis program.

short of this desirable scenario, and also it is not yet clear that one should always find a one-to-one matching between real-world objects and implementation objects in a design.

The normal means for describing this initial solution is by using free text (informal English for our purposes). For this example, the first attempt might consist of the following plan:

The program first reads through the input Pascal source file, and makes a list of the procedures that are declared in that program. It then reads the input file again and this time makes a note of each call that is made to any of the procedures that were previously identified, and also records the identity of the calling component. From these records it constructs a tree that shows the interdependencies of the different procedures, and finally prints out a table that represents the tree, by listing the called procedures and calling procedures in a suitable manner.

(This solution is not unlike that derived in Chapter 10 through the use of Data-Flow Diagrams, and so can be considered as derived from the use of Structured Systems Analysis during step 1 of the HOOD method.)

Step 3: Formalization of the strategy

In this step, the designer's objectives are to identify:

- the objects themselves;
- the operations associated with each object;
- the interrelations between the objects.

The initial list of objects is created by extracting the noun phrases in the initial outline design description, while the verb phrases help with identifying the operations performed on the objects.

Beginning with the noun phrases, there are some basic rules that we can apply during the analysis itself. Besides identifying the nouns, each noun can be analysed to determine whether it is

- a *common* noun – that is, a 'class' name, such as 'book', 'program', 'file', and so on, which in turn can help with identifying potential abstract data types, and any specific instances of these;
- a *mass* noun, which describes a unit of measure;
- a *proper* noun, used to identify a specific entity in the system.

In order to apply these rules to the example, we first go through it and identify the nouns and adjectives (these are numbered in order to aid reference during analysis):

The *program* (1) first reads through the *input Pascal source file* (2), and makes a *list* (3) of the *procedures* (4) that are declared in that *program* (5). It then reads the *input file* (6) again and this time makes a *note* (7) of each *call* (8) that is made to any of the *procedures* (9) that were previously identified, and also records the *identity* (10) of the calling *component* (11). From these *records* (12) it then constructs a *tree* (13) that shows the *interdependencies* (14) of the different *procedures* (15), and finally prints out a *table* (16) that represents the *tree* (17) by listing the *called procedures* (18) and *calling procedures* (19) in a suitable manner.

Within this we can identify several objects that appear to play a significant role in the solution. (One way of verifying ideas about the selected candidates is to outline the top-level algorithm again in terms of these objects alone; any difficulties that are encountered indicate where we may have failed to identify an object, and any ambiguities might suggest where there is some redundancy.) First, though, by going through the numbered items in the above solution, one by one, we can draw the following conclusions:

(1)   *Program* can be discarded, since it is simply a reference to the mechanism of the complete solution, and is not itself a part of the solution.

(2)   *Input Pascal source file* leads us to identify *source file* as an object that the program will operate on (with operations such as open, close, read) and which will possess attributes of some form.

(3,4)   *List of procedures* seems a good candidate for an object, since the program will perform operations on it (adding an item, searching for an entry, and so on).

(5)   *Program* is here simply a synonym for *source file*.

(6)   *Input file* is again a synonym for *source file*.

(7,8)   *Note* (of *each call*) might possibly be an object, but in this context, as it can be replaced with the action 'notes each call', it should be discarded as a candidate.

(9)   *Procedures* seems to be a reference to the object *procedure identifier*, which seems to be a candidate for an object (although the associated operations are unclear at this stage).

(10,11) *Identity* (of a calling *component*) seems to be a further synonym for *procedure identifier*, and in the light of the previous reference to 'notes each call' we can now see that 'calling' and 'caller' might be attributes of some kind.

(12)   *Record* is a synonym for *list*, as its context shows.

(13)   *Tree* suggests the presence of a new object, or, at least, of a new data structure constructed from existing objects. It therefore seems appropriate to keep it for now and review it later if necessary.

(14,15) *Interdependencies* is really another reference to the attributes of *procedure identifier* (the presence of the preposition 'of' makes this particularly evident).

(16)   *Table* could be an object, but it seems to refer to some structure that is constructed from existing objects and which has some association with *tree*.

(17)   *Tree* is simply a repeat of (13) above.

(18)   *Called (procedure)* is simply an attribute of *procedure identifier*.

(19)   *Calling (procedure)* is also an attribute of *procedure identifier*. (These attributes should remind the designer to consider how recursive calls to procedures will be handled in this solution – a good example of a situation where note-making by the designer should be encouraged.)

Examining the survivors in terms of the classification into class, mass and proper nouns, we find:

- the common (class) noun *procedure identifier*;
- no evident candidates for mass nouns;
- three specific objects (proper nouns) – *source file*, *list of procedures*, *tree of relations*,

having concluded that *table* should be rejected (and *tree* is a candidate for the same treatment, if further analysis concludes that it too has no real claim to being an object).

One obvious conclusion from the above is that it is difficult to systematically parse statements expressed in a natural language such as English. Features such as synonyms tend to add complications, and clearly the way that a solution is phrased can assist with or obscure the finding of a solution.

Continuing our analysis, we repeat the parsing of the rough design, but this time identifying the verbs and the adverbs.

The program *first reads* (1) through the input Pascal source file, and *makes* (2) a list of the procedures that *are declared* (3) in that program. It then *reads* (4) the input file again and this time *makes a note* (5) of each call that is *made* (6) to any of the procedures that *were previously identified* (7), and also *records* (8) the identity of the calling component. From these records it then *constructs* (9) a tree that *shows* (10) the interdependencies of the different procedures, and *finally prints out* (11) a table that *represents* (12) the tree by *listing* (13) the called procedures and calling procedures in a suitable manner.

(Note the use of *then*, *again* and *this time*, showing how adverbs and adjectives can provide additional information about timing constraints in the solution.)

This time, in going through the list, one can not only examine the credentials of an action but also try to link it to one of the candidates identified for the role of objects.

(1)   *Reads* is clearly an operation applied to the *source file* (ReadItem).

(2)   *Makes* (a list) becomes the operation of adding entries to the *list of procedures* (AddEntry).

(3)   *Are declared* is an 'existence' verb, and so is discarded (unless we decided that 'declared' should be an attribute).

(4)   *Reads (again)* has already been covered in (1).

(5)   *Makes (a note)* can be expressed more rigorously by regarding it as a synonym for the action of adding an attribute to *procedure identifier* (or modifying an existing attribute).

(6)   *Is made* simply identifies the attribute to be modified by the preceding operation.

(7)   *Were previously identified* can again be considered as an existence reference and discarded.

(8)   *Records* identifies the attribute of *list of procedures* that is to be modified.

(9)   *Constructs* is really an operation on *tree of relations*, or, more probably, a set of operations when expanded.

(10)   *Shows* is another existence reference, and so is ignored.

(11)   *Prints out* is an operation (or set of operations) applied to the *tree of relations*.

(12)   *Represents* is another existence verb, and so it is ignored.

(13)   *Listing* can be considered as an operation on an object that has not yet been considered, namely the *output file*. As a fairly minor object in the context of this solution, it can just be noted at this stage, but may require further consideration later. (Another example of where note-making may be needed in the design process.)

The result of these two processes is the summary shown in Figure 12.15, listing the objects with the initial set of operations that have been identified. Further consideration of the last two objects in the list suggests that one of these is transformed to create the other at some point, and so for our purposes they can be merged into some composite form that can be used to represent either. This therefore gives us a final list of four objects, and an initial set of operations associated with each of these.

A further issue that needs to be resolved by a consideration of the operations performed in a system is whether the associated objects are to be considered as active or passive. There is also some scope to consider the

Object	Operation
Procedure identifier	Add_Caller_Identity
	Add_Calling_Identity
Source file	Read_Item
Output file	Print_Item
List of procedures	Add_Entry
Tree of relations	Add_Relation
	Read_Node

Figure 12.15 Initial list of objects and operations extracted using the HOOD design step 3.

presence of concurrency at this stage, too. However, this relatively simple problem gives little scope for demonstrating either of these features.

Step 4: Formalization of the solution

This is largely concerned with what can be termed 'completion tasks'. In particular, these include

- providing formal definitions of the interfaces to the objects making up the system;
- identifying/defining the 'parent' object of the whole system.

For the present example, Figure 12.16 shows a more complete description of the final objects, and Figure 12.17 shows the corresponding HOOD diagram. The object that provides the parsed form of the input file is clearly a candidate for a further level of decomposition into a set of corresponding child objects. In this example, also, an arbitrary 'parent' object has been created to provide a coordinating role (rather as in Chapter 10, where it was necessary to create a central transform for this system in the absence of a suitable candidate among the operations identified for the problem).

As this example demonstrates, the noun–verb analysis *can* be made to work on problems of a nontrivial nature. However, in this case we are aided by the fact that the problem can to some extent be decomposed hierarchically: the design of the parsing task can be deferred until the overall design is established, and then used to refine one of the objects into a set of child objects and operations.

It is tempting at this point to seek to compare the solution generated in this chapter with that generated in Chapter 10. However, although each

Object	Attributes	Operations

Procedure identity	Procedure identifier
	Link to list of calling
	    procedures
	Link to list of called
	    procedures
		create_procedure_identifier
		add_caller_link
		add_called_link

Source file	File identifier Open/close End of file	read_token open_file close_file
Output file	File identifier Open/close	print_string open_file close_file
Table of procedures	Entries Entry relations	add_new_entry add_link_to_entry determine_level_in_tree

Figure 12.16 Attributes and operations for the four objects identified in the HOOD design process.

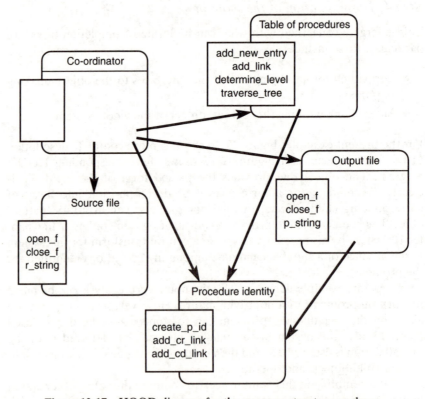

Figure 12.17 HOOD diagram for the program structure analyser.

is presented in terms of a structural viewpoint, the two viewpoints used capture rather different attributes of the design. For the SSA/SD solution, the Structure Chart emphasizes procedure hierarchy, and lacks any direct means of modelling shared data dependence (although, as previously observed, it can be included to some degree through the use of the supplementary table). In the case of the HOOD solution, there are no specific guidelines about decomposition of tasks into procedure, and all of the emphasis lies on encapsulation and modularity. So, while both of these are structural viewpoints, it is unreasonable to expect that design methods that place their decision-making emphasis upon such radically different subsets of attributes will produce solutions that are equivalent, even where both begin from the same structured analysis of the problem.

SUMMARY

When the object-oriented design practices presently available are examined using the same methodological approach that has proved valuable for the other methods surveyed in the preceding chapters, they prove to be difficult to classify and categorize in this manner. While in part this may reflect their relative immaturity, there may also be some deeper reason that is based in the nature of the object-oriented paradigm itself. Having observed throughout this book that the process of design never follows a prescriptive and tightly structured set of procedures, perhaps we need to accept that the diversity of viewpoints needed to describe an object-oriented design model and the interactions occurring between its elements means that no well-formed design process *can* be used.

This question of the balance between the viewpoints used for capturing the design model is one that may be particularly significant in explaining the difficulties of classification that we encounter. The 'classical' structured approaches to design generally use a *primary* viewpoint for constructing the design model, with any other viewpoints being used in *secondary* roles. (The SSA/SD process of Chapter 10 is an example of this: the primary viewpoint for modelling through the use of DFDs is a functional one, and any use of data-modelling or behavioural forms will be essentially secondary to this.) However, since the object-oriented model potentially involves all of the four major viewpoints, and imposes no order of precedence in their use, this may effectively render it impossible to devise any design practices that use a procedural form.

If this is so, it is also likely that one of the major potential strengths of the strategy will be severely diluted. Object-oriented practices are generally considered to provide potential for reuse of previously developed design elements (classes, objects, modules). However, without a procedural framework for the design process, it is unclear how this potential can be exploited in any systematic way. (Indeed, this particular claim should perhaps therefore be regarded as 'not proven' in terms of demonstrating design reuse in a general and repeatable way.)

However, none of these points concerning design *practices* can be considered as invalidating the object-oriented paradigm itself, and there can be little doubt that in the hands of experienced practitioners, object-oriented practices can provide a very effective approach to the design and implementation of complex systems. But for the object-oriented model to be convincingly demonstrated as having general applicability, and especially to large-scale systems, some means of transferring the available design expertise, or of helping to codify it, needs to be found. One role for a systematic design method is in helping a designer to build up expertise with a particular design strategy; it is this that at present is most noticeably lacking in the object-oriented domain, and which therefore needs to be addressed more effectively in order to fully establish the claims and expectations of this approach to software design.

FURTHER READING

Snyder A. (1993). The essence of objects: Concepts and terms. *IEEE Software*, January, 31–42

A very well-written and carefully produced summary of both the object concept and the ideas that go with it. The author writes on behalf of a 'task force' that has tried to provide a set of terms that help understanding of the concepts and communication among those who use the concepts. (The issue of communication is a particular problem for the object-oriented community, given the rather varied terminology that is used under this banner.) The paper defines a set of terms, and provides a taxonomy for their meanings; it is to be hoped that these will be widely adopted, not least because of the clarity they provide.

Booch G. (1991). *Object-Oriented Design with Applications*. Redwood City, California: Benjamin-Cummings

An authoritative description of the major features that form the object-oriented approach to design and construction of systems. In terms of design *practices*, however, while Booch suggests a number of techniques, he does not attempt to recommend any specific practices – a demonstration of honesty that greatly enhances the value of the book. This book is an invaluable source for anyone needing to get to grips with the essentials of object-oriented thinking.

Fichman R.G. and Kemerer C.F. (1992). Object-oriented and conventional analysis and design methodologies. *IEEE Computer*, **25**(10), 22–39

An extensive review of a number of object-oriented practices for both analysis and design, which draws some comparisons with 'conventional' practices. It provides good insight into the current state of development of object-oriented strategies, and identifies some of the weaknesses that need to be overcome if these are to be successful.

EXERCISES

12.1   In a simple banking system, one candidate for the role of an 'object' might be a customer account. Consider how each of the four major viewpoints might be used in modelling the operation of a bank account, and suggest forms that might be suitable for each viewpoint. (There is scope for using inheritance here, too, in that the bank may provide different forms of account, and although each will provide certain standard methods, the details of these might vary with the type of account involved.)

12.2   An issue records system for use in a public lending library is required (such as that modelled in Exercise 11.1 of Chapter 11). Suggest a set of suitable candidates for 'objects' in this system, and for each of these identify the major attributes and provided operations.

12.3   Consider the simple filling station that was used as an example in Chapter 9. Think how you might model the working of this in an object-oriented manner, and sketch a HOOD diagram to represent your ideas.

13 Some Other Systematic Approaches to Design

13.1 Systematic design methods in perspective
13.2 Traditional analysis revisited: SADT

13.3 Organizational design practices: SSADM
13.4 Designing real-time systems: MASCOT

The material of the preceding four chapters has been concerned with providing some insight into current design practices by means of examples. This has been achieved by presenting outline descriptions of a set of design practices that differ quite markedly from one another. In particular, they have exhibited a gradual increase in degree of complexity, both in the design models that they use and in the procedures that embody their design practices. Indeed, in Chapter 12 it was observed that the power (and corresponding complexity of form) of the object-oriented design model was such that no satisfactory form for a procedural approach to designing such systems had yet been identified, nor did it seem very likely that one would be devised. However, while these methods are relatively well established and can therefore be regarded as reasonably representative, they are far from being the only forms of design practice that are documented and available to the designer.

This chapter seeks to widen our survey of design procedures by reviewing three other systematic design methods, although of necessity these will be described in rather less detail than were those of the preceding chapters. Indeed, rather than trying to provide a comprehensive description of these methods, the chapter will concentrate on describing those features that make them particularly good examples of some other developments, in the form either of the design model or of the design practices incorporated in them.

13.1   Systematic design methods in perspective

The previous four chapters have been concerned with examining a set of software design methods that embody the principal systematic design strategies that are used in the development of software. In this chapter the focus is instead on some other, mostly more specialized, design methods that use these basic strategies in rather different ways. For that reason, the descriptions will be rather briefer, and will be mainly directed at examining those features of a design method that make it of particular interest in a methodological context.

The three methods selected for inclusion in this chapter are:

- SADT

- SSADM

- MASCOT

SADT is included because it provides a model for functional analysis and design that is somewhat different from that presented in Chapter 10; SSADM is an example of an 'organizational' design method; and MASCOT shows how the 'traditional' process model can be extended and adapted to meet the needs of real-time system design. Not surprisingly, they are all oriented towards functional decomposition as the basis for their strategies. This partly reflects the extent to which designers have accumulated experience with using this strategy and partly its relative ease of application.

The extent to which tutorial documentation describing these methods is available varies considerably, but all of them are at least adequately documented in the open literature. Certainly, though, none of them is as well supported by textbooks and examples as the methods examined in Chapters 9, 10 and 11.

As a final point: not all of these methods are as 'complete' as those already described. In some of them the process parts are less well evolved, or are more strongly weighted to one end of the design task. However, all are in reasonably wide use in the software development community and can therefore be considered as well 'proven' as any method can claim to be.

Each of the sections describing a method will again follow the general strategy used in the preceding chapters. Some general comments will be followed by: a review of the representation part; an outline of the process part; a description of any significant heuristics, where applicable; and a short concluding survey of any developments that may apply to a particular method.

13.2   Traditional analysis revisited: SADT

13.2.1   Some background to SADT

The Structured Analysis and Design Technique (SADT) is of a similar vintage to the SSA/SD method that was described in Chapter 10, and like SSA/SD it is based on a functional decomposition strategy. However, it makes use of a very powerful and detailed representation form in which the components are linked by function, using a hierarchical structure to describe the design 'model' that is developed. (This is in contrast to the model that is created by the use of the Data-Flow Diagram in Structured Systems Analysis. The functional 'bubbles' of a DFD are linked by data flow, which is not hierarchical in itself.)

It is a point open to debate as to how far one can regard SADT as a *design* method. Its prime emphasis is on building an 'organized sequence of diagrams, each with concise supporting text' (Ross and Schoman, 1977) by means of a well-structured process of analysis. In that sense, it is perhaps rather more of a technique for requirements analysis (or, in SADT terms, requirements definition) than a design method, and it provides no systematic forms of practice to produce the final detailed design of the system through any form of transformation. However, there are arguments to support the claim that SADT does not separate the tasks of analysis and design in the classical 'waterfall' manner, and so it is generally regarded as a useful tool for developing an architectural design for a system. In addition, as it is also an example of a method that uses a very different form to that of SSA/SD, it has been regarded in this chapter as a design method for the purposes of comparison.

A good outline of the SADT process, together with examples of the diagrammatical form, can be found in Birrell and Ould (1985), while a much more comprehensive description is given in Marca and McGowan (1988). (As something of a contrast to many other methods, it took a very long while before any form of textbook describing this method in detail became available.) Basic papers that provide good source material are those of Ross and Schoman (1977) and Ross (1977). For our purposes we will mainly consider the representational elements of SADT, since these provide some particularly distinctive features.

13.2.2   Diagrammatical forms for SADT

A box-form diagram is used in SADT to describe the decomposition of both function and data, since the SADT design process makes use of both the functional and the data-modelling viewpoints of a system. These diagrams are known as either 'actigrams' or 'datagrams', depending on whether they are used to describe function or data respectively. A fairly

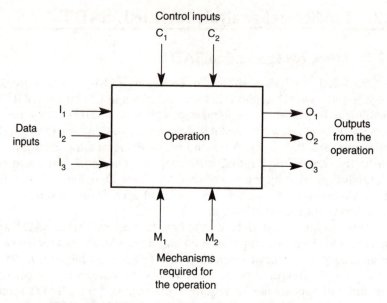

Figure 13.1   The basic SADT notation (actigram form).

strict set of rules is applied to the development of the hierarchy of diagrams that is typically used to describe the SADT model of a system.

   Figure 13.1 shows the basic form of the box notation as used in SADT (this particular illustration shows the actigram form). Each box represents a particular operation, and each side of the box is labelled with the details of one component of the information flow that is involved in performing the operation. These are organized as follows:

- the *input data* flows required for the operation are shown entering on the *left* side;
- the *control* flows are shown at the *top*;
- the *mechanisms* required are shown at the *bottom*;
- the *output* flows resulting from the operation are shown as emerging from the *right* side.

These operations can be linked in a network, with the outputs from one operation forming the inputs for another, as shown in Figure 13.2. Note that the outputs from any one operation can be used as either control or data inputs by another operation. Ross and Schoman (1977) have also observed that the arrow structure should be viewed as representing a *constraint* relationship rather than a flow of control or a sequencing of operations. Using this notation, a given box can be decomposed into a network of subordinate boxes, for which, of course, the external inputs and

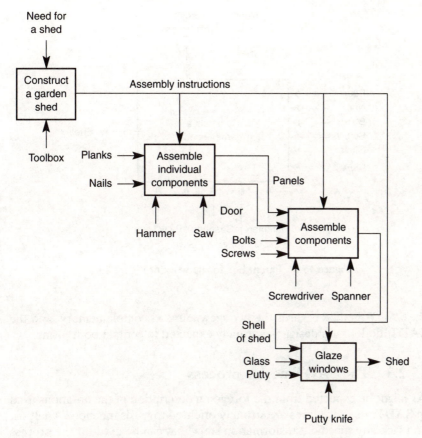

Figure 13.2 A simple network of operations (SADT).

outputs must correspond to those that flow in and out of the parent box. Figure 13.3 shows an operation that can be regarded as the parent of the network shown in Figure 13.2. Part of a more software-oriented operation is shown in Figure 13.4.

Further information can be added to a diagram in the form of 'notes', and diagrams can also be subject to 'activation rules', which define sequencing constraints on the input and output data flows of an operation. (In default of any such rules from a diagram, assume that all the outputs from an operation can be generated only if all the input flows and control flows are available.) A much fuller description of how such diagrams are organized and developed is given in Ross (1977).

Figure 13.5 shows the same form of notation being used to describe a data structure and its decomposition. While this can prove useful for modelling data elements, the emphasis on functional decomposition in the process means that the datagram plays a much less central role. However,

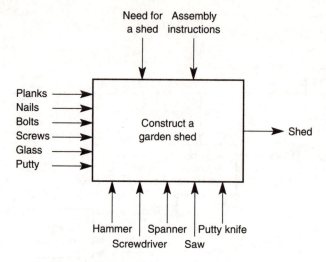

Figure 13.3   Parent box for network of Figure 13.2.

the SADT method regards the two viewpoints as complementary, and the SADT model for a design is normally expected to contain both forms.

13.2.3   The SADT design process

As might be expected from the foregoing description of the notations used in SADT, its procedures are strongly oriented towards functional analysis, and lack any specific transformation steps that can be used for the process

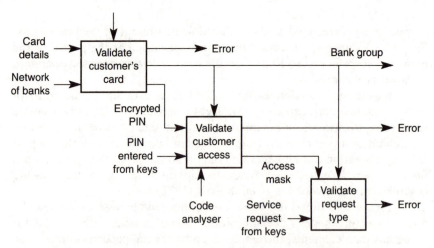

Figure 13.4   A software-oriented problem described using SADT.

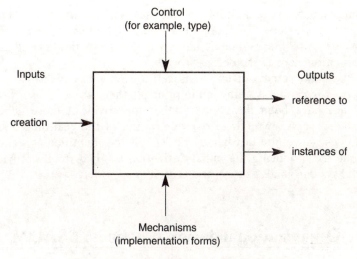

Figure 13.5   The datagram form of SADT.

of producing a physical design. (There is a very readable description of the use of SADT for analysis in Birrell and Ould (1985), and the design process is also described in Ross and Schoman (1977).) Indeed, the basic design process consists of a gradual refinement of the functional description until this reaches the stage where the operations can be mapped onto sub-programs within the system.

In this sense, therefore, the 'process part' of SADT is also different from those of the preceding examples, since it focuses more on the tasks the designer should perform than the procedures that should be followed to perform the tasks. It is worth noting that the main tasks are identified as:

- *context analysis* (the reasons for creating the item, boundary conditions that apply to it, and so on);
- *functional specification* (what the object should do, which may also lead to boundary conditions upon its behaviour);
- *design constraints* (identifying the boundary conditions on the form of the solution produced via the analysis).

So there is no scope for producing a 'transformation diagram' that can show the basic process model for SADT, using the same form as in the previous chapters.

13.2.4   The role of SADT

As a method, SADT has essentially retained a 'closed' form over the years: there are no methods that can be identified as having developed from the ideas encapsulated in it. In addition, the method itself has not evolved to any significant extent. The lack of a transformational structure for its process part also means that it has no major heuristics related to the transformation steps in the design process.

The main domain of use envisaged for SADT seems to have been data-processing systems, although in principle there are no reasons why it should not have been developed further to provide a more generally applicable process. Indeed, in our description of the real-time-oriented HOOD design method in Chapter 12, SADT was identified as a suitable technique for producing the initial design model. It certainly provides a powerful systems-analysis tool, and is used quite widely.

13.3 Organizational design practices: SSADM

13.3.1 Some background to SSADM

The Structured Systems Analysis and Design Method (SSADM) can be considered an example of what was earlier termed an 'organizational' method of design. This is because it has been strongly influenced by the need to fit the general needs and staff development practices of the user organization, in addition to the need to address the normal technical requirements of an actual problem. Methods of this form are attractive to international agencies, as well as to central and local government bodies, since these are major customers for software-based systems, ranging across a wide range of technical needs. Many of these systems are very large; they are difficult to specify; the requirements may change with technology and legislation; and they may be produced either by in-house teams or with the aid of outside contracting agencies.

A significant feature of such organizations is that traditionally, they have also provided their staff with career paths that are essentially independent of the needs of a software development project. In such an organization, the staff in a particular grade are likely to be given a number of different postings as a part of their career development, with each posting being for a fixed interval. So in such an organization it is quite possible that members of staff may be transferred in and out of project teams (and project management) at times that are determined by organizational factors, and that are wholly independent of the status of the project itself.

The organization-wide adoption of a 'standard' method for developing systems, such as SSADM, is therefore of benefit to such an organization. In particular, to meet the organizational needs for continuity, SSADM has been designed to encourage rigorous attention to the recording of design decisions, and provides relatively prescriptive ways of achieving these. It is thus much easier for staff who are involved in software development projects to hand their responsibilities over to others with a minimum degree of disruption, and it ensures that a change in the management of a project, or a change of team leadership, will not cause any alterations to the technical direction of the project.

SSADM was developed for the UK Central Computing and Tele-communications Agency (CCTA), which has traditionally been given responsibility for the oversight of all British government computer systems procurement. The developers of the method were Learmonth and Bur-chett Management Systems (LBMS), and the early versions of SSADM were based on their own in-house method, LSDM. However, the two methods have subsequently followed somewhat different lines of develop-ment.

SSADM was first introduced in 1981, and within the UK it became a mandatory standard for use in central government work in 1983. Since then it has been quite widely used for both local and central government projects, and in industry. SSADM probably achieved maturity with Ver-sion 3, which was the first version to be widely supported by textbooks, and the subsequent development of Version 4 has largely been concerned to consolidate its form and to fill in a number of gaps. This section will use the more established forms and terminology of Version 3, since Version 4 is still relatively new.

SSADM is targeted at large data-processing applications, and so it essentially uses a data-driven approach for its analysis and design forms. The basic strategy underpinning the method is that of top-down develop-ment through analysis to logical design and then to physical design, but this is extensively augmented through abstract modelling techniques. These techniques make use of multiple viewpoints to describe a system and its interactions, and encourage the developers to perform cross-checking between the viewpoints in order to ensure the consistency and complete-ness of the analysis and design models.

SSADM is not the only example of a method that has been developed with the wider needs of an organization in mind. The HOOD approach to design, described in Chapter 12, was partly intended to meet such a need, although with real-time systems in mind. Similarly, in the UK MASCOT (described in the next section of this chapter) has been in use for a good number of years in the development of real-time systems. In France, the MERISE method (Quang and Chartier-Kastler, 1991) per-forms a role equivalent to that of SSADM, and is also intended for use in the development of data-processing systems.

One aspect of SSADM that should be mentioned here is that it is essentially concerned with developing systems that embody established practices. That is, it is geared towards analysing existing practices (whether manual or automated) and then using this as the basis for designing a system to support such practices, rather than with providing insight into ways of redesigning or adapting the practices when developing a solution.

(To some extent this reflects the context in which it is expected that SSADM will be used, with the emphasis being placed upon the repeatability of the analysis and design processes.) Indeed, the analysis stages of SSADM are much more prescriptive and better supported diagrammatically than the design stages.

The creators of SSADM were well aware that designers and programmers are rarely keen on producing extensive quantities of text to describe their systems. So, wherever possible, SSADM recommends making use of diagrams and standard forms to capture the attributes of the analysis and design models and to capture the rationale behind any decisions. This approach is also intended to encourage the involvement of the end-users in the process of reviewing the ideas of the system developers by ensuring that these are presented in as clear a manner as possible. So while SSADM seeks to be 'prescriptive' about the design process as far as this is possible, the techniques used are also supported by a realistic approach to the documentation of design decisions and design structures.

SSADM has been relatively well documented, at least for Version 3, and as the differences caused by the developments of Version 4 are relatively minor, any textbook based on Version 3 is sufficient to provide a general understanding of the method. A useful overview is given in Ashworth (1988), and more comprehensive descriptions can be obtained from books such as Downs *et al.* (1988), Ashworth and Goodland (1990), and (for Version 4) Longworth (1992). The really determined reader can also obtain the complete (and voluminous) SSADM developer's documentation from the UK's National Computing Centre, based in Manchester.

13.3.2   The diagrammatical forms of SSADM

While neither the notations nor the procedures of SSADM are particularly innovative in a technical sense, its designers have made good use of a basic set of data description forms that have been well proven in use. Any innovative element in SSADM therefore lies more with the way that these are combined, rather than with the forms themselves. As mentioned earlier, SSADM uses three principal 'viewpoints' for modelling a system, and these are represented by three principal diagrammatical forms. This section gives a brief review of these viewpoints and of the corresponding diagrammatical forms.

The Entity–Relationship Diagram

In SSADM these diagrams are referred to as 'Structure Charts', but the term 'Entity–Relationship Diagram' is used throughout this section to avoid confusion with the Yourdon-style Structure Charts that were described in Chapters 6 and 10.

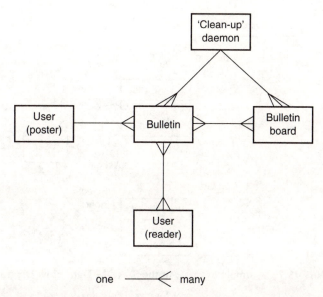

Figure 13.6 Example of SSADM 'Structure Chart' (Entity–Relationship Diagram). The example is based on an electronic 'bulletin board' system. Note that: the user may read and post many bulletins; bulletins may be read by many users; a bulletin board may contain many bulletins; a bulletin may be posted to more than one bulletin board; the daemon process may erase many bulletins on many boards.

These diagrams provide a static data-modelling viewpoint of the elements of the system, and are used for building entity models. Their purpose is therefore one of modelling the relationships that are expressed *in* the data itself. The form is not particularly original: an example of such a diagram is shown in Figure 13.6. In such a diagram the 'crow's-foot' symbol at the end of an arc is used to express one-to-many, many-to-one and many-to-many relationships between data entities.

The point about this viewpoint and the relationship that it describes is that it is independent of the way that a system functions or is organized. The data is described in an abstract form that does not consider in what ways the data will be used, or how it will be structured, transferred, and so on. This view of the design model is also essentially static, in that the relationships so described are not expected to undergo any significant changes over time.

The Data-Flow Diagram

This viewpoint *is* concerned with the organization of the eventual system and, in particular, with its dynamic behaviour. Unlike the previous form of DFD encountered in Chapters 6 and 10, this notation is concerned with providing a functional description of the *solution*, as well as being used for

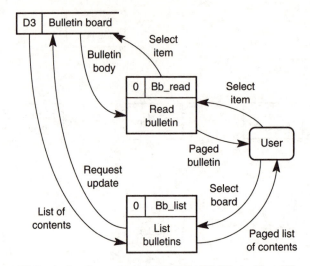

Figure 13.7 A simple example of the SSADM Data-Flow Diagram.

analysing the *problem*. As a result, its form is less abstract, and it possesses a more extensive and detailed syntax, than that of the Yourdon/De Marco techniques.

Figure 13.7 shows an example of such a Data-Flow Diagram. The major boxes that appear in this are termed 'processes', although they are likely to be eventually implemented as subprograms. Each has an identi-fication number and (optionally) a short identifier in the top section, together with a brief description of its function in the main body. Data stores are represented by labelled boxes that are open at one end. External entities (that is, those that are not modelled in the solution, but which provide inputs and receive outputs) are described using a box with rounded corners. The arcs between these elements are used to describe data flow in the 'normal' manner.

The Entity Life-History Diagram

To all intents and purposes this third (functional/behavioural) viewpoint has a form identical with that of the Entity–Structure Diagrams of JSD (in other words, an ELHD uses the form and syntax of a Jackson Structure Diagram), and its main purpose is for use in modelling the evolution of data entities over time. An Entity Life-History Diagram is shown in Figure 13.8.

A survey of the experiences of users of SSADM by Edwards *et al.* (1989) identified this viewpoint as the one that gave most difficulty to users, in that they found it difficult to develop these diagrams. While no specific reasons for this were identified, this viewpoint is certainly less 'physical' than that of the DFD, and the production of Entity Life-History

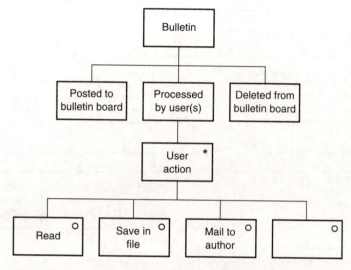

Figure 13.8 Example of an SSADM Entity Life-History Diagram.

Diagrams requires practice with selecting the 'right' abstractions. The next section outlines some of the techniques provided in SSADM, and it should be noted that one of these is specifically intended to assist with the production of this form of diagram.

13.3.3 The process part of SSADM

While the strategies involved in SSADM are not primary objects of interest for purposes of methodological study, their organization offers a much more interesting subject of study. We should also observe that, despite its title, SSADM is really much more concerned with analysis than with design; indeed, the design steps are relatively weak, and lack the degree of diagrammatical support that is provided for the analysis steps.

The basic SSADM process model is shown in Figures 13.9 and 13.10. There are three major 'phases' (the first of these, the 'feasibility study' is optional), which in turn are divided into six 'stages'. The stages are in turn divided into 'steps', with each of these encompassing a set of 'tasks'. The titles of the stages show that SSADM places major emphasis on developing a *logical* design, and its transformation into a *physical* design takes place only in the final stage of the method.

In terms of organizing the overall process of analysis and design in SSADM, the basic management component is the step. Figure 13.11 outlines the components that are involved in a step, while Figure 13.12 shows one of the standard steps. The example chosen here is not technically exciting, but it shows 'typical' entries for each of the four major

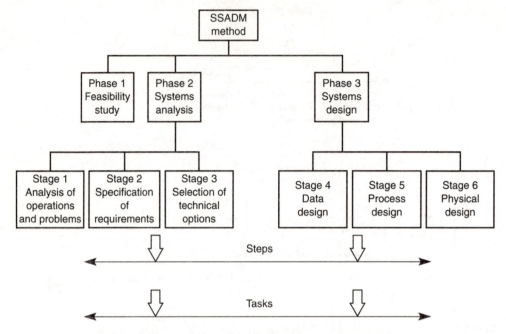

Figure 13.9   The sequencing of SSADM process components.

components of a step, and also illustrates the (excessive?) attention to detail that is a characteristic of the SSADM method.

It is intended that the tasks that are identified as part of a step should be capable of being performed by the techniques associated with the step. In the example of Figure 13.12, the techniques involved are not very profound or technical, but those that involve the production of diagrammatical forms do have associated techniques to assist with their production (these are outlined below). So while there is a general analysis and design process for SSADM itself, there are also a number of sub-processes in the method, which are followed in order to generate particular representations of the system model.

To return to the three major representations described in the preceding subsection: the techniques recommended for producing each of these are very briefly summarized as follows:

Entity–Relationship Diagrams

These reflect the logical data structures of the system, and they are produced through the use of the Logical Data-Structuring Technique (LDST), which is a recommended set of procedures. This technique is used in a wide selection of steps in the feasibility and analysis phases. The major steps of LDST involve:

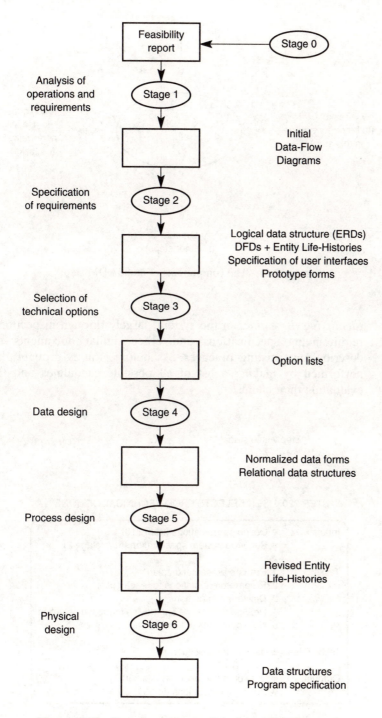

Figure 13.10   Transformation model of the SSADM process.

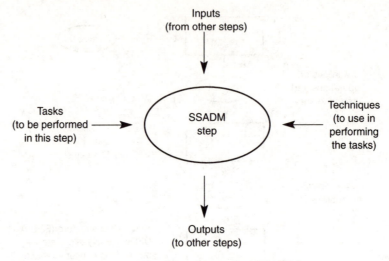

Figure 13.11 The components of an SSADM step.

(1) *Identifying the entities* in the system, largely through inspection of requirements specifications and other similar documents that describe any existing practices. As before, this is probably best performed by making a list of all possible candidates and then evaluating their claims.

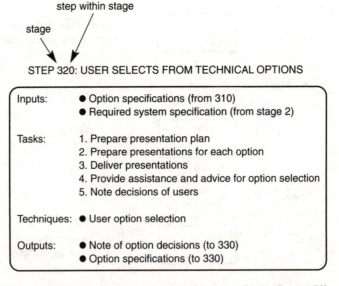

Figure 13.12 An example of an SSADM step (stage 3, step 20).

	Bulletin	Bulletin board	User (reader)	User (poster)	Daemon
Bulletin		*	*	*	*
Bulletin board					*
User (reader)					
User (poster)					
Daemon					

Figure 13.13   Example of LDST grid chart.

(2)   *Identifying the relationships* between the various entities (so giving a further opportunity for revising the list of entities). As a part of this task, the analyst is advised to draw up a grid (matrix) listing the entities along both axes and to examine every potential relationship. Figure 13.13 shows a simple example of such a grid chart, corresponding to the eventual diagram shown in Figure 13.6. (This step also requires the analyst to study the *nature* of each relationship.)

(3)   *Drawing the diagram*, which involves creating a box for each entity, and linking those that have been identified as related. The form of each link will be dependent on the further analysis performed in step 2 to identify whether relationships are one-to-one, one-to-many or many-to-many.

(4)   *Validation of the logical data structure*. This involves such issues as checking for redundant relationships, ensuring that the user agrees with the relationships identified by the analyst, and checking against the Data-Flow Diagrams to ensure that the access paths involved are able to provide the data required for each process box.

A particularly good description of the issues and tasks involved in LDST is provided in Ashworth and Goodland (1990).

Data-Flow Diagrams

These are produced by much the same techniques as are used for developing the De Marco form of DFD. There is no specially named technique in SSADM, although some guidance is provided. Once again, the initial DFDs are *physical* DFDs, which are then used to help with development of the *logical* forms.

ENTITIES	EVENTS					
	Post bulletin	List b-b contents	Read bulletin	Delete expired bulletin	Mail bulletin author	Save bulletin in file
Bulletin	*		*		*	*
Bulletin board	*	*				
User	*	*	*		*	*
Daemon				*		

Figure 13.14 Example of an Entity Life-History matrix.

Entity Life-History Diagrams

As with the production of logical data structures, the strategy recommended for developing these diagrams involves using a matrix or grid (the 'ELH matrix') that helps identify the basic links between system events and the individual data objects (entities). So the basic steps are:

(1) *Listing the entities.* This task has effectively been performed during the creation of the logical data structures. Indeed, one of the roles that ELHDs perform in SSADM is to provide a further degree of validation for the choice of entities.

(2) *Identifying and listing the events.* This is a task that normally involves an analysis of the DFDs produced for the system in order to extract the details of those events that are:

- *external* (caused by events outside the system);
- *temporal* (occurring at a particular point in time);
- *internal* (arising from a condition being satisfied within the system itself).

(3) *Creating the ELH matrix.* Figure 13.14 shows a simple example of such a matrix. Again, it is one that would be produced for one of the earlier examples, in this case that of Figure 13.8. The first substep in developing this is to identify links between events and entities; a further analysis substep is to determine whether a particular link leads to entry creation, modification or deletion, and hence provides further guidance on the development of the ELHD itself.

(4)   *Drawing the ELH diagram.* This is likely to involve several evolutionary stages for each such diagram. It has previously been observed that, while these diagrams are a powerful descriptive form, they can be difficult to create and so, even with the aid of the ELH matrix, there will often need to be many iterations in the development of the ELH diagram to resolve the structural issues that arise.

These outline descriptions should be sufficient to allow the reader to appreciate that these techniques seek to provide a degree of cross-checking between the three major viewpoints, and hence seek to avoid the possibility of any inconsistencies occurring between them in the model of the system. One other point to observe here is that all three of these techniques are essentially concerned with analysis tasks. This reinforces our earlier classification of the SSADM process as oriented more to analysis than to design.

13.3.4 SSADM in use

While SSADM has now been in use for some time, it has taken quite a while for its form to become fully established, and only since the late 1980s has it been seen as an important technique in its own right. Its use is now bolstered by requirements that trainers in SSADM should hold certificates, by the provision of a unit dedicated to maintaining SSADM, and by tools and other materials.

Edwards *et al.* (1989) surveyed the extent to which SSADM was used in 1987 in industry and in local and central government. Their survey drew some interesting conclusions about the areas of Version 3 that have given difficulty to users (some of these have been addressed in Version 4), and the extent to which only parts of the method have been used in practice.

Another interesting conclusion of the paper was the extent to which users seemed to have made use of JSP to augment the Physical Design stage of SSADM. It seemed that they generally saw it as a particularly weak stage in the method, and felt that JSP was capable of meeting some of the needs that this should address; or perhaps JSP was simply the detailed design technique most familiar to the developers of such systems.

At this point we have probably considered enough of the main features of SSADM, especially in the absence of any well-established heuristics concerning its use. It should, however, be noted that in the future some form of 'Euro-method' for software development may be required, and SSADM or MERISE are the most likely forms on which it could be based. However, as yet, this remains only a speculation.

13.4 Designing real-time systems: MASCOT

13.4.1 Some background to MASCOT

MASCOT (the acronym stands for 'Modular Approach to Software Construction, Operation and Test') originated in the UK defence industry during the mid-1970s (Simpson and Jackson, 1979; Simpson, 1982) and was devised in response to the growing difficulties that were being encountered in designing and constructing large and complex real-time systems. Until then, real-time systems had been largely developed using very low-level programming forms such as assembler code, with minimal operating-system support, and they sought to extract maximum performance from the hardware. However, the rapid advances in computer technology, together with a growing recognition that existing systems were exceedingly difficult to modify or maintain, made it evident that such an approach to real-time system development was fast reaching its practical limits, if it was not already past them.

The solution adopted in MASCOT was to use a modular philosophy to specify a relatively high-level virtual machine to provide the necessary level of abstraction from the hardware, while supporting the forms of behaviour that would be expected for real-time demands. Since real-time systems require close control of the time-ordered behaviour of a system, it was also necessary for any supporting implementation to have minimal and predictable overheads.

The 'MASCOT machine' was therefore based on the notion of a system as formed from a network of cooperating parallel processes (with no implicit assumptions as to whether the physical realizations of these would run on a single machine or a network of processors), using well-defined mechanisms for their interactions. The MASCOT 'run-time executive' provided a minimal operating system (Section 13.4.2) that was required to provide a standard set of primitive operations, enabling a designer to predict more readily the dynamic behaviour that the system corresponding to a given design would exhibit in specified circumstances.

As indicated above, MASCOT was devised at a time when CPU power was increasing rapidly and memory costs were falling steeply. It was therefore a little easier (but still not particularly easy) to sell the idea of the inevitable run-time overheads imposed by the extra layer of abstraction to the real-time community which has traditionally been concerned with squeezing maximum performance from systems by designing interactions in great detail, especially where interrupts were concerned. A degree of abstraction was already becoming acceptable, through the use of high-level programming languages such as CORAL-66 (Webb, 1978), RTL-2 (Barnes, 1976), and C (Kernighan and Ritchie, 1978), and so the use of MASCOT added the further run-time and constructional levels of abstraction that were increasingly required by real-time designers.

According to the definitions of 'method' that we have used so far, MASCOT cannot really be considered a fully fledged design method, for although it provides a design notation and a set of constructional forms that are used to specify the detailed mapping of a design into a system, it has always lacked a single well-defined process part. However, some procedural guidelines for developing MASCOT designs do exist, and the relatively extensive use of MASCOT, together with the general lack of well-developed real-time design strategies, means that it merits inclusion in this chapter.

In practice, while MASCOT proved quite successful (after some early adjustments), the diagrammatical notation in its orginal form was revealed to have limitations when it was used for describing large systems. This was chiefly because its form was essentially that of a single 'flat' diagram, and the single level of abstraction it provided did not give any scope for the designer to make use of the hierarchy of diagrams needed for the 'separation of concerns' and the layered abstraction required for the development of large systems. So the form of the diagram was revised extensively as part of the evolution of a new standard that became known as MASCOT 3 (SEJ, 1986).

This section will examine both the original form of the MASCOT notation (which will be termed 'MASCOT 2' where it is necessary to make the distinction) and the developments that were incorporated into MASCOT 3. This is partly because the original form possessed an elegance that was to some degree lost when it was extended, and also because it is still sometimes used for the initial architectural design phases, before being translated into MASCOT 3. (One of the criticisms of MASCOT 3 is that while the new notation allows for a better description of large systems in terms of detail and of a hierarchy of abstraction, it has also had the effect of reducing the ease with which the basic architecture of a design can be understood.)

13.4.2 The MASCOT notation

We will begin with a brief review of the original MASCOT notation, followed by a description of the MASCOT 3 forms. Because the interpretation of the diagrams depends upon an understanding of the rules imposed by the run-time executive, the details of the executive will also be reviewed as a part of this description.

The MASCOT system elements

In its original form, the 'MASCOT machine' supported three basic abstract system elements:

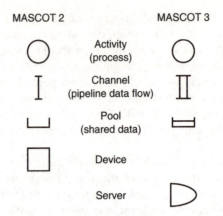

Figure 13.15 The basic system elements in MASCOT.

- An *Activity* is a schedulable process that provides a single 'thread' of execution. It performs the algorithmic functions of the system, and is constructed as a single sequential task with no internal concurrency. One consequence of this is that an Activity will be unable to access data objects in any other Activity.

- A *Channel* provides a 'pipeline' mechanism that is used for the transmission of data (messages) between Activities. Data in the buffer of a Channel is normally regarded as being transient; once a message has been read by an Activity it is considered to have been 'consumed', and the buffer space again becomes available for use.

- A *Pool* provides a mechanism by which Activities can access shared information of a more 'static' form. Information in a Pool normally continues to be available to be read by Activities until it is expressly deleted or overwritten.

However, even before the development of MASCOT 3, this set of elements proved to be inadequate, and the external 'device' providing input to and output from the system frequently became an *ad hoc* fourth system element.

Figure 13.15 shows the basic symbols used for these system elements in both MASCOT 2 and MASCOT 3. For the moment, though, we will concentrate on describing MASCOT 2, in which the Activity is denoted by a labelled circle, the Channel by a vertical bar and the Pool by an open box. Both Channels and Pools are also labelled, although finding sensible identifiers for all the Channels in a large system can become a rather difficult exercise.

The Channels and Pools are known collectively as Intercommunication Data Areas (not surprisingly, this is usually shortened in use to 'IDAs'). IDAs usually contain one or more data buffers, together with a

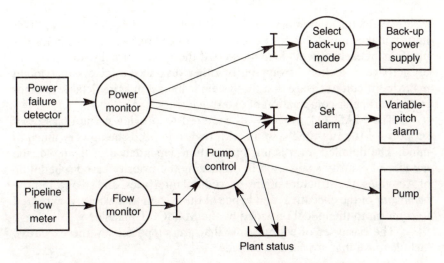

Figure 13.16 A segment from a MASCOT 2 ACP diagram.

set of Access Procedures that provide the external interface used by Activities. These Access Procedures further support the use of information-hiding, by concealing the internal structures of the IDA's buffers.

The network diagram that shows the flow of information between the system elements is known as an ACP diagram (for Activity, Channel, Pool). A particularly important rule in an ACP diagram is that Activities may communicate only through IDAs, and may not be linked in any direct way.

Figure 13.16 shows an example of a simple MASCOT ACP diagram. While this has some similarity in appearance to the De Marco Data-Flow Diagram described in Section 6.2, it is much more formal in style, and is concerned with forming a model of the solution to a problem, rather than with describing the problem itself. It also shows explicit threads of concurrency, where this is instantiated through the Activities.

To fully understand an ACP diagram, however, it is necessary to consider the form of the underlying executive, since this creates some 'implicit rules' that will determine how the system actually behaves.

The run-time executive

For a real-time system, the run-time executive provides a set of services for the real-time processes that are somewhat akin to those provided by an operating system. Essentially, therefore, it provides a level of abstraction between the application software and the underlying hardware.

The need for a real-time system to respond predictably and rapidly to asynchronous events means that it is normal to consider the MASCOT system elements as memory-resident, although this is not mandatory. This in turn makes it possible for the executive to be configured exactly for the numbers of each system element, so that there are normally no overheads of 'garbage-collection', swapping or other disk-access factors that might make it difficult to ensure that the system will react in a predictable manner to any particular combination of external events.

The MASCOT executive is required to provide certain classes of support for the run-time system, with real-time needs being very much in mind. The detailed form is implementation-dependent (for example, the number of priority levels used in organizing the priority-based scheduling of Activities, the structure of any procedural interfaces, and so on), but the *behaviour* of the executive, and hence of the system as a whole, is expected to conform to the model provided by the MASCOT machine.

The basic set of system calls that are supported by the executive include those that are used to provide:

- Activity execution control (the delay, suspend, and endroot primitives);
- timing information (timenow, and delay);
- synchronization and mutual exclusion (the join, leave, stim, wait, check, and waitfor operations);
- monitoring and recording options;
- Subsystem control (in MASCOT 2, the Subsystem construct was chiefly used for initialization, with the system elements in a group of objects being initialized together; MASCOT 3 has extended the role of the Subsystem very considerably);
- interrupt handling (the stimint, connect, and disconnect primitives).

As indicated above, while the behaviour of these primitive operations is expected to conform to the structure defined for the MASCOT machine, their detailed form (such as that of the procedural interface, or the units used for time intervals) could vary with an implementation.

A very significant point about the MASCOT philosophy is that a system is composed of *cooperating* parallel processes (Activities). This means that an Activity may only have direct control over its own actions, and may not directly control the behaviour of any other Activities. An Activity may use the primitive operations of the executive in order to defer its own execution for a period (delay), or surrender the CPU to another Activity of equal priority (suspend), but it cannot cause another Activity to defer execution or to transfer control of the CPU. There is therefore no control hierarchy in MASCOT: the only hierarchy is that of scheduling priority, which is primarily considered to be a means of fine-tuning performance.

INITIAL STATE		FINAL STATE			
		join	wait	leave	stim
Queue available (not stimmed)	1	2	*	*	5
Queue claimed (not stimmed)	2	□	3	1(or2)	4
Queue claimed (waiting)	3	□	*	*	2
Queue claimed (stimmed)	4	□	2	5(or4)	▽
Queue available (stimmed)	5	4	*	*	▽

* illegal operation

□ 'nil effect': the calling Activity is suspended on a list of Activities waiting to join the control queue

▽ 'no effect'

Figure 13.17 The five-state control queue transitions.

A consequence of this cooperative structure is that all coupling that exists between the system elements is explicitly shown in the ACP diagram. There is no hidden control coupling: interprocess communication is only possible by means of message-passing, and this is shown explicitly on the diagram by means of the data-flow arcs.

A distinctive feature of the MASCOT machine is the mechanism used for managing the sychronization and mutual exclusion needs. This mechanism is known as the 'control queue', and the control queues used to protect access to buffers within an IDA are normally regarded as being a part of the data structures of the IDA, since they are manipulated by the Access Procedures associated with that IDA.

Synchronization is provided via the primitive operations stim and wait (there is a further waitfor primitive in MASCOT 3). Mutual exclusion is handled via the join and leave operations (extended to include check in MASCOT 3). A widely adopted model for the control queue in MASCOT 2 used a five-state form: Figure 13.17 shows the details of the states and of the transitions that occur when the main four primitives are used. A distinctive feature of the control queue is that it does not preserve any sense of 'history' of events (unlike the semaphore), and so multiple stims on a control queue that does not have an Activity waiting on it will have the same effect as a single stim.

The principal developments in MASCOT 3

Some of the major reasons for the evolution in the form of MASCOT, eventually leading to MASCOT 3, were based on experience with using MASCOT in the late 1970s and early 1980s. It was recognized that MASCOT had the following shortcomings:

- The 'flat' form of the ACP diagram made it difficult to manage and comprehend the designs for large systems, owing to the complexity of the diagrams. It was generally recognized that some form of hierarchy was needed within the diagram structures.

- Some adjustments to the primitive operations of the executive were needed. In particular, the form for handling interrupts needed to be standardized, and the primitives available for handling inter-Activity communication required to be augmented.

- Facilities to allow systematic design elaboration were required. While MASCOT 2 had both a graphical representation and forms for specifying how construction was to be organized, these were not closely linked.

The final form of the MASCOT 3 standard was published in 1987, and sought to address these issues. In doing so, it considerably strengthened the constructional aspects of MASCOT; one criticism is that this consideration was perhaps too dominant when the graphical forms and other structures were being revised.

The rest of this subsection will concentrate on examining the extensions to the MASCOT notation, since this is the aspect that is most relevant to the general theme.

The basic system elements in MASCOT 3 are still largely recognizable as those that proved to be so successful in MASCOT 2. The main extension was the addition of the server as a fourth basic system element. In keeping with its intermediate role, having characteristics that are partly those of an Activity and partly those of an IDA, it has been assigned a semi-elliptical shape as its symbol. As shown in Figure 13.15, all the established system elements have also had some revisions to their symbolic forms, in order to reflect the increased information content required in a MASCOT 3 diagram.

The most significant change to the diagrammatical notation was the extensive development in the role of the Subsystem. In MASCOT 2 this had a role that was almost entirely concerned with initialization and control at run-time. In MASCOT 3 it was 'promoted' to become a composite form of system element that could be used as a design object.

The Subsystem is denoted by a box with rounded corners, and it may contain any mix of the four basic system elements together with further

Subsystems. It has therefore provided the means of including a hierarchy of diagrams within the ACP diagram structure.

One consequence of this has been that, where a data-flow path is indicated between Subsystems, there is no way of identifying whether the data is being 'pushed' or 'pulled', and hence which of the Subsystems contains the IDA and which contains the Activity. We can determine this only by tracing down through the hierarchy of Subsystems to find the eventual Activity–IDA link. To indicate the 'control' aspects of data flow, therefore, the MASCOT 3 notation includes a symbol at each end of a data-flow arc, which is used to indicate whether this is the active end or the passive end. The active end is denoted by a 'port' (for which the symbol is a round black dot), while the passive end is denoted by a 'window' (for which the symbol is a black bar). Ports are normally positioned within Activities or Subsystems, but for certain purposes it is also possible for a port to be included in an IDA.

Together with this extension on the graphical front, there has been an extension in the amount of detailed textual information that needs to be provided in an ACP diagram. Critics have argued that this lowers the level of abstraction unnecessarily, and it certainly appears that many designers do not follow the full MASCOT 3 standards in this matter until they begin to reach a relatively detailed level of design.

Figures 13.18 and 13.19 show examples of two levels of hierarchy in an ACP diagram, using the MASCOT 3 notation.

13.4.3 The MASCOT design process

One of the features that has perhaps restricted the extent to which MASCOT has been adopted beyond the immediate real-time domain is that there has never been a single recommended set of design practices forming a 'process part' to accompany the very powerful MASCOT notation – a feature for which it has sometimes been criticized. The DARTS system, which has many similarities with MASCOT, has attempted to provide more extensive guidance in this particular area, chiefly by using derivatives of the SSA/SD strategy (Gomaa, 1986).

On those occasions where a design procedure has been identified, the basic architectural strategy adopted has been to use functional decomposition to divide the system into major subsystem units, and it is likely that the same strategy has generally been used for the design of the detailed network. MASCOT encourages designers to separate out the concurrent threads of processing, by realizing them as Activities; the strong emphasis on modularity in all forms provides a means of ensuring that there are no potential cross-effects arising through ill-conditioned forms of interaction between system elements.

The MASCOT emphasis on separation of concerns, and the scope that the IDAs provide for information-hiding, suggest that there is scope to

Main system

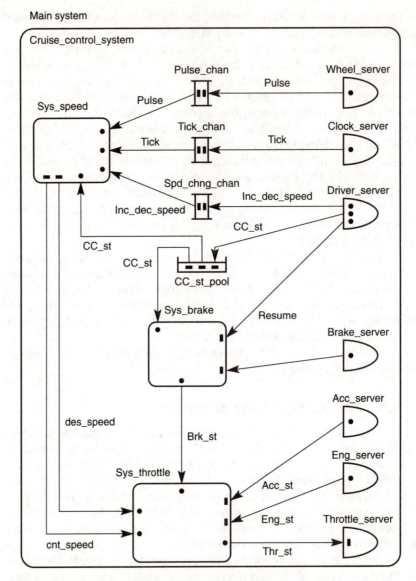

Figure 13.18   An example MASCOT 3 diagram. Note: some of the annotation has been omitted for clarity.

use some form of object-based design strategy with MASCOT. However, the strong process-centred form of MASCOT, in which the Activities form the principal algorithmic units, rather inhibits this, so accounting for the predominance of the functional decomposition strategy to date.

This lack of a recommended set of 'design procedures' also means that there are no particular guidelines for handling the 'nonfunctional'

Sys_speed

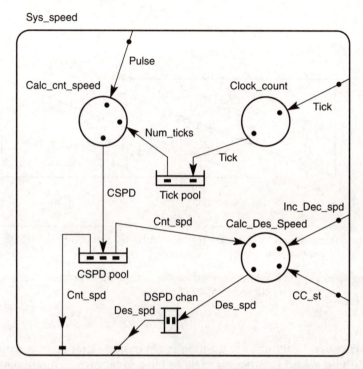

Figure 13.19 A MASCOT 3 subsystem. Note: the ports and window symbols have not been labelled in this example (each should have a unique label).

aspects of design that are so important in real-time systems. To some extent this is understandable, since this aspect of the design process is very problem-specific. Perhaps the main strength of MASCOT in this area is that the provision of a standard form of run-time executive enables the designer to make reliable predictions of system behaviour in different operating scenarios.

It is interesting to make some comparisons with another design process that seeks to support the development of systems based on parallel processes, namely JSD. Any comparison that we can make here is essentially subjective in nature, but one such is shown in Figure 13.20 which seeks to contrast the support that the two methods provide for different tasks in the development life-cycle.

This shows that JSD provides detailed support and guidelines for the early stages of analysis and model development, but much weaker guidelines for the later tasks such as physical design. MASCOT, on the other hand, provides a philosophy that is almost diametrically opposite, giving very little support to the early stages, beyond the ACP diagram notation, but extensive support for the later (constructional) tasks.

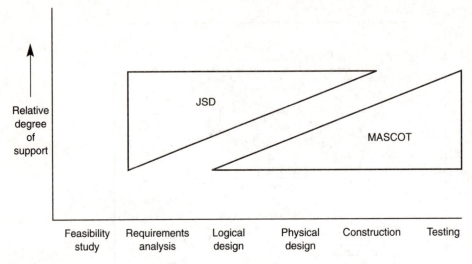

Figure 13.20 Comparison of the support provided for the development process stages by JSD and MASCOT.

However, although the diagram might indicate that there is scope to 'splice' these methods, attempts to do so have so far proved disappointing. The underlying virtual machine models prove to be less compatible than they may appear on the surface and, indeed, the whole question of bringing design methods together is one that needs to be investigated further.

13.4.4 MASCOT developments

At various times considerable efforts have been made to link MASCOT to Ada, in the hope that it could aid the process of design (Jackson, 1986). However, the differences in the run-time virtual machine models have so far rendered this generally unsatisfactory. In particular, the Ada task model permits tasks to share types, constants and variables within the same compilation unit (usually the package), which contradicts the total separation of Activities imposed in MASCOT. The rendezvous used for inter-process communication is also incompatible with the model of mutual exclusion and synchronization used in the MASCOT machine. It is interesting to note that much the same type of effort has gone into attempting to extend the DARTS model (Gomaa, 1989), with no clear evidence of any greater success.

In concluding this review, it should be observed that the MASCOT model has proved to be highly successful in use. Indeed, the elegance of the original MASCOT 2 formulation has almost been counterproductive: its very success led to a demand to extend the form of MASCOT, and then, in providing this, something of the simplicity and power of the model seemed to get lost.

One of the attractions of MASCOT has been that it has a published standard, and hence has been relatively free of any significant attempts to develop variant forms.

The lack of a well-defined process part means that there has been considerable use of design heuristics. Unfortunately, these often seem to have been regarded as proprietary, or company-specific, and so there has been no successful compilation of the hard-won experiences of MASCOT designers. Of course, this also reflects something of the very application-specific nature of real-time design – although, as the very success of MASCOT has itself shown, this can sometimes be overstated.

SUMMARY

The selection of design practices described in this chapter was made with the intention of illustrating something of the extent to which design 'models', procedures and notations can vary between different methods, even where they notionally address the same problem domain. The selection also provides an illustration of an 'organizational' design method, as well as an example from the rather specialized real-time domain. Other design practices could have been chosen for the purpose of comparison, and so we have by no means exhausted this particular seam.

FURTHER READING

Ross D.T. (1977). Structured Analysis (SA): A language for communicating ideas. *IEEE Trans. Software Eng.*, **SE-3**(1), 16–34

A discussion of the analysis part of the SADT method, providing a number of useful illustrations of the notation.

Ashworth C.M. (1988). Structured Systems Analysis and Design Method (SSADM). *Information and Software Technology*, **30**(3), 153–63

A concise and useful review of the main features of Version 3 of the SSADM method from a technical viewpoint.

SEJ (1986). Special issue on MASCOT 3. *Software Eng. J.*, **1**(3)

Contains a set of papers that range from the introductory to the highly detailed, describing the application of MASCOT to real-time problems.

EXERCISES

13.1   Use the SADT actigram notation to describe the process of constructing a garden shed (assembling panels from a set of beams and planks; assembling the panels; glazing windows; hanging the door; and felting the roof).

13.2   The SSADM Entity Life-History matrix is a useful means of identifying the components of an Entity Life-History Diagram, although, of course, it does not help much with the task of determining any sequencing that might be involved. Construct a matrix, and hence an Entity Life-History Diagram, to describe the entity 'book' within a library system. (Suggestions for other entities might include 'catalogue', 'issue record system' and 'records list'; while possible events might include 'purchase', 'issue to borrower', 'return from loan' and 'dispose'.)

13.3   Sketch out a design for a MASCOT 3 Subsystem that can be used to control a bank autoteller machine used for issuing cash and providing an optional receipt for each issue.

14 A Formal Approach to Design

14.1 The case for rigour

14.2 Model-based strategies

14.3 Property-based strategies

The design representations and methods that have so far been described in this book have largely been *systematic* in nature, lacking formal mathematical underpinnings (the main exceptions have been the Statechart and Petri Net description forms). While the informal syntax and semantics of systematic forms of notation can assist the designer with exploring and developing ideas about a design, their lack of rigour can sometimes create difficulties for such tasks as those involved in verifying a design, or communicating ideas about it to the implementors.

The topic of the so-called 'formal methods' is a very large one, and can only be treated fairly briefly in this text. This chapter therefore concentrates on examining how the mathematical underpinnings provided by such techniques can help to overcome such problems as those described above.

14.1 The case for rigour

The role of so-called 'formal methods' in the sofware development process
is a large topic, and one that is still developing and evolving. This chapter
will chiefly be concerned with describing the forms of notation and the
procedures that they employ, and with considering how their application
fits within the framework for the software design process that was
developed in Chapter 8. Taken together, these will allow us to make some
comparisons with the properties of the systematic methods that were
described in the previous chapters.

The systematic software design methods, such as those described
and analysed in the preceding chapters, all make use of graphical representation forms, supported to varying degrees by structured text and free
text. One problem with these notations is that they generally lack any
rigorous syntactic and semantic foundations, and so it is difficult to reason
about them in any 'formal' manner. In particular, to understand the
meaning of any diagram we may well need to resolve ambiguities of
interpretation by consulting the textual components. (This is not to say
that *all* diagrams have no well-defined syntax and semantics. Jackson's
Structure Diagram form has a very well-defined syntax, together with
some semantic content, while the Statechart and Petri Net described in
Chapter 6 can certainly be regarded as more rigorous, since they are
based on mathematical formalisms and are therefore unambiguous in
nature.)

The problems caused by this lack of a firm syntax and well-defined
semantics for many of the diagrammatical notations used in systematic
design practices can easily be seen when we consider issues such as design
verification. In many of the forms considered so far, it is virtually impossible to perform any kind of verification operation to make a comparison
between the eventual design and the initial requirement. This is because
the design transformations have so changed the forms of description (or
their interpretation), that there is little or no scope to perform such checks
in a rigorous manner, or to reason analytically about the properties of the
design itself. As a result of these transformations, the design virtual
machine that is used in the early stages of the design process is unlikely to
be compatible with that which is used in a later stage.

Formal methods seek to overcome this problem through the use of
formal specification languages, based on mathematical structures. The use
of such forms permits the application of mathematical techniques in reasoning about a design and its properties. In return, there is of course a
corresponding reduction in terms of the powers of abstraction that are
offered by such notations when compared with the systematic forms of
diagram. In seeking to remove ambiguity, the penalty incurred is to reduce
abstraction and enforce a greater attention to detail than may always be
desirable in terms of the needs of the design process.

The role of formal methods can therefore be summarized as being to provide mathematically based techniques that can be used for describing system properties – remembering, though, that the notations can still be diagrammatical in form, as in the example of the Statechart.

In terms of the framework for describing a 'method' used in this book, the formal methods are skewed in a very different manner to the systematic methods, in that they have:

- fairly simple process parts;
- relatively few well-established design heuristics;
- but (in compensation) very powerful representation parts.

For this reason they are often termed 'Formal Description Techniques' (or 'FDTs' for short) and, where appropriate, this term will be preferred in the descriptions of this chapter.

While FDTs can be used almost anywhere in the software development process and life-cycle, the tasks for which they are best suited are:

- specifying system properties during requirements specification;
- specifying the detailed form of a solution in the detailed design stages.

Both of these tasks are enhanced by the FDTs' power of detailed notation. In contrast, the operations involved in making what we might term the *architectural* design decisions (concerned with such issues as the choice of modules and the division of function between them), in which the designer needs to manipulate relatively abstract concepts, are much less well suited to such forms. Figure 14.1 suggests how FDTs might be employed for the main stages of the software life-cycle introduced earlier, in Chapter 3.

Although a number of FDTs are very well developed, their industrial use has so far been limited, although it is undoubtedly growing, as is the scale of problem for which they have been used (Hall, 1990). Some of the reasons for the relatively slow adoption have been identified by authors such as Sommerville (1992) and Hall, and these include:

- The conservative approach of many project managers (like most software engineering techniques, FDTs require long-term 'up-front' investment in training and in project development time). The same problem may also affect the expectations of customers, who may have a reluctance to adopt 'unfamiliar' techniques and notations.
- The use of FDTs requires some familiarity with logic and with discrete mathematics (Gibbins, 1988).

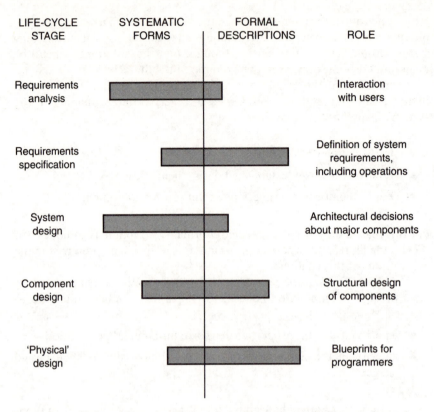

Figure 14.1 Roles of formal and systematic description techniques and notations in the software development life-cycle.

- The existing forms are not suited for use with all problems. Such aspects as Human–Computer Interaction (HCI), some features of parallelism, the nonfunctional elements of real-time systems, all present difficulties for these forms of description.

- Only limited tool support is currently available (perhaps aggravated by the rather varied forms of mathematical symbols used too, presenting difficulties for the simple word processor).

- There has been a degree of overselling on occasion, leading to unreasonably high expectations and subsequent disillusionment. (This is nothing new of course: the history of software engineering has many examples of genuine technical advances that have been unfairly criticized when they did not prove to be universal panaceas!)

Despite this, Hall (1990) notes that FDTs have been used on a reasonably large number of real projects, especially for key (usually safety-critical) components of systems. The increased trend towards making FDTs mandatory for certain tasks is also likely to increase interest in their use.

The second of the points in the above list perhaps merits a brief discussion. Without a doubt, the effective *use* of FDTs does require a good grounding in the appropriate mathematical techniques. What is much less clear is the extent to which this level of training is necessary to be able to *understand* formal descriptions. (We have previously encountered this issue of the distinction between the skill levels needed to *create* as opposed to those required to *understand*.) There seems to be good reason to think that a much less extensive degree of training will be needed for the latter where FDTs are concerned. The staff on a project who need the higher skill levels are likely to be considerably fewer than those who need only enough knowledge to understand formal specifications, and it may well be that the 'formal methods community' have unwittingly created a barrier to wider acceptance by failing to make this distinction clearer.

The more general issues involved in the use of FDTs have been well reviewed in a paper by Gerhart (1990), in which she addresses such topics as the factors affecting the wider adoption of these techniques. In particular, Gerhart points out that there are cultural differences between Europe and the USA, which can be summarized as:

- developments in Europe are based on exploiting the powers of formal specification, using languages such as VDM and Z to reason about the properties and behaviour of the end-system, and making only limited use of tools;
- in North America the focus is much more on program-proving techniques, aimed at verifying a solution against a requirement and supported by software tools.

So while both approaches seek to use mathematical forms and techniques to specify behavioural and structural properties of a system, the two communities are working from quite different starting points.

It has been observed that a formal specification language provides the following features (Wing, 1990):

- a notation (the 'syntactic domain');
- a universe of objects (the 'semantic domain');
- a rule stating which objects satisfy each specification.

The formal techniques that are in current use can also be grouped into two principal categories:

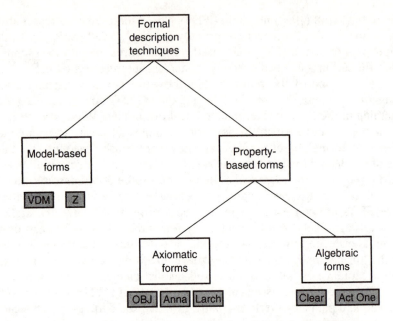

Figure 14.2 General categorization of formal methods.

(1) The *model-based* forms, in which the specifier defines the behaviour of a system by constructing a 'model' of the system using structures such as sets, functions, tuples and sequences. Notable examples of these forms are VDM and Z (the latter is pronounced 'zed').

(2) The *property-based* forms, in which the specifier defines the behaviour of a system indirectly, by stating a set of properties that it must satisfy. There are two further subcategories of these:

    (a) *Axiomatic* forms use *procedural* abstractions based on first-order predicate logic. Examples of these are OBJ, Anna and Larch.

    (b) *Algebraic* forms model *data* abstractions using axioms in the form of equations. Examples of such forms include Clear and Act One.

This division is summarized in Figure 14.2.

This general classification of form provides the basis for the structure that has been adopted for this chapter. This introduction is followed by two major sections that respectively examine the nature of the model-oriented and property-oriented forms.

Two further classifications that can be applied to FDTs, and which extend beyond these, while being related to them, are as follows:

- *Visual languages* use graphical forms for their syntactic content. Statecharts and Petri Nets have already been mentioned in this context.
- *Executable forms* use specifications that can be 'executed' via an interpreter. The requirement that their functions must be computable restricts the scope of these to a greater degree than the non-executable forms, and their role and scope are still subjects of debate (Hayes and Jones, 1989). Examples include me too (Alexander and Jones, 1990), Prolog and PAISley (Zave, 1984).

The form and application of formal methods are very wide subjects, and it is well beyond the scope of this book to attempt to describe any of these methods in detail. Greater detail and a fuller context are provided in Cohen *et al.* (1986), while Wing (1990) provides a useful framework and a brief example. Good reviews of the strengths and weaknesses of these methods are provided in both Gibbins (1988) and Hall (1990), and the latter cites some useful examples of application. The collection of papers in Gehani and McGettrick (1986) are mostly 'classical' rather than recent, but they do provide a valuable introduction to the subject of specification forms and the thinking behind them.

This chapter is concerned less with the detailed nature of the forms used in a given category of method than with the question of how to describe them within our present model of the design process. As observed earlier, formal methods generally combine very strong representation parts with quite weak process parts, with the latter usually involving some form of stepwise refinement. (The use of the term 'specification' in describing these forms places a not inappropriate emphasis on representation as against procedural content.) As such, therefore, the creative design component is apt to get pushed to a very early stage (usually the development of the basic model). Also, the roles and uses of design heuristics are harder to identify; this point will be examined a little more in each of the next two sections.

One question that is raised by the use of such forms is whether formal methods are essentially domain-specific, in that some problems lend themselves more readily to the use of this type of design process. This is a rather wide question, but it will be examined a little further when specific forms are considered.

14.2 Model-based strategies

14.2.1 Overview

In the previous section, model-based specification forms were described as those in which the specifier uses various mathematical forms to construct a 'model' of the system, and then uses this as the basis for reasoning about the properties and behaviour of the system. We begin a rather more detailed discussion of these design strategies by examining one of the methods using such an approach. It has features that will be readily recognizable to anyone with experience of imperative programming forms (although the analogy should be treated with due caution). It is also closer than the property-based forms to the approach used in the systematic methods described in the preceding chapters, in both its philosophy and its features; since the property-based forms concentrate more on describing the external features of a system than on the mechanisms that are used to produce these features.

The particular example used in this section is VDM (Vienna Development Method), which was developed in IBM's Vienna Research Laboratories during the 1970s. The original purpose of VDM was to aid the definition of programming languages, but subsequently its use has extended to encompass a much wider range of applications.

In this section we can examine only the main features of this method. A more detailed (and very readable) description is available in Cohen *et al.* (1986), while Jones (1980) is generally regarded as the definitive work on VDM. More examples of its use are given in Jones (1986). An important contribution by Jones has been to emphasize the use of mathematical *rigour*, in preference to complete formality; that is, while the framework used is a formal one, intuition is often enlisted to help with providing correctness arguments, with full formal verification being applied where absolutely necessary.

The design process of VDM is directed towards developing a sequence of models, beginning with a very abstract model of the overall system and ending with detailed models of the individual design components. These models are based on an explicit model of the state of the system, and make use of data objects that are used to represent the state of the system, as well as any inputs and outputs, and the operations that are used to manipulate these. The operations can be specified either implicitly (using preconditions and postconditions), or constructively (using recursive functions), with most textbooks seeming to prefer the former style.

Jones (1986) has argued that it is in the *specification* of data objects and types that VDM differs most strongly from property-oriented techniques. He argues that while the property-oriented style offers mathematical tractability, this is gained at the expense of limiting the ability to handle the full range of data types needed for problems in computing science.

The design process involved in VDM is relatively simple in form, being primarily one of refinement of the data structures by gradually adding detail to them; it can be summarized algorithmically as follows (Hekmatpour and Ince, 1988):

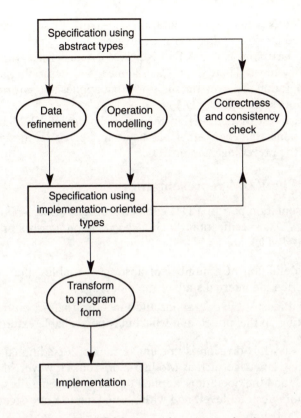

Figure 14.3   The VDM approach to system development.

specify the system formally;
prove that the specification is consistent;
repeat
    refine and decompose the specification (realization);
    prove that the realization satisfies the previous iteration of the
    specification;
until the realization can be implemented as a program;
revise the above steps.

This shows that the emphasis is placed on ensuring that each elaboration of
the design model is consistent with the previous (more abstract) version of
the model.

    This process is termed 'reification'; Figure 14.3 provides a schematic
and more abstract description of the transformations involved. (The iteration involved in this fairly simple process has of course no firm 'stopping
rule', which was a general design problem that was identified back in
Chapter 1.) So while at the top level of abstraction the properties of the
system might be described using very abstract data forms such as sets, at

the lower levels (where implementation is in sight), these are likely to have been refined into trees, linked lists or arrays.

One last point is that VDM is primarily concerned with describing sequential systems. There is no specific means of describing any form of parallel operation. This restriction is one that applies to the formal description techniques generally.

In the rest of this section the general form of VDM is described using the same framework that has been applied to the design methods studied in the preceding chapters.

14.2.2 The VDM representation

The representation part of VDM can be regarded as corresponding to the form of a VDM specification. Such a specification consists of two major components, which are:

- the definition of a number of abstract 'variables' that are used to describe the internal state of the model;
- definitions of the operations and functions that act on the variables making up the model, and which may be available externally.

(In some ways this division is not unlike that of a traditional imperative programming language such as Modula-2 or Ada. However, the variables themselves, and the operations applied to them, are generally described at a rather more abstract level, and without making use of assignment operations.)

We shall begin by examining the variables and the forms that these can take. The typographical conventions that have been used for printing the details of VDM specifications are:

- user-defined *OPERATIONS* are printed in upper-case serif italics;
- the identifiers of *types* are printed in serif italics;
- identifiers of variables are printed in serif roman type in declarations;
- identifiers of **keywords** are printed in bold sanserif type;
- type identifiers begin with an upper-case letter, followed by a sequence of lower-case letters;
- the constants of scalar types are named using upper-case serif *italic* letters only;
- extensions such as -set or -list are printed in a sanserif typeface.

Data forms

These are briefly reviewed below. For our purposes, we will look at the simple types, at the use of variables, and (briefly) at some of the more powerful types that are used in VDM.

Simple types   A number of 'built-in' types are predefined in VDM; some examples of these are *Int*, the set of integers, and *Nat0*, the set of non-negative integers (including zero). (Unlike the implementation of similar types in a programming language, these are essentially infinite in range, although it might be convenient to define subtypes.)

Another simple type is the set. Sets of scalar values may be introduced by using a type definition such as

$$Position = \{NORTH, SOUTH, EAST, WEST\}$$

Variables   Again, the form of definition is very similar to that used in many programming languages, with a variable being defined in terms of its identifier and type, as in the example

currentlocation : *Position*

More powerful types   At the abstract level of specification, there are a number of forms that can usefully be manipulated to describe the properties of a model.

One such form comprises sets and combinations of sets (states of a model may well be formed by combining a number of states of the sub-components). VDM allows the use of variables of a 'set type', for which the value will be a set, and provides operations such as set union, difference and intersection. Again, these features are not unknown in programming languages such as Modula-2 (Budgen, 1989).

Another powerful abstraction is the idea of the list (sometimes also referred to as a 'sequence' or a 'tuple'). Basic operations that are supported are those of hd (returning the first element of a list) and tl (returning the last), len to obtain the size of a list, and elems which returns a set made up of the elements of a list (this removes duplicates). Individual elements of a list can be obtained in the normal manner by indexing.

Both set types and list types can be created from a basic type by adding the suffix -set or -list to the identifier of the type. (The set type so created is termed the 'powerset'.)

Continuing the analogy with some of the data types that will be more familiar to programmers using imperative programming languages, we can also define record types, which combine variables of different types within a single structure. An example of such a definition is:

Turret :: height : *Nat0*
　　distance : *Nat0*
　　orientation : *Position*-set

so that in describing a turret (say of a fortification), one needs to specify its height and position (in terms of distance and bearing) with regard to some datum point within the structure. (The last component provides some scope for ambiguity, as it is a set type, and so it is likely that not all combinations of elements will be legal.)

The final data form is the mapping, which is a special form of function that can be used to map the elements of one set (termed the 'domain') to a second set (termed the 'range'). We will not discuss this form in this section.

Operations and functions

At this point, the similarity with imperative programming forms disappears, which is quite appropriate, since the operations in a programming language are often closely related to the structures of the underlying machine (as in the operation of assignment), rather than to the structures of the problem.

In VDM, the operations and functions of a system are usually defined through the standard operators of predicate logic. These include:

$\sim$	not
$\wedge$	and
$\vee$	or
$\equiv$	is equivalent to (iff)
$\rightarrow$	implies
$\forall$	for all (universal quantifier)
$\exists$	there exists (existential quantifier)
$\exists!$	there exists exactly one (existential quantifier)

In addition, the use of a 'let clause' allows a section of an expression to be 'named' in order to simplify the overall form, rather as one may choose to do when manipulating complex algebraic expressions.

Since VDM models a system using a state-based form, it is necessary to relate the effect of an operation to its effect on a particular state of the system. So the first element of a VDM specification provides a model of the relevant data using the VDM data types that were described above. This model is termed the 'system state', and it is used when defining the operations that will be provided for users of the 'system'.

In structure, therefore, a VDM model has some similarity to the concept of the 'object' that was so central to the forms described in Chapter 12: these too had the concept of an object state, and of a set of operations that could be used to modify the state. (At a less elaborate level, it is also akin to the idea of the abstract data type.)

Figure 14.4 shows part of a VDM specification for a simple record base for an Air Traffic Control system. In this system, new entries are added when an aircraft enters the airspace, and entries are removed when an aircraft leaves the airspace. While within the airspace an aircraft is

Airspacestate:: inflight : *Aircraft*-set
onground : *Aircraft*-set

Aircraft:: callsign : *Callsignformat*
flightnumber : *Flightcode*
height : *Nat0*
distance : *Nat0*
bearing : *Angle*
speed : *Nat0*
direction : *Angle*

ENTERSPACE(a : *Aircraft*)

ext wr inflight : *Aircraft*-set
  rd onground : *Aircraft*-set

pre $a \notin inflight \wedge a \notin onground$

post $inflight = inflight' \cup \{a\}$

LAND(a : *Aircraft*)

ext wr inflight : *Aircraft*-set
  wr onground : *Aircraft*-set

pre $a \notin onground \wedge a \in inflight$

post $inflight = inflight' - \{a\}$
       $onground = onground' \cup \{a\}$

TAKEOFF(a : *Aircraft*)

/* same form as for landing */

LEAVESPACE(a : *Aircraft*)

/* same form as entering the airspace */

INIT( )

ext wr inflight : *Aircraft*-set
  rd onground : *Aircraft*-set

post $inflight = \{ \}$
       $onground = \{ \}$

Figure 14.4   A section of a VDM specification for the record base (track table)
used in an ATC system.

recorded as either in flight or on the ground (clearly, both of these states can subsequently be further refined). Other basic operations involve landing and taking off, and refinements of these will be likely to identify the need for further operations.

Each operation defined for this system is structured in three parts (although not all of the parts need be present), labelled as follows:

- **ext** (for 'external') is a clause describing those parts of the state that are accessed in the operation. The further keywords **rd** and **wr** are used to indicate read only and read/write access. In our example, the operation of *ENTERSPACE* will require write access to the 'inflight' variable (to add a new entry), but only requires read access to 'onground' (for checking).

- **pre** is a precondition forming a predicate over the values of the input parameters together with the initial state when the operation occurs. This determines the conditions under which the operation is defined to have an effect. Again, for *ENTERSPACE*, the precondition is used to specify that the aircraft should not already be present in the airspace; the later stages of refinement will need to determine what action should be performed if an aircraft entering the airspace has an identical call-sign or flight number to one already present.

- **post** is a 'postcondition' showing how the values of the variables in the state are to be modified, and how the values of the output parameters are to be generated. Since the condition may need to be expressed in terms of the values of the variables both before and after the operation has occurred, the values of variables in the initial state are distinguished by using a prime on the variable name. For the *ENTERSPACE* operation, the new aircraft will simply be added to the 'inflight' set.

Further properties may be defined through the use of *invariants*, which are predicates used to define additional constraints on the values that the variables may assume. As an example of an invariant that applies to Figure 14.4, we can observe that no aircraft should be both in flight and on the ground at any time. This is clearly an invariant condition (it should be physically impossible for this condition to be broken), and may be expressed by adding the following predicate to the specification:

$$inv\text{-}State = inflight \cap onground = \{\}$$

to show that the intersection of the sets of aircraft that are in flight and on the ground must be the empty set – that is, no aircraft can be both in flight and on the ground.

The use of invariants forms an important topic, since it is necessary for the designer to ensure that any operations will preserve the invariant properties of a system. This is a good example of how the mathematical properties of a VDM specification can be utilized to assist with producing a design for a system that will maintain a consistent description of the model.

Another important feature of a VDM specification, not really brought out in this example, is the use of comments. While formal descriptions offer the benefits of mathematical reasoning, they also need to be related to the corresponding real-world problems, and their features may need to be explained to the reader. The use of comments provides this important link between the powerful but terse notation of mathematics, and the need to relate a design description to the problem and the final system. (This issue will arise again when we look at the property-based forms, for which it is generally recognized that there is a need to include textual comments for the purposes of explanation and clarification.)

The above description of the VDM representation is fairly simplistic in nature, and inevitably it omits some important features, but it does serve to demonstrate some of the main elements used in such a form and some of the ways in which the mathematical model may be used.

14.2.3 The VDM process

The process of developing a VDM specification is not structured in the same manner as is generally the case for the systematic approaches to design, with separate steps that involve quite distinct operations. The basic VDM strategy is one of decomposition, although, as in many methods, this is influenced by other factors. In this case, a major consideration concerns the abstract data types used in the model.

The overall development process has already been described in Figure 14.3: rather than a sequence of transformations, it consists of repeated iterations of the same operations. The process of reification basically consists of adding more detail to a specification in terms of both the data structures (for example, sets being developed into trees) and the operations performed on the data structures, until an 'implementation' level of specification is considered to have been reached. We have already observed that, as in other design strategies, this process has no specific stopping rule, and so, despite the formality, it has the same basic limitations found in any other software design process.

The VDM process does not seek to prescribe how each refinement should itself be structured, and it can be argued that this is where the designer is given the opportunity to make the type of choices that are required by the whole concept of design. (This point is made in Jones (1986).) However, by the nature of the overall strategy, the designer is likely to find that the scope for choice is quite limited at each step – although this can be considered as a strength in terms of ensuring a consistent design strategy.

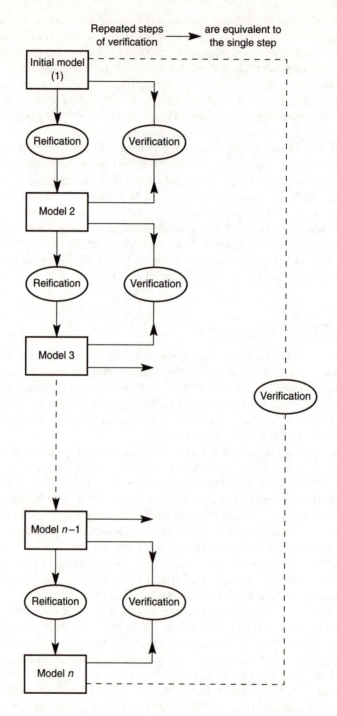

Figure 14.5 The verification operations in VDM.

For each stage in the refinement of the model, the method encourages the designer to verify that the reified operations correctly model those of the (more abstract) level above. It is here that the formality of the method becomes strongly evident.

The basic strategy adopted for the task of verification is that the designer should use formal 'proofs' at each step in refinement, so keeping these as simple as possible. As a result of this, the final proof steps used to validate the implementation against the specification as a whole need only be conducted in terms of the least abstract level of the specification (Figure 14.5).

The nature and form of the proof techniques used to demonstrate consistency at each stage of reification are large topics in themselves, and they are outside the scope of this text. A short example of their form is given in Jones (1986), and the VDM method as a whole is described much more fully in Jones (1980).

14.2.4 VDM heuristics

In our study of the systematic approaches to design, we have observed a number of examples of the roles that can be performed by design heuristics in such methods, almost all of which are concerned with the way in which the design *process* steps are to be structured. For VDM, and for the formal methods in general, any heuristics that might exist are more likely to be applied to such operations as the choice of data structures and the application of proofs to development steps. So when using a formal approach to design, we can expect to find a rather different form for any design heuristics that might be in use.

While it seems very likely that practising designers do apply a number of heuristics in using VDM, so far no heuristic techniques have been identified from the prescriptions of the method and none have been codified by the practitioners themselves. Once again, this probably reflects the much weaker process component of such methods, since this is where heuristics are most readily recognized and adopted into common practice.

14.3 Property-based strategies

14.3.1 Overview

The model-based specification form of FDT that was described in the previous section is concerned with specifying *how* a system is to operate. The property-based approach that is described in this section is more concerned with identifying the external properties of a system, and hence with codifying *what* the system is to do.

It could therefore be argued that the model-based strategy comes somewhat closer to supporting the activities of *design*, while the property-based strategy is closer to meeting the needs of *requirements specification*. While this view is undoubtedly over-simple, it does emphasize the difference between these strategies: one emphasizes the properties of the system, whereas the other focuses on its workings. For that reason, we should not expect the property-based forms to use an explicit model of system state, such as was used in the model-based example of VDM.

In this section the general characteristics of algebraic specification will be examined, as being sufficiently representative of the property-based approach for our needs.

In this context, algebraic specification can be regarded as a technique whereby an object class or type is specified in terms of the relationships between the operations defined on that type. For purposes of illustration, it is most easily demonstrated using abstract data types for the objects, but it should be recognized that the technique is not restricted to this form alone. Once again it can be seen that some elements of the general 'object model' are reflected in this form of description. Even though the concept of state might be absent, an algebraic specification is able to capture many of the external properties of an object, including the uses relationship, the inheritance hierarchy, and the provision of operations for use by other objects.

As in the previous section, most description and discussion will be centred on examining the form and properties of the representation part used for algebraic specification. Again, this emphasis is really a reflection of the major strengths of the formal techniques in this area.

14.3.2   Algebraic specification: representation part

One of the less attractive features of the formal techniques is the relative complexity of their notations! In this section a relatively simplified form will be adopted, based closely on that employed in Sommerville (1992) for the same purpose of describing the general approach used with these forms. An alternative example of a fairly simple form is used in Bradley (1989).

A term that is widely used in algebraic specification is **sort**. An entity (or object) is regarded as being an instance of a sort, and so this is a concept that is essentially related to the idea of a type or class. Strictly speaking, a sort is a set of objects, but we will not be exploring this aspect particularly closely in this section.

An algebraic specification usually consists of the following four main parts (these are shown schematically in the example of Figure 14.6):

- *Introduction*. This specifies the entity being defined, together with its sort and the names of any other specifications that are needed for its description.

	OBJECT	
Introduction	External features, details of the **uses** relations
Informal description	English text description
Signature	Operations **provided** by this object
Axioms	Definitions of the operations

Figure 14.6 Schematic of an algebraic specification.

- *Informal description*. This is an English description of the entity and of the operations performed upon it.
- *Signature*. This defines the names of the operations, and provides the details of any parameters that they require.
- *Axioms*. This part actually defines the operations and the relations that exist between them.

Each of these will now be described a little more fully, using the specification of a simple structure. This is the 'aircraft table' used in an Air Traffic Control system to maintain a run-time record of aircraft in the airspace or on the ground. (For those who like to have a more concrete picture of the behaviour of this abstract data type, it will essentially correspond to that of a hash table.)

The introduction

The heading of the introduction identifies the 'entity' (or 'object' according to preference) that is to be described. The exact syntax for this varies according to the preferred method. Figure 14.7 shows the heading parametrized by a set of elements, where the type of the elements is specified externally. So specific a parametrization is not essential, since we are only describing the external behaviour of an object, and could use a more general parameter (such as Elem) to emphasize this. (That is, in Ada terms, we can describe a generic form that will eventually need to be 'instantiated' for a specific type.)

The sort of the entity is also described in this introduction; in this case it is simply 'aircraft_table'.

AIRCRAFT_TABLE(AIRCRAFT_DETAILS)

Introduction

sort aircraft_table

imports integer, aircraft_track, aircraft_details

Figure 14.7 A simple algebraic specification (1).

The third part of the introduction is used to identify both the other object sorts or types that are used in the definition and the way in which they are used. Broadly speaking, there are two ways in which a specification can make use of other types/sorts:

- *Importing* a sort and its operations brings them into the scope of the new specification, so that they can be used within it, but do not become a part of it. (This roughly corresponds to the IMPORT mechanism used in Modula-2, and as with Modula-2, it may sometimes be necessary to qualify the identifier of an operation with its sort, in order to make clear the particular instance of the operation that is required.) The specification of Figure 14.7 uses 'aircraft_track' (which may eventually be of type integer, but not necessarily so), and also 'aircraft_details'.

- *Enrichment* allows a new sort to be defined that inherits the operations and axioms of another specification. (In some cases, new operations may be defined that will in effect overwrite some of these.) This concept is obviously closely related to the inheritance mechanism used in object-oriented programming.

The present example is too simple to make use of enrichment, but it does import the sort integer, since this is required in the later definitions.

The informal description

The previous section discussed the importance of textual comments used to explain the mathematical formalism and to relate this to the real-world entities where appropriate. The same purpose is performed by this section of the specification in the case of the property-oriented forms. In Figure 14.8 this is added to the introduction provided in Figure 14.7.

The signature

The purpose of the signature is to define the external 'appearance' of an object, by describing its basic properties using a set of operations. These operations usually fall into two groups:

Introduction

AIRCRAFT_TABLE(AIRCRAFT_DETAILS)

sort aircraft_table

Introduction

imports integer, aircraft_track, aircraft_details

The aircraft_table is used in an Air Traffic Control system to record the details of sets of aircraft within the airspace controlled by the system. (These aircraft may be in flight or on the ground.) The size of an aircraft_table has an upper bound (discovered by operation last), and individual elements are accessed via their 'track number' (which may actually be a combination of letters and digits).

Informal description

The operation **create** takes the size of the new table as its parameter, and initializes the value of the table to *Undefined*. The operation **insert** creates a new table where the selected element has been assigned a value, and **eval** reveals the value of a specified entry in the table. The operation **remove** creates a new table where the entry for the specified element has been reassigned to a value of *Undefined*.

Figure 14.8   A simple algebraic specification (2).

- *Constructor* operations are used to create and modify entities of the defined sort. These will typically have identifiers such as **create**, **update**, **add**.

- *Inspection* operations are used to evaluate the attributes of the entity's sort.

(In the case of our example, we now see why it was necessary to import the sort integer, since this is needed to provide an upper bound to the size of the table.)

While the constructor operations are fairly standard. regardless of the sort of the entity, the inspection operations are obviously very sort-specific. Figure 14.9 shows the example extended to include the signature. The operations **create**, **insert** and **remove** are obviously constructor operations, while **last** and **eval** are inspection operations.

The axioms

It is here that we get into the use of mathematical notation. Basically, this section provides the definition of the inspection operations in terms of the constructor operations. Indeed, the construction of these definitions can be regarded as the main technical problem of developing an algebraic specification, and is discussed further in the next section. Essentially, though, a set of equations is developed that gives mathematical expressions defining

---

AIRCRAFT_TABLE(AIRCRAFT_DETAILS)

Introduction

sort aircraft_table

imports integer, aircraft_track, aircraft_details

Informal description

The aircraft_table is used in an Air Traffic Control system to record the details of sets of aircraft within the airspace controlled by the system. (These aircraft may be in flight or on the ground.) The size of an aircraft_table has an upper bound (discovered by operation last), and individual elements are accessed via their 'track number' (which may actually be a combination of letters and digits).

The operation **create** takes the size of the new table as its parameter, and initializes the value of the table to *Undefined*. The operation **insert** creates a new table where the selected element has been assigned a value, and **eval** reveals the value of a specified entry in the table. The operation **remove** creates a new table where the entry for the specified element has been reassigned to a value of *Undefined*.

Signature

create(integer) --> aircraft_table
insert(aircraft_table, aircraft_track, aircraft_details) --> aircraft_table
remove(aircraft_table, aircraft_track) --> aircraft_table
last(aircraft_table) --> integer
eval(aircraft_table, aircraft_track) --> aircraft_details

Figure 14.9   A simple algebraic specification (3).

these relationships. These are shown for our example in Figure 14.10, which now provides a fully expanded definition for the aircraft_table, using this simplified form of algebraic notation.

In the example of the aircraft_table, each of the inspection operations can be related to each of the constructor operations. So, for example, the inspection operation **last** is first related to the operation **create**, by stating that **last** will return a value that corresponds to the upper bound used in the **create** operation. **last** is then related to the **insert** and **remove** operations using a recursive form of definition.

The **eval** operation can also be related to each of the constructor operations. The axiom used to relate it to **create** can be interpreted as meaning: 'inspecting any element in a newly defined table will result in an undefined result'. This makes sense, since no values will have been inserted into the table at the point of its creation, and so attempting to read from it will have undefined effects.

This (and the next relation between **eval** and **insert**) should make the interpretation of these axioms somewhat clearer. The axioms define the effect of performing the operation on the object when the object is in a particular state. However, rather than using an explicit model to define the

Introduction

AIRCRAFT_TABLE(AIRCRAFT_DETAILS)

sort aircraft_table

imports integer, aircraft_track, aircraft_details

Informal
description

The aircraft_table is used in an air traffic control system to record the
details of sets of aircraft within the airspace controlled by the system.
(These aircraft may be in flight or on the ground.) The size of
an aircraft_table has an upper bound (discovered by operation last), and
individual elements are accessed via their 'track number' (which may
actually be a combination of letters and digits).

The operation **create** takes the size of the new table as its parameter, and
initializes the value of the table to *Undefined*. The operation **insert** creates
a new table where the selected element has been assigned a value, and
eval reveals the value of a specified entry in the table. The operation
remove creates a new table where the entry for the specified element has
been reassigned to a value of *Undefined*.

Signature

create(integer) --> aircraft_table
insert(aircraft_table, aircraft_track, aircraft_details) --> aircraft_table
remove(aircraft_table, aircraft_track) --> aircraft_table
last(aircraft_table) --> integer
eval(aircraft_table, aircraft_track) --> aircraft_details

Axioms

last(create(x)) = x
last(insert(x, n, y)) = last(x)
last(remove(x, y)) = last(x)
eval(create(x, y), n) = undefined
eval(insert(x, n, y), m) = **if** m > last(x) **then**
                                        undefined
                                else
                                    if m = n **then** y **else** eval(x,m)
eval(remove(x, n), m) = **if** m > last(x) **then**
                                        undefined
                                else
                                    if m = n **then** undefined **else** eval(x, m)

Figure 14.10 A complete algebraic specification.

state (as would be used in VDM), it is defined in terms of the constructor
operations. So each axiom relates the effect of one of the inspection
operations on the aircraft_table after it has been modified by a constructor
operation.

The axiom used to relate **eval** and **insert** therefore first tells us that if
the aircraft_track value is greater than the size of the table (however these
are defined), the result will not be specified by these relationships. It then
goes on to show that if a particular value of aircraft_details has been inserted
for the chosen track, then the details of this will be retrieved by **eval**.

Failing such a correspondence, the rule will need to be applied to another element.

The relationships between **eval** and **remove** are similar. Again, the second of these observes that if a particular aircraft_track has been deleted from the table, then attempting to read this will produce an undefined result.

Having examined, therefore, something of the general form of such a specification, we now need to consider briefly how this might be developed.

14.3.3   Algebraic specification: process part

Once again, the algebraic formal description technique really lacks any 'process part' of the form that is provided by the systematic design methods, and most of the literature is more concerned with describing the form of a specification than its derivation. As with the object-oriented strategies, the form of the specification makes it equally well suited for use with a top-down or bottom-up development strategy. Features such as the **uses** mechanism also aid the designer in the task of partitioning the functionality of a system.

In the absence of any overall strategic guidelines on how a system should be structured, there are various guidelines for the more detailed task of constructing the specification of an object, or a set of objects. The techniques for ensuring that the set of axioms is complete and correct are also well established, and to the practising engineer they have the particular attraction of using more familiar mathematical forms and techniques (algebra). An added useful side-effect is that the task of generating the axioms also effectively generates a set of guidelines for testing the eventual implementation (Bradley, 1989).

The strategy for developing algebraic specifications is more flexible than that of VDM, since it readily encompasses both the top-down and bottom-up strategies. But it is probably more difficult to construct this form of specification for a very large system without very extensive experience of its use.

14.3.4   Heuristics for property-based specification

One thing that the algebraic form currently lacks is a good tutorial textbook along the lines of those now available for VDM. Partly as a result of this, there are no well-documented heuristics for algebraic forms, although, as for VDM, this is not to imply that none have been developed by the practitioners.

SUMMARY

This chapter has only skimmed the surface of a large and technically complex topic, and one that is still a major area for research. However, it should have provided sufficient detail to give the reader an appreciation of why some familiarity with the strengths and limitations of formal methods is an important part of the software designer's repertoire. There are times when a more rigorous approach to specification of behaviour, or of component structures, is needed, and it is important to appreciate that there are techniques that can provide support when this arises.

What does emerge from the material covered in this chapter is that formal descriptions can provide a very powerful aid to developing a design, especially when issues such as consistency and verification are considered. However, the *design* techniques needed for the derivation of a formal specification (as opposed to the *mathematical* techniques) are much less well developed. This leaves open the question of when to make use of these techniques and on what scale. There is relatively little documented use of formal methods for the development of very large systems and, indeed, this may not be the best way of making use of their strengths. There is evidence of increasing use for the development of high-integrity systems – or at least, of those parts of a large system that may require high integrity (including those often termed 'safety-critical'). It is here that we may well find that these techniques can make their largest contribution.

FURTHER READING

Hall A. (1990). Seven myths of formal methods. *IEEE Software*, **7**(5), 11–19

A highly-acclaimed paper written by an industrial practitioner and providing a refreshingly unbiased appraisal of what such approaches can provide, and where their limitations lie.

Gibbins P.F. (1988). What are formal methods? *Information and Software Technology*, **30**(3), 131–7

Provides rather more technical examples than the paper by Anthony Hall and, as such, provides a useful short sampler of the forms and notations used by some of the major techniques.

Bradley I.M. (1989). Notes on algebraic specifications. *Information and Software Technology*, **31**(7), 357–65

A tutorial approach to one of the property-based strategies, based on a number of relatively familiar examples.

Cohen B., Harwood W.T. and Jackson M.I. (1986). *The Specification of Complex Systems*. Wokingham: Addison-Wesley

A slim textbook that gives a very good tutorial introduction to the general issue of using mathematical notations, supported by examples from both model-based and algebraic forms. Perhaps the main criticism would be that it is really a bit too slim, and leaves the reader wanting to know just that little bit more.

EXERCISES

14.1 For the simple VDM specification given in Figure 14.4:

(a) add the bodies of the *TAKEOFF* and *LEAVESPACE* operations;
(b) consider how you might add a variable that would report the state of the runway at any time, where this could be any of the following:

- available for take-off
- available for landing
- available for take-off or landing
- in use

14.2 Write a simple VDM specification (similar to that of Figure 14.4) that describes the top-level operation of a bank autoteller machine.

14.3 For the example algebraic specification provided in Figure 14.7, add an operation that updates the aircraft details for a given track, so that the signature will now include:

    update(aircraft_table,aircraft_track,aircraft_details) --> aircraft_table

15 The Evolution of Software Design Practices

15.1 Experiences from the past   15.3 Future developments
15.2 Present practices

This final chapter seeks to review and draw together some of the ideas that underpin the examples and illustrations of software design practices that have been provided in the preceding chapters. In particular, it reviews the progress of software design technology to date, and identifies how this might proceed in the future.

15.1 Experiences from the past

The era of the digital computer now spans nearly half a century, and hence so also does our experience of developing software. So it might be expected that our techiques for software design would have begun to mature a little.

Unfortunately, such a view is rather misleading, since only in the last 20 years or so have there been sufficient powers of abstraction available in software tools and environments for a truly general problem-solving discipline to begin to develop. Prior to that, the nature of the tools available (assembler code, early versions of FORTRAN, and so on) meant that software design objectives were essentially confined to algorithm design alone (a worthy enough subject in itself), and the limited power of hardware also meant that efficiency was the dominant criterion in assessing design quality.

So it is perhaps not so surprising that relatively general-purpose systematic practices for software design emerged only during the 1970s. The greater emphasis that these placed on the use of abstraction and on data-structuring also encouraged the development of diagrammatical forms that could be used to capture the relevant attributes of a system. (Before this time, the flowchart was generally regarded as adequate for the documentation of software, although some might dispute its adequacy even for this purpose!)

The previous chapters have therefore chronicled something of the accumulated thinking of the past 20 years, although this in turn contains elements of the experiences and the baggage of nearly 50 years. In the early chapters we examined some ideas about the design process in general, its nature, and the attendant constraints. These ideas were then used to make a methodological study of some of the software design techniques that have been developed as the means of assisting with the development of software-based systems. The development of ideas about software design has not been systematic, nor has it been continuous, and it has not been based upon one agreed set of criteria that can be used for identifying 'good' design forms and practices. In many ways it has itself been a prototyping experience, gradually edging forward, adding new experiences and new ideas at each step, and in the process occasionally discarding some that were previously more highly prized.

During this time, too, the 'ground rules' for what is expected of a system have also changed. In the 1950s and 1960s, the primary criterion for evaluating the design of any system was likely to be 'efficiency' in some form or other, whether it be efficiency of operation, memory use, or secondary storage. To some extent this is now perhaps even underrated as a measure, with the relative cheapness of primary and secondary memory and the wide availability of high-speed processors. Our thinking has moved on to such criteria as modularity, reuse, separation of concerns, information-hiding, and the like. Software design methods have sought to move along in concert with this, although generally lagging well behind, and growing ever more complex in form.

Certainly any consideration of the present and future states of the software design art needs to consider the experiences and lessons of the past, short though that past has been. So in the remaining two sections of this chapter, we try to assess the current state of software design practices, and to identify some of the more promising trends in our thinking about their future development.

15.2 Present practices

Since this topic has formed the main theme of this book, one might reasonably expect that all that should be necessary at this point would be to provide a summary of the points covered in the preceding chapters. However, since each 'method' chapter has focused largely on examining the features of a particular design method, at this point we should try to draw together something of our observations from these, and to set these into a wider context.

A key aspect of software design is the designer's identification of the most suitable (or 'right') set of abstractions to describe the entities used in the solution and to capture the nature of their interactions. A design method therefore provides a particular framework that can be used to help with identifying these abstractions – perhaps by considering the 'functions' of the system, or 'modularity', or 'behaviour' – and thereby provides the basis for what we have termed the design 'model'.

Those whom we consider to be 'good' designers are often those people who have the gift of identifying the 'right' abstractions, whether by experience or by the skilful use of a method. Studying the actions of designers may therefore be a valuable way of helping to determine just how they make their selection of abstractions (and relationships) for a particular problem – and also how they develop these.

The major purpose of a design method can therefore be considered as being to provide an alternative source of design knowledge to that available from a designer's personal experience, so allowing him or her to draw on the experiences of others. Figure 15.1 illustrates this by summarizing the principal influences on the design process. This transfer of design experience is generally achieved by capturing these experiences as a set of 'rules' (or procedures), possibly supported by a set of rules of thumb that we have termed 'heuristics'. This implies that:

- It is doubtful whether there can ever be a 'right' method that would be appropriate for all problems (and suited to all designers).

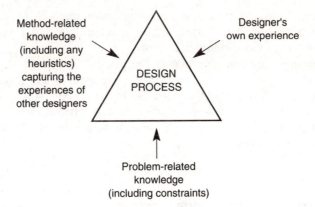

Method-related
knowledge
(including any
heuristics)
capturing the
experiences of
other designers

DESIGN
PROCESS

Designer's
own experience

Problem-related
knowledge
(including constraints)

Figure 15.1 Influences on the software design process.

- There is a need for measures of design quality that can be used to assist with determining when a 'good' solution has been identified.

As a subsidiary question, we might also ask why some forms of abstraction and viewpoint would appear to be more readily used in an 'intuitive' manner, and whether this renders them 'stronger' in any way.

Between them, the *representation* part and the *process* part of a software design method define the set of abstractions that go to make up its particular form of design model. The resulting abstractions, and their related attributes and relationships, are therefore method-related in their turn.

One possible criterion for a 'good' design solution, although it is probably currently beyond our means to achieve it in any systematic manner, would be to identify this as any solution for which a change in the problem description would require only minimal changes to the abstractions forming the solution. (This would be rather akin to the physicist's principle of least action.)

If we look therefore at the development of software design practices as exemplified in the methods described in the previous chapters, we can identify a number of trends, at least in terms of the abstractions used. These can be summarized as follows:

- The use of an increasing number of *viewpoints* within the design model itself. Earlier methods, such as JSP and SSA/SD, tended to require the designer to perform a sequence of operations on a principal viewpoint of the problem, transforming this as appropriate, but nevertheless maintaining one major viewpoint throughout this process. In the evolution of more specialized adaptations of SSA/SD, and in later design methods, one can observe an increased complexity in the form of the model, culminating in the 'object-oriented' forms, which require a balanced use of all four of the primary viewpoints (function, behaviour, structure and data-modelling).

- A corresponding increase in the complexity of the *process parts* of such methods, as they attempt to specify how a particular form of design model should be developed and transformed, in order to maintain consistency between the viewpoints themselves.

- A reduction in the degree to which *heuristics* can be relied on. One of the major roles these play is to reinforce the method as a means of transferring experience between generations of designers. With an increasing complexity of model, it becomes correspondingly difficult to identify and codify some of the practices that we might consider to form the heuristics associated with a particular method.

All the design methods that we have examined so far can also be considered as *procedural* in form. In other words, the process parts are expressed as a sequence of operations and actions that the design should perform, modifying and adapting these as necessitated by the form and nature of the particular problem in hand. From the trends identified above, we can see that this procedural approach begins to break down when the designer is required to manipulate an increasingly complex model of a system.

Unfortunately, moving away from a well-established approach, in which design practices are described and taught using a procedural form, leads to other problems, not least because of the difficulty of describing non-procedural forms. While we may recognize that practising designers do deviate from set plans in an opportunistic manner, it appears that they largely do so on the basis of their own past experience, rather than by using any practice that could be captured and codified. (At the programming level, an analogy might be the far greater complexity that is required in the structure of a program that is to operate in a window-based and event-driven mode, compared with that of a program requiring only a simple sequential form of interaction with its environment.)

Related to this increasing degree of complexity in design procedures is the question of how design activities might themselves be supported by using the power of the computer. The subject of CASE (Computer-Assisted Software Engineering) tools encompasses a wide range of support forms. (The forms of CASE used for the early tasks of analysis, specification and design are often referred to as 'upper-CASE' forms, while those concerned with constructional issues are described as 'lower-CASE'.) Support for software design through the use of CASE has traditionally involved providing graphical editors to capture the representational part of a given design method, together with some means of checking consistency between diagrams and viewpoints wherever possible.

Although it may not always be recognized, CASE tools may themselves implicitly encourage a designer to follow particular practices, largely through the form of user interface that they provide. For example, the user interfaces provided with graphical editors may well enforce certain sequences (draw this form of diagram before that one, ensure that this diagram is syntactically correct so that it will be accepted in the archive, use this particular naming convention, and so on). Indeed, many design support tools effectively limit the designer to developing a design in a top-down manner, providing little scope for opportunistic deviations, or for developing a part of the design separately and then inserting it as a set of components within the fuller design.

CASE tools may also bind the user to themselves, particularly where rather complex notations are involved (we saw some examples of such notations when examining the issues involved in object-oriented forms of software design). Specialized notations that are tedious to draw by hand, and which cannot be approximated fairly easily and unambiguously, should perhaps be viewed with a degree of suspicion. Indeed, it might well be posited that a designer should seek to use only those representations that can be easily drawn with a pencil. We should recognize that any move away from this principle both binds a designer to using particular proprietary tools and reduces the ease with which design reviews and walkthroughs can be carried out around a whiteboard.

This last point raises one other feature of CASE tools that still needs to be more fully explored. Design is often a group activity, particularly in the early stages, and there needs to be a willingness on the part of the design team to make quite extensive changes. CASE tools may actually act as barriers to communication (although not necessarily), and the effort involved in creating a 'neat' diagram may make its producer reluctant to modify it extensively. (We can see the same effect with text-processing tools, where the ability to explore visual effects produced by alterations of font and layout can distract from the real need, which might be to rewrite an item of text in its entirety!)

The above points are not intended as arguments against the use of CASE tools. The benefits of such tools are much too great for that, especially in terms of recording decisions, consistency-checking, versioning, and so on. However, not all such tools may be suitable for supporting the detailed processes of software design, and like design methods themselves, they are no substitute for creative thinking about how a problem is to be solved.

15.3 Future developments

Predictions about technologically based futures are notoriously unreliable, not least because technological changes tend to occur in quantum steps rather than as some continuous flow of development. (An excellent example of this is Rudyard Kipling's short story *With the Night Mail*. This was published in 1908, and quite accurately envisaged extensive air travel in the year 2000 – but expected that this would be in airships!)

However, in making any predictions, we are likely to see little change in the general *nature* of the problem, which has been so well captured by Fred Brooks Jr (1987) in his observation that:

> 'The complexity of software is an essential property, not an accidental one. Hence, descriptions of a software entity that abstract away its complexity often abstract away its essence.'

On this basis then (and it would be difficult if not impossible to contradict this quotation on present evidence and experience), software design methods will probably need to find more powerful paradigms rather than to look for simpler ones.

One view that I would like to advance here is that we are now seeing an evolutionary trend towards the development of systematic design methods that stretch procedural practices very hard, and that further development may well need to explore other directions, such as:

- Finding mechanisms for encapsulating the design expertise embodied in a design method that have forms other than 'perform step 1, then step 2, then step 3', which is currently the normal form for expressing the process part of a method (Harel, 1992).

- Achieving a corresponding advance in design support tools, so that they can do more 'intelligent' things than simply recording diagrams and checking them. Such tools will need to 'know' about more than the syntax rules for a representation – they will somehow have to embody semantic 'knowledge' about the design or problem, and make use of such knowledge to help designers assess the consequences of their decisions.

Neither of these developments is likely to be achieved through a process of evolution from current practices. Both are of the revolutionary form of development that may well be needed for the next quantum step in the development of systematic design practices. Such approaches to designing software may also make greater use of formal descriptions in order to reduce ambiguity. Even then, they may not necessarily provide a *large* step in terms of improving the quality of our designs, since, as the quotation from Brooks emphasizes, software systems are inherently complex, and no amount of improved design technology can remove that complexity. However, we can be certain that without such developments, or similar ones, we are unlikely to do more than contain the levels of complexity that presently exist.

This position should not be regarded as unduly pessimistic. Current software design technology still has plenty of scope for improvements of an evolutionary kind. The object-oriented methods may yet be able to provide more balanced guidance to the designer than has emerged so far, and the science of measurement as applied to design descriptions is still in its infancy, relatively.

One thing we can be sure of, though: software design will remain one of the most creative and exciting forms of design activity, and the search for ways of improving our techniques will continue to be a vital part of it.

SUMMARY

This chapter should serve as a reminder of the intrinsically complex nature of the software design process, and hence of the limitations that this creates for any design method. One conclusion that can be drawn from our study of current software design methods is that future methods may need to move away from procedural forms in order to achieve any significant steps forward.

FURTHER READING

Since each of the chapters has suggested further ideas for reading based on its particular subject matter, this section simply identifies some rather more general reading about software design. The domain-related nature of software design means that more advanced reading really needs to be driven by particular needs. But for more general reading in the area of information systems, *Information Systems Methodologies*, by Olle *et al.* (1991), addresses the relevant issues in a non-method-specific manner. For real-time systems, Allworth and Zobel (1992) have produced a slim volume, *Real-Time Software Design*, that similarly addresses general issues within a domain, rather than describing specific methods.

Bibliography

Abbott R.J. (1983). Program design by informal English descriptions. *Comm. ACM*, **26**(11), 882–94

ACM (1990). *Comm. ACM, Special Issue on Object-Oriented Design*, **33**(9)

Adelson B. and Soloway E. (1985). The role of domain experience in software design. *IEEE Trans. Software Eng.*, **SE-11**(11), 1351–60

Akin O. (1990). Necessary conditions for design expertise and creativity. *Design Studies*, **11**(2), 107–113

Alexander H. and Jones V. (1990). *Software Design and Prototyping using me too*. Prentice-Hall

Allworth S.T. and Zobel R.N. (1992). *Real-Time Software Design* 3rd edn. Macmillan

Ashworth C.M. (1988). Structured systems analysis and design method (SSADM). *Information and Software Technology*, **30**(3), 153–63

Ashworth C.M. and Goodland M. (1990). *SSADM: A Practical Approach*. McGraw-Hill

Baker F.T. (1972). Chief programmer team management of production programming. *IBM Systems J.*, **11**(1), 56–73

Barnes J.G.P. (1976). *RTL/2 Design and Philosophy*. Heyden Press

Barnes J. (1989). *Programming in Ada*. Addison-Wesley

Batini C., Ceri S. and Navathe S.B. (1992). *Conceptual Database Design*. Benjamin/Cummings

Birrell N.D. and Ould M.A. (1985). *A Practical Handbook for Software Development*. Cambridge University Press

Boehm B.W. (1981). *Software Engineering Economics*. Prentice-Hall

Boehm B.W. (1988). A spiral model of software development and enhancement. *IEEE Computer*, 61–72

Booch G.R. (1983). *Software Engineering with Ada* 1st edn. Benjamin/Cummings

Booch G.R. (1986). Object-oriented development. *IEEE Trans. Software Eng.*, **SE-12**(2), 211–21

Booch G.R. (1987). *Software Engineering with Ada* 2nd edn. Benjamin/Cummings

Booch G.R. (1991). *Object-Oriented Design with Applications*. Redwood City, California: Benjamin/Cummings

Bradley I.M. (1989). Notes on algebraic specifications. *Information and Software Technology*, **31**(7), 357–65

Branscomb L.M. and Thomas J.C. (1984). Ease of use: A system design challenge. *IBM Systems J.*, **23**(3), 224–35

Brooks F.P. Jr (1975). *The Mythical Man-Month*. Addison-Wesley

Brooks F.P. Jr (1987). No silver bullet: Essence and accidents of software engineering. *IEEE Computer*, 10–19

Brough M. (1992). Methods for CASE: a generic framework. In *Advanced Information Systems Engineering* (Loucopoulos P., ed.), Lecture Notes in Computer Science No. 593, 524–45. Springer-Verlag

Budde R., Kuhlenkamp K., Mathiassen L. and Zullighoven H. (1984). *Approaches to Prototyping*. Springer-Verlag

Budgen D. (1989). *Software Development with Modula-2*. Addison-Wesley

Budgen D. and Friel G. (1992). Augmenting the design process: Transformations from abstract design representations. In *Advanced Information Systems Engineering* (Loucopoulos P., ed.), Lecture Notes in Computer Science No. 593, 378–93. Springer-Verlag

Budgen D. and Marashi M. (1988). Knowledge-based techniques applied to software design assessment. *Knowledge-Based Systems*, **1**(4), 235–9

Buhr R.J.A. (1984). *System Design with Ada*. Prentice-Hall

Cameron J.R. (1986). An overview of JSD. *IEEE Trans. Software Eng.*, **SE-12**(2), 222–40. Reprinted in Cameron (1988a).

Cameron J.R. (1988a). *JSP and JSD: The Jackson Approach to Software Development* 2nd edn. Los Alamitos, California: IEEE Computer Society

Cameron J.R. (1988b). The modelling phase of JSD. *Information and Software Technology*, **30**(6), 373–83. Reprinted in Cameron (1988a).

Chen P.P. (1976). The entity–relationship model: Toward a unified view of data. *ACM Trans. Database Systems*, **1**(1), 9-37

Coad P. and Yourdon E. (1991a). *Object-Oriented Analysis* 2nd edn. Prentice-Hall

Coad P. and Yourdon E. (1991b). *Object-Oriented Design*. Prentice-Hall

Cohen B., Harwood W.T. and Jackson M.I. (1986). *The Specification of Complex Systems*. Addison-Wesley

Connor D. (1985). *Information System Specification and Design Road Map*. Prentice-Hall

Conte S.D., Dunsmore H.E. and Shen V.Y. (1986). *Software Engineering Metrics and Models*. Benjamin/Cummings

Cross N. (ed.) (1984). *Developments in Design Methodology*. Wiley

Curtis B. and Walz D. (1990). The psychology of programming in the large: Team and organizational behaviour. In *Psychology of Programming* (Hoc J.-M., Green T.R.G., Samurçay R. and Gilmore D.J., eds.). Academic Press

Curtis B., Krasner H. and Iscoe N. (1988). A field study of the software design process for large systems. *Comm. ACM*, **31**(11), 1268–87

Davies S.P. and Castell A.M. (1992). Contextualizing design: Narratives and rationalization in empirical studies of software design. *Design Studies*, **13**(4), 379–92

Davis A.M., Bersoff E.H. and Comer E.R. (1988). A strategy for comparing alternative software development life-cycle models. *IEEE Trans. Software Eng.*, **SE-14**(10), 1453–60

De Marco T. (1978). *Structured Analysis and System Specification*. Yourdon, Inc.

Denning P.J., Comer D.E., Gries D., Mulder M.C., Tucker A., Turner A.J. and Young P.R. (1989). Computing as a discipline. *Comm. ACM*, **32**(1), 9–23

Downs E., Clare P. and Coe I. (1988). *Structured Systems Analysis and Design Method: Application and Context*. Prentice-Hall

Edwards H.M., Thompson J.B. and Smith P. (1989). Results of survey of use of SSADM in commercial and government sectors in United Kingdom. *Information and Software Technology*, **31**(1), 21–8

ESA (1989). *HOOD Reference Manual* Issue 3.0. European Space Agency

Fenton N.E. (1991). *Software Metrics: A Rigorous Approach*. Chapman & Hall

Fichman R.G. and Kemerer C.F. (1992). Object-oriented and conventional analysis and design methodologies. *IEEE Computer*, **25**(10), 22–39

Floyd C. (1984). A systematic look at prototyping. In *Approaches to Prototyping* (Budde R., Kuhlenkamp K., Mathiassen L. and Zullighoven H.), pp. 1–18. Springer-Verlag

Floyd C. (1986). A comparative evaluation of system development methods. In *Information Systems Design Methodologies: Improving the Practice* (Verrijn-Stuart A.A., Olle T.W. and Sol H.G., eds.), 19–54. North-Holland

Friel G. and Budgen D. (1991). Design transformation and abstract design prototyping. *Information and Software Technology*, **31**(9), 707–19

Gane C. and Sarsen T. (1979). *Structured Systems Analysis: Tools and Techniques*. Prentice-Hall

Gehani N. and McGettrick A.D. (1986). *Software Specification Techniques.* Addison-Wesley

Gerhart S. (1988). Applications of formal methods: Developing virtuoso software. *IEEE Software*, 7–10

Gibbins P.F. (1988). What are formal methods? *Information and Software Technology*, **30**(3), 131–7

Gladden G.R. (1982). Stop the life-cycle, I want to get off. *ACM Software Engineering Notes*, **SE7**(2), 35–9

Gomaa H. (1986). Software development of real-time systems. *Comm. ACM*, **29**(7), 657–63

Gomaa H. (1989). Structuring criteria for real-time system design. In *11th International Conference on Software Engineering*, pp. 290–301. Los Alamitos, California: IEEE Computer Society

Gomaa H. (1993). *Software Design Methods for Real-Time Systems.* Addison-Wesley

Guindon R. and Curtis B. (1988). Control of cognitive processes during software design: What tools are needed? In *Proceedings of CHI '88*, 263–8. ACM Press

Hall A. (1990). Seven myths of formal methods. *IEEE Software*, 11–19

Hall N.R. and Preiser S. (1984). Combined network complexity measures. *IBM J. Research and Development*, **28**(1), 15–27

Halstead M.H. (1977). *Elements of Software Science.* North-Holland

Harel D. (1987). Statecharts: A visual formalism for complex systems. *Science of Computer Programming*, **8**, 231–74

Harel D. (1988). On visual formalisms. *Comm. ACM*, **31**(5), 514–30

Harel D. (1992). Biting the silver bullet: Toward a brighter future for system development. *IEEE Computer*, **25**(1), 8–20

Harel D., Lachover H., Naamad A., Pnueli A., Politi M., Sherman R.,Shtull-Trauring A. and Trakhtenbrot M. (1990). STATEMATE: A working environment for the development of complex reactive systems. *IEEE Trans. Software Eng.*, **SE-16**(4), 403–13

Hatley D.J. and Pirbhai I. (1988). *Strategies for Real-Time System Specification.* Dorset House

Hayes I.J. and Jones C.B. (1989). Specifications are not (necessarily) executable. *Software Engineering J.*, **4**, 330–8

Hekmatpour S. and Ince D. (1988). *Software Prototyping, Formal Methods and VDM.* Addison-Wesley

Henderson P. (1986). Functional programming, formal specification, and rapid prototyping. *IEEE Trans. Software Eng.*, **SE-12**(2), 241–50

Henderson-Sellers B. and Constantine L.L. (1991). Object-oriented development and functional decomposition. *J. Object-Oriented Programming*, **3**(5), 11–17

Henderson-Sellers B. and Edwards J.M. (1990). The object-oriented systems life-cycle. *Comm. ACM*, **33**(9), 142–59

Henry S. and Kafura D. (1984). The evaluation of software systems' structure using quantitative software metrics. *Software Practice and Experience*, **14**, 561–73

Hoare C.A.R. (1978). Communicating sequential processes. *Comm. ACM*, **21**(8), 666–7

Humphrey W.S. (1991). *Managing the Software Process.* Addison-Wesley

Ingevaldsson L. (1986). *JSP – A Practical Method of Program Design.* Chartwell-Bratt

Ingevaldsson L. (1990). *Software Engineering Fundamentals – the Jackson Approach.* Chartwell-Bratt

Jackson K. (1986). Mascot 3 and Ada. *Software Eng. J.*, **1**(3), 121–35

Jackson M.A. (1975). *Principles of Program Design.* Academic Press

Jackson M.A. (1983). *System Development.* Prentice-Hall

Jones C.B. (1980). *Software Development: A Rigorous Approach.* Prentice-Hall

Jones C.B. (1986). *Systematic Software Development using VDM.* Prentice-Hall

Jones J.C. (1970). *Design Methods: Seeds of Human Futures.* (Revised edn. 1981.) Wiley-Interscience

Kernighan B.W. and Ritchie D.M. (1978). *The C Programming Language.* Prentice-Hall

King M.J. and Pardoe J.P. (1985). *Program Design Using JSP: A Practical Introduction.* Macmillan

Kitchenham B., Pickard L.M. and Linkman S.J. (1990). An evaluation of some design metrics. *Software Eng. J.*, **5**(1), 50–8

Koepke D.J. (1990). The evolution of software design ideas. In 'Anecdotes' (Tomayko J.E., ed.), *Annals of the History of Computing*, **12**(4), 269–76

Lee J. (1991). Extending the Potts and Bruns model for recording design rationale. In *Proceedings of the 13th International Conference on Software Engineering*, pp. 114–25. Los Alamitos, California: IEEE Computer Society

Lehman M.M., Stenning V. and Turski W.M. (1984). Another look at software design methodology. *ACM Software Engineering Notes*, **9**, 38–53

Lientz B.P. and Swanson E.B. (1980). *Software Maintenance Management*. Addison-Wesley

Littman D.C., Pinto J., Letovsky S. and Soloway E. (1987). Mental models and software maintenance. *J. Systems and Software*, **7**, 341–55

Longworth G. (1992). *Introducing SSADM Version 4*. Blackwell

Longworth G., Nicholls D. and Abbott J. (1988). *SSADM Developer's Handbook, Version 3*. Manchester: National Computing Centre

Marca D.A. and McGowan C.L. (1988). *SADT: Structured Analysis and Design Technique*. McGraw-Hill

McCabe T.J. (1976). A complexity measure. *IEEE Trans. Software Eng.*, **SE-2**(4), 308–20

McCracken D.D. and Jackson M.A. (1982). Life-cycle concept considered harmful. *ACM Software Engineering Notes*, **SE7**(2), 29–32

Miller G.A. The magical number 7 plus or minus 2: some limits on our capacity for processing information. *Psychological Review*, **63**, 81–97

Mills H.D. (1988). Stepwise refinement and verification in box-structured systems. *IEEE Computer*, 23–36

Mills H.D., Linger R.C. and Hevner A.R. (1987). Box-structured information systems. *IBM Systems J.*, **26**(4), 395–413

Olle T.W., Hagelstein J., Macdonald I.G., Rolland C., Sol H.G., Van Assche F.J.M. and Verrijn-Stuart A.A. (1991). *Information Systems Methodologies*. Addison-Wesley

Page-Jones M. (1988). *The Practical Guide to Structured Systems Design* 2nd edn. Prentice-Hall

Parnas D.L. (1972). On the criteria to be used in decomposing systems into modules. *Comm. ACM*, **15**(12), 1053–8

Parnas D.L. (1979). Designing software for ease of extension and contraction. *IEEE Trans. Software Eng.*, **SE-5**(2), 128–37

Parnas D.L. and Clements P.C. (1986). A rational design process: How and why to fake it. *IEEE Trans. Software Eng.*, **SE-12**(2), 251–7

Parnas D.L. and Weiss D.M. (1987). Active design reviews: Principles and practices. *J. Systems and Software*, **7**, 259–65

Peters L.J. (1981). *Software Design: Methods and Techniques*. Yourdon Press

Potts C. (1989). A generic model for representing design methods. In *Proceedings of the 11th International Conference on Software Engineering*, Pittsburgh, pp. 217–26. Los Alamitos, California: IEEE Computer Society

Potts C. and Bruns G. (1988). Recording the reasons for design decisions. In *Proceedings of the 10th International Conference on Software Engineering*, Singapore, pp. 418–27. Los Alamitos, California: IEEE Computer Society

Pressman R.S. (1991). *Software Engineering: A Practitioner's Approach* 3rd edn. McGraw-Hill

Quang P.T. and Chartier-Kastler C. (1991). *MERISE in Practice*. Macmillan

Rentsch T. (1982). Object-oriented programming. *ACM Sigplan*, **17**(9), 51–7

Rittel H.J. and Webber M.M. (1984). Planning problems are wicked problems. In *Developments in Design Methodology*. (Cross N., ed.), pp. 135–144. Wiley

Robinson P.J. (1992). *Hierarchical Object-Oriented Design*. Prentice-Hall

Rochfeld A. and Tradieu H. (1983). MERISE: An information system design and development methodology. *Information and Management*, **6**, 143–59

Ross D.T. (1977). Structured analysis (SA): A language for communicating ideas. *IEEE Trans. Software Eng.*, **SE-3**(1), 16–34

Ross D.T. and Schoman K.E. Jr (1977). Structured analysis for requirements definition. *IEEE Trans. Software Eng.*, **SE-3**(1), 6–15

Royce W.W. (1970). Managing the development of large software systems: Concepts and techniques. In *Proc. Wescon*. (Also available in *Proceedings of ICSE 9*. Los Alamitos, California: IEEE Computer Society.)

Sanden B. (1985). Systems programming with JSP: Example – a VDU controller. *Comm. ACM*, **28**(10), 1059–67

SEJ (1986). Special issue on MASCOT. *Software Eng. J.*, **1**(3)

Shepperd M. and Ince D. (1989). Metrics, outlier analysis and the software design process. *Information and Software Technology*, **31**, 91–8

Shlaer S. and Mellor S. (1988). *Object-Oriented Systems Analysis: Modeling the World in Data*. Yourdon Press

Simon H.A. (1984). The structure of ill-structured problems. In *Developments in Design Methodology* (Cross N., ed.), pp. 145–66

Simpson H.R. (1982). Act parallel: use MASCOT. *Computer Bulletin*, 6–9

Simpson H.R. and Jackson K. (1979). Process synchronisation in MASCOT. *Computer J.*, **22**(4), 332–45

Smith M.F. (1990). *Software Prototyping: Adoption, Practice and Management*. McGraw-Hill

Snyder A. (1993). The essence of objects: Concepts and terms. *IEEE Software*, 31–42

Sommerville I. (1992). *Software Engineering* 4th edn. Addison-Wesley

Stevens W.P. (1991). *Software Design: Concepts and Methods*. Prentice-Hall

Stevens W.P., Myers G.J. and Constantine L.L. (1974). Structured design. *IBM Systems J.*, **13**, 115–39

Sutcliffe A. (1988). *Jackson System Development*. Prentice-Hall

Sutcliffe A. (1991). Object-oriented systems development: Survey of structured methods. *Information and Software Technology*, **33**(6), 433–42

Thimbleby H. (1990). *User Interface Design*. Addison-Wesley

Troy D.A. and Zweben S.H. (1981). Measuring the quality of structured designs. *J. Systems and Software*, **2**, 113–20

Visser W. and Hoc J.-M. (1990). Expert software design strategies. In *Psychology of Programming* (Hoc J.-M., Green T.R.G., Samurçay R. and Gilmore D.J., eds.), pp. 235–49. Academic Press

Walker I.J. (1992). Requirements of an object-oriented design method. *Software Eng. J.*, **7**(2), 102–13

Ward P.T. (1986). The transformation schema: An extension of the data-flow diagram to represent control and timing. *IEEE Trans. Software Eng.*, **SE-12**(2), 198–210

Ward P.T. and Mellor S.J. (1985). *Structured Development for Real-Time Systems*, Vols 1–3. Yourdon Press

Warnier J.D. (1980). *Logical Construction of Programs*. Van Nostrand

Wasserman A.I., Pircher P.A. and Muller R.J. (1990). The object-oriented structured design notation for software design representation. *IEEE Computer*, **23**(3), 50–63

Webb J.T. (1978). *CORAL 66 Programming*. Manchester: National Computing Centre

Webster D.E. (1988). Mapping the design information representation terrain. *IEEE Computer*, 8–23

Weinberg G.M. (1971). *The Psychology of Computer Programming*. Van Nostrand Reinhold

Weinberg G.M. and Freedman D.P. (1984). Reviews, walkthroughs and inspections. *IEEE Trans. Software Eng.*, **SE-10**(1), 68–72

Wing J.M. (1990). A specifier's introduction to formal methods. *IEEE Computer*, 8–24

Wirth N. (1971). Program development by stepwise refinement. *Comm. ACM*, **14**, 221–7

Woodman M. (1988). Yourdon data-flow diagrams: A tool for disciplined requirements analysis. *Information and Software Technology*, **30**(9), 515–33

Yourdon E. (1979). *Structured Walkthroughs*. Yourdon Press

Yourdon E. (1989). *Modern Structured Analysis*. Yourdon Press

Yourdon E. and Constantine L.L. (1979). *Structured Design*. Prentice-Hall

Zave P. (1984). The operational versus the conventional approach to software development. *Comm. ACM*, **27**(2), 104–18

Index

A

abstract data type 265–7, 269, 277, 280, 348, 351, 354
abstraction 18, 19, 62, 68, 82–5, 102, 120, 129, 143, 148, 184–6, 190, 228, 262, 270–1, 277, 287, 324–5, 327, 338, 364–6
access procedure 73, 327, 329
ACP diagram 327, 329–31, 333
Act One 342
actigram 307–9
active object (in HOOD) 280–3, 287
Activity (in MASCOT) 328–8, 330–1
Ada (programming language) 36, 70, 71, 110, 111–5, 150, 258, 266, 276–7, 279–83, 286, 290, 334, 346, 355
adaptive maintenance 49
Adelson, Beth 28, 31, 42
ADT *see* abstract data type
algebraic form (of formal method) 342, 354–60
algorithm (design of) 180–1, 188, 190, 201, 211, 364
ambiguity (in design representations) 338, 348
analysis 314, 317, 323
Anna 342
application domain *see* problem domain
architectural design 27, 28, 149, 216, 293, 307, 325, 331, 338
artifacts (design of/software as) 4, 6, 58
attributes (of design entities/actions) 60, 64, 67–76, 83, 85, 105–6, 251, 254, 314

axiom 355, 357–60
axiomatic form (of formal method) 342

B

backtracking
  (in JSP) 191–2
  (in JSD) 260–1
batch systems 154, 225
behaviour 16, 272
behavioural (description forms) 85, 87, 88, 97, 118, 125, 127, 131, 134, 260, 269, 286, 341
blueprint 9, 10, 27
Boehm, Barry 44, 49, 54
Booch, Grady 270, 277, 280, 284, 302
Boochograms 277
boundary clash *see* structure clash
Brooks, Frederick P. Jr 26, 39, 42, 369
Buhr, Ray 111

C

Cameron, John 263
CASE 64, 93, 367–8
CCTA 313
central transform 218–21, 231–3
Channel (in MASCOT) 326–7
Chen, Peter 105
chief programmer 39
child objects (in HOOD) 281–3

class   268, 272–3, 280, 287
  diagrams   289
  hierarchy   272–4, 287
Clear   342
cliché   *see* design heuristics
cohesion   71–2, 220, 222
communicating sequential processes   240
compiler (design of)   153–4, 172
complexity   2, 68, 108, 369
compositional (design strategy)   164, 168–9,
    178, 186, 206, 214, 239–40, 262
concurrent systems   154–5, 207, 240, 258, 327
    see also parallel
Constantine, Larry   206
constraints   9, 11, 29, 35–7, 88
constructor (operations)   357–9
context diagram   214, 225
Control Flow Diagram   211
control queue   329
cooperating parallel processes   324, 328
coordinating control coupling   71
coroutines   199–201, 260
corrective maintenance   50
coupling   70–1, 220, 222, 329
criteria (for design decisions)   10–1, 17, 142
cross-checking (between viewpoints)   313
Curtis, Bill   29, 30, 40, 42
Cyclomatic Complexity   61

D

DARTS   331, 334
data dictionary   208–9, 215, 228
data-flow stream (in JSD)   245, 252, 256, 260
Data-Flow Diagram   97–104, 207–21, 315–6,
    321–2
data forms (in VDM)   346–8
data modelling (viewpoint and description
    forms)   86, 88–9, 97, 106, 118, 168, 269,
    286, 307, 315
data processing   153–4, 178, 207, 239–40, 258,
    312–3
datagram   307–9
De Marco, Tom   98, 206, 215
decision criteria   *see* criteria
decompositional (design strategy)   164, 166–8,
    206, 214, 343, 351
derived viewpoint   86

design
  artifacts   *see* artifacts
  attributes   *see* attributes
  audit   37
  documentation   51, 75, 78, 147, 150, 170,
    224, 284, 312, 314
  heuristics   33, 144, 145, 171, 175, 189–201,
    221–2, 258, 260–2, 286, 312, 335, 339,
    343, 353, 360, 365, 367
  methods   18, 29, 32, 52, 82, 142–53, 175, 365,
    369
  metrics   60–4
  model   18, 26, 27, 30, 32, 37, 75, 76, 83–5,
    104, 160, 168, 265, 365
  process   4, 5, 8, 58
  rationale   314
  representations   *see* representations
  reuse   29, 171–3, 364
  review   48, 74–6
  strategy   144, 159–73, 262, 317
  team   38–40, 147, 150, 368
  trade-offs   18
  transformations   30, 32, 34, 35, 338 *see also*
    transformational model of design
  virtual machine   147–51, 153, 160, 164, 338
detailed design   27
DFD   *see* Data-Flow Diagram
diagrammatical (descriptions)   90–2, 96, 364
    see also representation part
divide and conquer   211 *see also*
    decompositional design strategy
documentation   *see* design documentation
domain knowledge   31, 32, 33, 77, 78, 147
dynamic (properties)   85
dynamic (relationships)   88

E

efficiency   66, 73
encapsulation   269–71, 277, 287 *see also*
    information hiding
enrichment   356
entity   60, 105–6, 126, 168, 242–5, 247, 250–4,
    261, 269, 320–2, 355, 365
entity model   315
Entity Life-History Diagram (ELHD)   316–7,
    322–3
Entity Life-History Matrix   322–3

Entity–Relationship Diagram 97, 104–8, 208, 211, 314–5, 318
Entity–Structure Diagram (ESD) 242–4, 247, 252, 255–6, 260
ERD *see* Entity–Relationship Diagram
error handling *see* exception handling
ESD *see* Entity–Structure Diagram
European Space Agency 280
event 322, 328
event (driven) 123, 125, 127, 130, 280, 282
event partitioning 206, 214
evolutionary prototype 53
exception handling (in design) 165, 220, 252
executable specification 53, 343
experimental prototype 53, 78
experimental studies (of design) 28, 30, 31
exploratory prototype 53, 78

F

factoring 221–2
feasibility study 53
Fenton, Norman 79
finite state machine/automaton 88, 123, 127
fitness for purpose 18, 59, 61, 64
flow of information *see* information flow
flowchart 90, 91, 364
Floyd, Christiana 53, 78
Formal Description Technique (FDT) 339, 341–2, 369 *see also* formal method
formal design 30
formal method 144–5, 337–62
formal specification 341
function 16
functional analysis 310
functional (viewpoint/description forms) 85, 88, 97, 118, 122, 207–8, 260, 269, 286, 307, 315
functional decomposition 166–7, 206, 267, 281, 284, 306–7, 309, 331–2 *see also* decompositional design strategy

G

generic mechanism (in Ada) 277
graceful degradation 66

H

Harel, David 93, 127
HCI *see* human–computer interaction
heuristics *see* design heuristics
hiding, information *see* information hiding
hierarchical forms 100, 108, 110, 127, 130, 160, 218, 220, 257–8, 307–8, 325, 330–1
Hierarchical Object Oriented Design method *see* HOOD
hierarchy 270–6, 325, 328
high-integrity systems 361 *see also* safety-critical)
Hoare, C.A.R. 240
Hoc, J.-M. 29, 31
HOOD 171, 278–87, 290, 293–301, 312–3
human–computer interaction 67, 165, 172, 340
Humphrey, Watts 76, 79

I

IDA 326–7, 329–31
ilities 61, 64–7
ill-structured problems 20
implementation 15, 36, 47, 48, 73
implementation stage (of JSD) 241, 250, 258–60, 261–2
importing 356
information flow 97, 206, 211, 215, 218, 220
information function step (of JSD) 254, 256
information hiding 72–4, 111, 115, 164, 169, 220, 266, 269, 271, 276, 327, 331, 365
inheritance 88, 150, 272–4, 278, 280, 287, 289, 356
initial model 8, 10, 164–5
initialization (design for) 191, 220
inspection operation 357–9
interactive function step (of JSD) 254–6
Intercommunication Data Area *see* IDA
invariant condition 350–1
inversion *see* program inversion
invocation (hierarchy) 87, 108, 111, 210, 220
iteration (description of) 115–20
iteration (in design) 8, 11, 15

J

Jackson, Michael 178, 196, 202, 240

Jackson Structured Programming *see* JSP
Jackson System Development *see* JSD
Jones, Cliff 344
Jones, J. Christopher 5, 6, 8, 13, 22
JSD 119, 163, 168, 239–64, 267, 279, 333
JSP 119, 145, 154, 168, 177–202, 256, 260, 323, 366

L

Larch 342
levelling 207, 221
lifecycle, software 14, 20, 44, 49, 51, 52
Logical Data-Structuring Technique (LDST) 318–21
logical design 27, 317
logical DFD 103–4, 215

M

magic number seven 90
maintainability 67
maintenance 37, 49, 50, 108, 111, 146–7, 170
MASCOT 171, 246, 258, 306, 313, 324–35
mathematical (description forms) 92, 96, 144
McCabe, Thomas 61
me too 343
measurement (of design properties) 60–4, 69–76, 370
mental models 29, 47, 64, 67, 147
MERISE 171, 313, 323
method *see* design method
methodology 142
metric *see* design metric
mini-specs *see* P-specs
model 5 *see also* design model
model-based (formal methods) 342–53
modelling stage (of JSD) 240, 248, 250–1
modularity 13, 69, 72, 164, 169, 181, 270–1, 277, 287, 324, 331, 364
module
    concept 164, 167
    diagram 290–1
multiple viewpoints (in design) 169
multithreading clash *see* structure clash
mutual exclusion 328–9, 334

N

n-ary properties 105–6
network stage (of JSD) 241, 250, 252–8
non-functional (design properties) 332–3, 340
note-making (by designers) 29, 227–9, 309
noun–verb analysis 277, 286, 295–9

O

OBJ 342
object 265–303, 348, 355
    classes 289, 354
    diagrams 290
    model 270, 274–6, 354
object-based 240, 274, 279–87
object-oriented 92, 108, 164, 168, 206, 265–303, 366, 368, 370
    analysis (OOA) 269, 279
    design (OOD) 267
object-oriented programming structures 267
OOPS *see* object-oriented programming structures
operating system 324
opportunistic 31, 32, 76, 147, 367
ordering clash *see* structure clash
organizational (design strategy) 165, 170–1, 306, 312–23
orthogonality 130 *see also* parallel

P

P-specs 208–9, 214–5
package (in Ada) 112–3, 150
Page-Jones, Meilir 97, 206, 215, 219, 236
PAISley 343
parallel 130, 134
parent-child decomposition 282, 287
Parnas, David L. 38, 72, 79, 157, 174, 269
passive object (in HOOD) 280–3
perfective maintenance 49, 150
Petri Net (Graph) 97, 131–5, 338, 343
physical design 27, 149, 258, 262, 291, 317, 323, 333
physical DFD 102–4, 215, 321
place (in a Petri Net) 132–3
Pool (in MASCOT) 326–7
postcondition 132, 344, 350

precondition 132, 134, 344, 350
predicate logic 348
prescriptive (design approaches) 143, 145,
    152, 178, 240, 253, 256, 260–1, 314
priority 256, 328
problem domain 30, 144–5, 147, 152–5, 172,
    207, 240
procedural (form of method) 367, 370
process *see* sequential process
process part (of method) 32, 33, 144, 149, 160,
    175, 181–9, 211–21, 247–60, 283–6, 310–1,
    317–23, 331–4, 339, 343, 351–3, 360, 366–7
process specifications *see* P-specs
program inversion
  in JSD 260–1
  in JSP 196–201, 222
program proving 341
programming in the large 29, 40, 146
Prolog 343
property-based (formal methods) 342, 344,
    353–60
prototype 45, 48, 49, 51–4, 78
provided operations (in HOOD) 281–2
pseudocode 97, 111, 120–2, 181, 210

Q

quality 13, 37, 57–79, 220, 366
quality attributes 58, 67–76
quality concepts 60–1, 67 *see also* ilities

R

reactive 123, 127, 130–1, 154
read-ahead (in JSP) 190–1
real-time 21, 61, 123, 126, 153, 155, 207, 211,
    223, 239–40, 306, 324–5, 327–8, 331, 333,
    335, 340, 370
re-entrancy 261
reification 345, 351–3
relational model (databases) 104, 108
relationship 105–6
reliability 65, 66
rendezvous (in Ada) 113, 334
Rentsch, Tim 266
representation 8, 9, 10, 16, 18, 82–93, 95–136

representation part (of method) 32, 33, 143,
    175, 179–81, 207–11, 242–7, 280–3, 307–10,
    325–31, 339, 343, 346–51, 354–60, 366–7
requirements
  analysis 15, 46, 47, 48, 53, 307
  document 250, 341
  specification 17, 27, 172, 354
reuse (of design) *see* design reuse
reverse engineering 224
Rittel, Horst 19, 22
rough-merge (in JSD) 246, 252
run-time executive 324, 327–9, 333

S

SADT 284, 306–12, 335
safety-critical (systems) 66, 146 *see also*
    high-integrity
scheduling (of processes) 257–8
selection 115–20
semaphore 329
separation of concerns 67, 69, 224, 271, 331,
    364
sequence 85, 88, 90, 97, 102, 115–20, 121, 178
sequential process 242, 253, 256, 258 *see also*
    cooperating parallel processes
signature 355–7
Simon, Herb 20, 22
simplicity 68
simulation 29
Software Process Maturity Model 76
Soloway, Elliott 28, 31, 42
solution space 35–6, 48, 51, 142, 211
sort 354–7
specification 15, 20, 47, 48, 53, 344 *see also*
    requirements specification
spiral model 45–6, 51, 54
SSA/SD *see* Structured Systems
    Analysis/Structured Design
SSADM 90, 98, 108, 119, 145, 168, 171, 306,
    312–23, 335
SSD *see* System Specification Diagram
state 124–33
Statechart 97, 127–31, 338–9, 343
State Transition Diagram 97, 123–7, 129–31,
    211
state vector (in JSD) 245, 247, 252, 256, 258
state vector separation (in JSD) 260–1

static relationships 87, 104
STD *see* State Transition Diagram
stepwise refinement *see* decompositional design strategy
stopping rule 20, 166, 345, 351
strategy 9
structural (representations/viewpoint) 85, 87, 97, 260, 269, 280, 286, 301, 341
Structure Chart 97, 108–11, 207, 210–1, 216–21, 270, 314
structure clash (in JSP) 192–202, 256
Structure Diagram 97, 115–20, 128–9, 179–202, 242, 316, 338
Structure Graph 97, 111–5, 281, 290–1
Structured Analysis and Design Technique *see* SADT
Structured Design 206–7, 212, 229–36, 270
Structured Systems Analysis 206–7, 212–6, 225–9, 236, 284, 295
Structured Systems Analysis/Structured Design 102, 108, 123, 167, 205–36, 366
stylized design *see* design reuse
subsidiary viewpoint 108
Subsystem (in MASCOT) 330–1
Sutcliffe, Alastair 263
synchronization 328–9, 334
synonyms *see* noun–verb analysis
System Specification Diagram (SSD) 245–7, 252, 255–6, 260
system state (in VDM) 348
systematic (methods) 30, 145, 306, 338, 344, 364, 366, 369

T

task (in Ada) 113, 150, 350
team (of designers) *see* design team
template 277, 283
template-based design strategy 165, 171–3, 224 *see also* design reuse
testing 15, 47, 48
textual descriptions 89–90
time-ordering (of operations) 202, 240, 242, 250–1
token (in a Petri Net) 133
top-down (design strategy) 31, 206, 211, 214, 225, 313 *see also* decompositional design strategy

transaction
    analysis 216–8, 229
    components of 216–8
transform analysis 218–20, 229–33
transformational model (of design) 144, 160–3, 181, 212–3, 241, 258–9, 284–5, 311–2
transitions (between states) 123–6, 128–33
tree (structure) 116
type 88, 272

U

uses hierarchy 70, 87, 114–5, 272, 279, 281
uses relationship 272, 281, 360

V

validation 15, 49, 59, 321, 353
VDM (Vienna Development Method) 341–2, 346–53
verification 49, 59, 169, 181, 187, 338, 353, 361
Vienna Development Method *see* VDM
viewpoint 17, 83, 85–9, 102, 106, 108, 111, 143, 168–9, 175, 314, 316, 323, 366
virtual machine 148, 324, 334
Visser, Willemien 29, 31, 157
visual language 343

W

walkthrough *see* design review
waterfall model 14, 44, 51
Weinberg, Gerald 39
wicked problem (design as) 19–21, 44, 166
Wirth, Niklaus 164, 173

X

X (Window System) 172

Y

Yourdon, Ed 167, 236

Z

Z (specification language) 341–2